HOW MAKE IT IN THE CITY

DEBBIE HARRISON

Virgin

First published in Great Britain in 2001 by
Virgin Publishing Ltd
Thames Wharf Studios
Rainville Road
London W6 9HA

A catalogue record for the book is available
from the British Library.

ISBN 0 7535 0548 7

Designed and typeset by Roger Kohn Designs
Printed and bound in Great Britain by
Mackays of Chatham

ABOUT THE AUTHOR

Debbie Harrison first published at eighteen when she made an outstanding contribution to the Dennis the Menace Fan Club page in the *Beano*. By the time she finished her career as a full-time student and queen of sex, drugs and rock and roll (she has always denied the rock and roll), she was totally unfit for a City career, so she became a journalist. After a stint on *Target Gun* and *Trout & Salmon*, it was only a matter of time before she was discovered by the Financial Times Group and was asked to contribute to the Pink Paper itself on technical investment and tax issues (you can see the natural progression here).

Today Debbie is horrified to realise she has eighteen years of grown-up journalism behind her. She has won lots of awards for her work and is a regular contributor to the *FT*, *Bloomberg Money* and *Investment Week*. Her consumer books include *The Money Zone, Pension Power, First Time Investor* and *Personal Financial Planner*, all published by Financial Times Prentice Hall. She specialises in UK and international pension fund issues and is the author of five *Financial Times* Management Reports on this subject.

Debbie lives in a spooky old house with her husband, two children and three cats. She still reads the *Beano*.

CONTENTS

ACKNOWLEDGEMENTS

The author would like to thank the following organisations for their contributions to this book: The specialist graduate recruitment and careers organisation GTI (doctor job.com and the Target publications), plus Prospects/the Association of Graduate Careers Advisory Services. Other recruitment organisations that provided information include the Recruitment & Employment Confederation, Michael Page City, Reed, Harrison Willis and Vault.com.

Many employers provided case studies and information on graduate training courses. These include Accenture, Arthur Andersen, Baker & McKenzie, Barclays Capital, the BBC, Bear Stearns, Bloomberg, Cap Gemini Ernst & Young Group, Chase Manhattan Bank, Credit Suisse First Boston, Deutsche Bank, Dresdner Kleinwort Benson, Ernst & Young, Goldman Sachs International, HSBC Investment Bank, J.P. Morgan, Lehman Brothers, KBC Financial Products, London Business School, William M. Mercer, Merrill Lynch Europe, Morgan Stanley Dean Witter, N. M. Rothschild, Polhill Communications, Reuters, Royal Bank of Scotland, PricewaterhouseCoopers, Schroder Salomon Smith Barney, Schroders, Standard Chartered Bank, Towers Perrin, UBS Warburg, Watson Wyatt, Zurich Financial Services.

The regulators that provided details about employment and policing the City include the Financial Services Authority, the Investment Managers Regulatory Organisation, the Securities and Futures Authority, and the Securities Institute.

The professional bodies and trade associations that contributed information on careers and professional examinations include the Association of British Insurers, the Association of Chartered Certified Accountants, the Association of Insurance and Risk Managers in Industry and Commerce, the Association of Private Client Investment Managers and Stockbrokers, the British Bankers Association, the Chartered Insurance Institute, the Faculty and Institute of Actuaries, the Institute of Chartered Accountants in England and Wales, the Institute of Management Consultancy, the Institute of Investment Management and Research, the Institute of Personnel and Development, the International Underwriting Association of London, the Law Society, the London Investment Banking Association, the National Association of Pension Funds (NAPF), the Royal Institution of Chartered Surveyors, and the UK Society of Investment Professionals.

Finally, the following City institutions provided material on their important role in the financial services sector and, in some cases, as employers: the Bank of England, the Baltic Exchange, the International Petroleum Exchange, the London International Financial Futures Exchange, Lloyd's of London, the London Clearing House, the London Metal Exchange, the London Stock Exchange, the London Securities and Derivatives Exchange, and the London Underwriting Centre.

AND A GOLDEN HELLO TO YOU!

Mention a career in finance and you immediately think of the City of London. Mention a career in the City and you immediately think of massive salaries, unbelievable bonuses and share options the size of a planet. You might also think of heart attacks, liver damage and cocaine addiction – but hey, this is a stressful place to work!

When City employers moan about the 'war for talent', smile. The talent in question is you. The war started in the 1990s and represents a fierce competition between employers to attract and retain the brightest graduates. And the price tag for the right sort of talent? Well, how does a starting salary of £35,000 sound? Plus a golden hello of up to £10,000. Plus an annual bonus, of course. And when you're a little bit older you might even get the golden handcuffs (but don't get the wrong idea).

Unlike most employment myths these remuneration systems really do exist. The City is, after all, *the* place to be if you want to go into investment banking, insurance, accountancy or management consultancy. It also houses some of the most eminent law firms and information technology consultants in the world.

Before you investigate your own price tag in the City job market, here are a few helpful tips.

HELPFUL TIP NO. 1

It may sound like an obvious point but City employers are not charities. The jobs pay extraordinarily well because they expect you to break certain delicate parts of your anatomy in the course of duty. If you are a market trader your day starts so early you will be eating breakfast the night before. Even the temps and secretaries work harder in the City than they do elsewhere in the country. So, if you want laid-back, consider earning a City salary vicariously and marry an investment banker. For *really* laid-back, look for your partner in the personal columns of *The Actuary*.

HELPFUL TIP NO. 2

The second point is that, although all the investment banks do pretty much the same thing, they get a bit testy if you point this out. The same is true of the professional services firms (previously known as chartered accountants), the private wealth managers (previously known as stockbrokers), and the management consultants (previously known as God). So, if you have an interview with three different banks for the same sort of job, check out their websites and memorise the 'what makes us special/different/best' stuff.

Companies call this their 'unique selling points', and you've got to believe in them or at least give a very convincing impression of 'sincere' and 'impressed'. Practise in front of the mirror. Make like it's a marriage proposal. Don't kneel, though. (Actually, you *could* try this with the Japanese banks.)

YOUR TICKET TO SUCCESS

Getting into the City is a tough process. Employers say they judge graduates on their independence of mind and their ability to work as part of a team. This is, of course, a complete contradiction in terms.

Oxbridge degrees still count with the blue-blooded fund managers, while a minority of firms will be irritatingly interested in your family background and, alas, the sports you play. Fortunately, the Americans dominate the City now, and they are very willing to swap good parentage for naked ambition and the ability to work 24 hours a day, eight days a week (more if you are crossing time zones regularly).

Apart from remembering the unique selling points of each firm, you need to get to know the jargon. Remember, the terms 'passive' and 'active' refer to styles of investment management and not to your personality. This is important.

Passive managers invest only in the stocks in an index. It doesn't matter if they hate the company for the way it treats fluffy bunny rabbits or if they think the MD is off his rocker. If it's in the index it must be in their fund. Computers do most of the work, so these managers charge less than the active variety, which has made them jolly popular with big institutional money like the multimillion-pound pension funds. This popularity has been largely justified by the fact that the passives have outperformed the more expensive actives in recent years. At the interview you can smile wryly at the irony of this, but don't push your luck – active managers are making a comeback.

Active managers are supposed to 'add value' by deviating from the index.

If you want to do the active thing you will need to know a bit about the UK and international economies, market cycles, which countries or geographical regions are emerging from the antediluvian swamp (these would be the ones we used to call Third World), and which are taking a nosedive back in (that would be us). You also need to know quite a lot about individual companies and be able to read company accounts, understand something called P/E ratios, and other information not to be found in FunFacts.

If you become a fund manager, the 'professionals' – and we use the term loosely – you'll have most contact with are the brokers who buy and sell equities and bonds on your instructions. While one wouldn't wish to spread gossip, nevertheless it is a fact that the big debate over clean (up-front) and dirty (downright obscure) fund management fees is largely focused on what goes on between the managers and brokers. More of this anon.

You might also have to meet prospective clients. In this case you need to practise a sympathetic expression for trustees of pension funds who think they know a thing or two about investments and will want to impress you. Trustees are likely to ask you to explain what you do for a living. *Never* tell the truth. A few charts with zigzagging lines, a spot of economic theory, the outlook for price inflation (as opposed to the slightly higher wages inflation) and your views on production possibility curves for the rubber industry should stem their thirst for knowledge. If not, move on to derivatives.

WHY YOU NEED THIS BOOK

This book provides a handy guide to the City and its golden careers. There are other guides, of course, but frankly they are either not so good or too big. This one tells you everything you need to know without overtaxing your attention span. It gives you lots of information about the jobs themselves, how to apply, and where to find out more details from recruitment consultants, professional bodies, specialist publications and employer websites.

To be completely straight from the outset, this book is aimed mainly at graduates because graduates are what most City firms want. Even if they don't need them. Call it snobbery if you like, but the reality is you stand a better chance of getting in with a first in zoology than good A levels and five years' practical experience running a high-street bank.

However, we do include a few jobs that target those with A levels and we take a quick saunter through the lively world of temping, which is either a brilliant way to find out about lots of different companies or the biggest pain in the backside you ever suffered. Success as a temp apparently depends on a sunny disposition and an ability to suffer fools gladly.

So, onward! It's time to explore the hub of the financial universe.

HOW TO USE THIS BOOK

Over one hundred City employers and dozens of employees contributed ideas, advice and comments for this book. We suggest you read through Parts 1 and 2 and then dip into the jobs outlined in Part 3 to suit your taste. Where a company was happy to be quoted we have included its name, but in some cases we simply refer to the type of organisation – for example, invest-ment bank, market trader, and so on. We refer to employees by their first name and where requested we have changed these to preserve their identity.

You'll find that the book is littered with summaries, cross-references and useful contacts for further infor-mation. The amount of information available on the Internet is phenomenal, and we hope that the legwork undertaken here on your behalf will speed up your search.

PART 1: GETTING STARTED

Part 1 explains how to identify and approach prospective employers in the City.

● **Chapter 2** provides a useful A–Z of job titles and their synonyms.

● In **Chapter 3** we consider different ways to get work experience in the City – for example, temping, internships and sponsorship.

● **Chapter 4** provides some useful tips on getting an interview and securing that job offer. These are based on the experience of dozens of City employees.

● In **Chapter 5** we take a look at your CV, interview technique and dress code.

● **Chapter 6** is your treasure trove of websites. Here we list tried and tested sites dedicated to helping you find your first job. This chapter also lists the websites for top recruitment consultants and key City institutions, including the professional bodies, the regulators and those employers who support the Women in Banking initiative.

● **Chapter 7** is all about money. Yours. It explains why, when you come to look at your job offer, you need to examine the small print beneath the headline salary. Benefits like share options, bonuses and pensions can add several thousand to your annual remuneration.

● Finally, in **Chapter 8** we run through some of the most relevant qualifications you are likely to be asked to pursue once you start your new job.

PART 2: ESSENTIAL INFORMATION

Read Part 2 to get a basic understanding of how the City works and how the different professions interrelate. Useful contact addresses and websites are provided for those who want to find out more about a specific institution.

Financial jargon is an integral part of City life, and while it doesn't do to show off at an interview, if you are interested in fund management it certainly helps if you understand the different characteristics of, say, the basic asset classes such as equities, gilts and property, while those interested in

stockbroking should know the difference between, say, discretionary and execution-only services.

The most common buzzwords are explained at the beginning of each section in Part 3 and again in the Appendix. This isn't just a polite afterthought. Unless you get a grip on some of the basic jargon you will have trouble knowing what different employers do.

HEGEMONY IN THE CITY

To be fair, some of the largest employers are themselves hard pressed to define precisely what it is they do. To cover up this embarrassment, most of them claim to do everything, and those that clearly can't do everything call themselves 'niche' players. This habit has become more noticeable over the past few years as the lines have blurred between professional firms of chartered accountants, management consultants, actuarial consultants and law firms. Even the investment banks have gone in for a bit of hegemony. Talk about greed.

The big consultancy firms now do everything from investment advice to employee benefits, and from taxation to law. The firms we used to know as chartered accountants (Pricewater-houseCoopers, Arthur Andersen, Deloitte and Touche, Ernst & Young, KPMG) are now 'professional services organisations' and have thrown down the gauntlet to the actuarial consultants on pensions and investment work, while hanging on to their traditional strengths in tax and accounting.

Investment banks used to be known as merchant banks while their offspring, the stockbrokers, now refer to themselves as private client services (PCS) firms or private wealth managers. This attempt to overcome the pin-striped, old-boy-network image has been only partially successful.

To overcome confusion over job titles we have set out the descriptions of careers and jobs under their generic headings in Parts 2 and 3, but in the introduction to each section in Part 3 we list the most common synonyms as well.

PART 3: YOUR GUIDE TO CAREERS IN THE CITY

Part 3 describes in more detail specific career paths and explains what the job entails, the salary and benefits package, the qualifications you need in order to get in, and much more.

We have divided the jobs into four broad categories:

● Banking and investment
● Professional services and consultancy
● Pensions and insurance
● Media and information services

Some of the careers span more than one category, so the boundaries are rather arbitrary.

This blurring of boundaries between jobs is inevitable. If you are unsure where to look, check Chapter 2, which lists job titles, provides a brief explanation and tells you where to find out more.

We introduce each section in Part 3 with a guide to the jargon, and at the end of each chapter we list further sources of information so you can pursue your own lines of enquiry.

PART 1
GETTING STARTED

'The main thing is to have money. I've been rich and I've been poor. *Believe* me, rich is better.'

The Big Heat, 1953

1
LIFE IN THE FAST LANE

Before you start looking at any specific jobs it is helpful to understand the nature of the environment in which you intend to work. Despite all the apparent complexity, the City is really very simple. But don't ever tell an interviewer you think so.

THE CITY AS A MARKETPLACE

Think of the City as a large marketplace. The product it deals in is money and the market operates on the usual principles of supply and demand. So, the City is where those who need to raise money for business find willing lenders and investors. The organisations that lend money are clearly taking a risk that the borrower might default – that is, not be able to pay the interest and/or the capital debt – and so they seek compensation for this risk by charging a rate of interest. This covers their costs, inflation, tea and sticky buns all round on a Friday, and gives them a nice fat profit. Investors take a risk in the hope that the value of their shareholding will grow in line with the company itself and the economy as a whole. That way they get a nice fat profit too, and everybody is happy.

The City is also a marketplace for insurance, where those who want to protect a financial risk can find a willing underwriter. Instead of charging interest on a loan, under-writers charge a premium that, when combined with all the other premiums, pays for any claims that arise – and gives them a nice fat profit. I hope you are getting the hang of this.

Supply and demand are affected by risk. Actually it doesn't really affect supply – it just puts up the price. The higher the risk of default on a loan or an insurance claim being made, the greater the interest rate or insurance premium.

A GAMBLER'S PARADISE

The City operates as a secondary market for the original loans, investments and underwriting. In this way it behaves rather like a betting shop. Ace Engineering goes to the primary market and raises capital by selling shares in its business. Those shares, which are listed on one of the FTSE UK indices, can be bought and sold in their own right. The price will fluctuate according to supply and demand, which in turn will depend on the analysts' views on how well that company is likely to perform in future, among other factors.

In the same way, Farmer Giles agrees to sell vast quantities of wheat to Jones the Baker in six months' time. Jones and Giles are happy, and in the meantime the City has a bit of fun buying and selling the contract, pushing the price up and down according to the latest weather forecast for the prairies and the reproductive activity of the weevil or whatever it is that eats crops.

IT'S A HI-TECH WORLD

In the old days most of the trading was conducted through the outcry system. A few exchanges still use this today. You can tell which by the hollering. Those with something to sell shout out their wares to attract those who want to buy. If your bananas are bigger than the bloke's on the stall opposite you yell out this information. Before the City was regulated you might even have lied about the size of your bananas. And got away with it.

Today most of the exchange floors have swept away the gentlemen in top hats and the wide boys in bright blazers. In their place are hundreds of computer screens that show up-to-the-minute news and price information from around the world to the buyers and sellers so they can get together, electronically speaking, and make many a mutually satisfactory deal.

WHY LONDON?

London is neatly situated between two important time zones – Tokyo and New York – so it provides the link between the three most important global financial centres and covers the stretch between the close of business in Japan and the opening of business in the US. Although the UK's domestic stock market is smaller than those in the US and Japan, London remains the most international of the three markets.

A useful booklet published by the Association of Graduate Careers Advisory Services (AGCAS), *City Institutions and Financial Markets*, highlights the following international features of the City, which are worth remembering for those chatty 'this is

not really an interview' moments at the bar with your prospective boss. If you don't understand any of the terms, see our jargon buster in the Appendix. For further information on how the City works, see Part 2 of this book.

TEN THINGS TO REMEMBER ABOUT THE CITY

● There are more foreign banks in the City – over 550 according to the Bank of England – than in any other financial centre in the world.

● Allegedly there are more American banks in London than in New York.

● London ranks as second to the US in exchange-traded financial derivatives.

● London is the world's second-largest market in international insurance.

● The biggest shipbroking market in the world is based in London at the Baltic Exchange.

● The London Metal Exchange is regarded as the primary base metals market in the world. Its prices are used as an international benchmark.

● The International Petroleum Exchange is Europe's only energy futures exchange.

● London is the world's most liquid spot market for gold and gold lending. It is also the global clearing centre for worldwide gold trading.

● 60 per cent of international bonds are issued in London; 70 per cent of subsequent dealing in these bonds is also carried out in London.

● 55 per cent of the world's securities trading is carried out in London. More foreign companies are listed on the London Stock Exchange than on any other exchange.

QUALIFICATIONS AND ENTREPRENEURSHIP GO HAND IN HAND

If you are a high-flier and set to get a first or upper second honours degree, the City is your oyster. Given the current boom in investment banking, the blue chip institutions are competing fiercely for the privilege of employing top graduates and MBAs. In the City it's not just indispensable senior executives who enjoy lucrative golden hellos. Top graduates in 2001 can expect a substantial 'sign-on' bonus of up to £10,000 and a salary worth up to £35,000. Not bad for a 21-year-old with no work experience.

Clearly, qualifications are important in your choice of career. But don't worry if you are not a pure maths student. While some jobs require very specific degrees in law, maths or information technology, others simply require a strong academic background. For example, if you apply for a graduate trainee position with the large professional services firms, consultants and investment banks, you are as likely to be accepted with a first in sociology and anthropology as in maths. The quality of your academic credentials is the important issue. The rest is down to your personality, which may or may not be a good thing.

Fancy certificates aren't everything. Entrepreneurship was born and bred in the City and, despite the rise in the number of young people with qualifications to die for, if your face fits and you have plenty of initiative, determination and charm, and a thick skin, you can get to the top.

So, apart from your existing qualifications from school, college, university or on-site training, it is important to be sure you have the right personality and drive for the career you have in mind. It also helps if you are interested in finance and can cope with long hours, commuting and a highly stressful job environment.

A CLOSE-KNIT COMMUNITY

The City adds a whole new dimension to the word 'compact'. The residential population is only about 3,000, but half a million commuters spend hours each day on the germ-fests run by London and regional transport.

Part of the attraction of the City is the sheer scale of opportunity within handshake or spitting distance. Do remember, though, that information technology has done more than just reduce the audible volume in the City. It is also largely responsible for spreading the boundaries of the Square Mile. An increasing number of major players in City finance have left EC1 for the open spaces (comparatively speaking) of Docklands, Canary Wharf, Victoria and even the West End.

If insurance or investment is your chosen career, don't overlook the other important financial centres in the UK. In particular, Edinburgh is home to many leading insurance and investment companies, while Dublin's young International Financial Services Centre is positively booming. In terms of youth culture and lifestyle both cities have much to offer. Expats from the City suggest that Edinburgh is the stronger financial centre but that Dublin is a tad warmer and generally more fun if you are under 30 and enjoy Guinness. However, this is just hearsay – go and take a look for yourself. *En route* you might visit the big regional financial services communities like Bristol and Glasgow – and draw your own conclusions as to where you want to live and work.

Even if you start in London, any institution with the adjective 'global' attached to its name is likely to send you off to New York, Tokyo or anywhere else in the world for that matter. Possibly even Wales.

HOW FAST AND FURIOUS DO YOU WANT?

There is nowhere between London and New York to rival the City if you fancy the fast and furious lifestyle of the securities traders or the corporate finance wheeler-dealer. However, there are less comfortable issues to consider here. Some of the exchanges and trading firms are about as far from the Civil Service style of job security as you can get this side of prostitution and murder. Once you're in a major financial institution your career can rocket ...

... And just as easily it can plummet. If you are after a job for life, don't bother to read on. In many of the careers outlined in this book your reputation will hang on the latest deal you stitch together. It will also depend on the whim of financial markets. Specialisation is the name of the game, but always remember that this year's dot.com expert is next year's South Sea Bubble has-been. The mega-mergers and frenzied corporate activity that fuel huge bonuses and expansions can dry up overnight. Contracts are often short-term, and in some jobs you are too old by the time you reach 35. It's a bit like Hollywood, except in the City you can't fix a flagging career with a facelift.

A JOB OR A LIFE?

City jobs are renowned for their high stress levels, and although employers now pay more attention to the overworked-to-burn-out syndrome, you really do have to watch your own back in this business. No amount of salary is worth total exhaustion – the reason given by the press for 31-year-old star investment manager William Littlewood's resignation in May 2000 from Jupiter Asset Management.

Currently the heavyweight US investment banks are the biggest recruiters of top graduates. Competition is fierce, and if you are offered the equivalent of a ransom to join, as far as the bank is concerned it has bought you body and soul. So, no matter how attractive the salary, make sure you like the corporate ethos and the people, because you are about to get married.

Joining in the corporate lifestyle is no longer just a question of learning golf. You will be expected to take part in lots of jolly bonding activities like paintballing, charity events and other corporate equivalents of sports day and feasts in the dorm. If the mere thought makes you want to heave, then for goodness' sake steer clear of the mega-firms and look for a smaller operation that is happy just to buy your mind and leave your soul virtually intact.

Don't be fooled by the apparently

relaxed atmosphere of the modern investment bank, or by the high levels of oxygen generated by the trees in the atrium. Even dressing down is fiercely competitive. Simon, a partner in a top City consultancy, says, 'I thought dressing down was just a case of leaving off the tie and wearing a blazer instead of a suit jacket. I was wrong. The dress code for "casual" is far stricter than on the formal suit days.' Little wonder, then, that those who are supposed to enjoy wearing cashmere jumpers, silk jackets and chinos have been caught reminiscing about the good old days of suits and ties as they sit in the Slug and Lettuce of a Friday evening and drink their spritzers (that's wine shandy to you and me).

Women in the City argue that barriers to promotion still exist. Most institutions are making a genuine effort to overcome career blocks and the uncomfortable working environment of traditionally male-dominated sectors, such as securities trading. However, do be practical here. If you have a thin skin as far as boorishness goes, don't take on the obviously male fraternities. The colourful jackets of the futures traders have disappeared from the exchange floor, but if you frequent the bars and cafés in the Cannon Street station area you will notice that the colourful language remains. Women who feel strongly about having their bottoms pinched might like to follow up the list of institutions that have joined together to launch the 'Women in investment banking' initiative (see page 38).

GET PASSIONATE ABOUT FINANCE

Keeping well informed is imperative if you have set your sights on a career in finance. You can forget Jane Austen, the Fabian Society and Greenpeace, although it's worth hanging on to your GCSE notes on Shakespeare in case your prospective employer pays lip service to culture through sponsorship of the Globe Theatre.

What you really need is a passion for things financial that borders on the obsessional. If you don't already peruse the *Financial Times* (aka the Pink Paper or just the Pinkie), then start reading it immediately. You will soon get a feel for the slant you need to apply to world events at interviews.

While some might register shock at the human cost of a breakdown in Middle East peace talks, you will calmly discuss the impact on oil prices. Your sad but well-intentioned friends might hail the overthrow of a petty dictator in eastern Europe as a victory for human rights, but your priorities must be the investment opportunities for emerging market fund managers and the prospects for corporate clients seeking access to cheap labour.

If you get the picture and are still keen, read on!

2
YOUR A–Z JOB GUIDE

● **ACCOUNTANT**

Traditionally this term referred largely to taxation and auditing roles, but the big professional services organisations now offer virtually every area of financial and technology consultancy. See Chapter 30.

● **ACTUARY**

The actuary has a mathematical and statistical background and is the brains behind the underwriting of major risks. His or her role is to assess the risk and enable the insurance company to price the premiums so that they are competitive but still generate a profit. Actuaries are often involved in the design of new financial products. See Chapter 37. Also Chapters 32, 38 and 39.

● **ADVISER**

This term covers a wide range of jobs. Corporate clients need advice on raising finance (through issuing debt or equity instruments) and corporate activities such as mergers, acquisitions and management buyouts. For corporate finance advisers, see Chapters 21 and 26. For financial advisers to individual investors, see Chapters 27 and 40.

● **ANALYST**

If you want to research companies, countries, governments, geographical areas and sectors, see Chapter 23. You might also consider news and information services in Chapter 45.

● **BANKING**

This covers a huge range of opportunities and job profiles, but the basic division is between investment banks – which look after corporate clients – and the retail banks, which deal with private individuals and small partnerships. See Section A in Part 3.

● **BROKING**

This job title has several meanings. You could be the person who buys and sells securities (Chapter 28) or who operates in the retail market as a financial adviser (Chapters 27 and 40). Only Lloyd's registered brokers can go to the Lloyd's syndicates to place business. See Chapter 13.

● **CLAIMS ASSESSORS**

Assessors are employed by insurance companies to investigate claims and to report on whether they are justified or not. Independent assessors are known as loss adjusters. See Chapter 39.

● **CORPORATE BANKING**

Aka institutional banking, this deals with the more traditional banking needs of medium-sized companies – for example, cash management and treasury services and finance packages typically in the £10m–£15m bracket. Corporate banks also dominate the global custody market. See Chapter 26.

● **CUSTODY**
The safe-keeping of assets – for example, for pension funds. Global custody is a huge business and is dominated by the corporate banks. See Chapter 26.

● **DEALER**
See **Market maker**.

● **EMPLOYEE BENEFITS**
This covers salary, pensions and a host of other products that are offered by employers to attract and retain the best staff. Your job, therefore, is likely to involve designing – or in most cases redesigning – the most appropriate benefits scheme for a client, negotiating the most competitive deals with providers of the benefits, and communicating the benefits to the workforce. See Chapter 38.

● **FUND OR INVESTMENT MANAGER**
Here you invest money on behalf of clients who could be the large multimillion pension funds or a collection of individuals in a pooled fund. Life offices run huge pooled funds for pension schemes as well as a wide range of 'single premium' (lump sum) and regular savings schemes. Fund management within an insurance company is very similar to the role of investment manager for an investment bank or unit trust group. See Chapter 22.

● **INDEPENDENT FINANCIAL ADVISER**
IFA is the term used to describe the role of the intermediary in the life,

pensions and investment market. Independent financial advisers (IFAs) are independent of any one company. Tied agents and sales people also give advice but they only sell the products of the company for which they work. See **Adviser**.

● **INSURANCE**
This covers a huge area, including underwriting, risk management and risk consulting. See Chapters 13, 14, 34 and 39

● **INSURANCE ACCOUNT HANDLER**
This is the title given to the person who looks after the brokers and financial advisers who sell the company's products. See Chapters 39 and 40.

● **INVESTMENT ADVISER/CONSULTANT**
For the corporate work, see Chapter 32. For individuals see Chapters 27 and 40.

● **INVESTMENT BANKER**
If you want to take companies apart and stitch them back together again, this is the place to be. See Part 3, Section A.

● **JOURNALIST**
Consider both PR and journalism – see Part 3, Section D.

● **LEGAL WORK**
You can work either as a solicitor or a barrister, or you can use your law degree to work for any of the professional firms. See Chapter 15, and Part 3, Section B. You could also

consider regulatory work. See Chapter 41.

● MANAGEMENT ACCOUNTING

A well-paid and highly skilled job for the mathematically minded who want to work in investment banking, for example. See Chapter 24.

● MANAGEMENT CONSULTANT

Management consultancy is primarily concerned with initiating and implementing change, whether a change in the technology a company uses, its management or organis- ational structure, or in the attitude and behaviour of staff. See Chapters 31, 33 and 34.

● MARKET MAKER/DEALER/ BROKER

The companies and individuals that make markets in securities – that is, buy and sell on behalf of their own bank or their clients. See Chapter 28.

● OPERATIONAL SUPPORT

This is the 'back office' function of an investment bank which ensures that deals are settled. It includes both administrative and IT positions. See Part 3, Section A, and Chapter 32.

● PUBLIC RELATIONS

Consider both PR and journalism – see Part 3, Section D.

● RESEARCH

See Research analyst, Chapter 23, and On-line information services, Chapter 45.

● RISK MANAGEMENT

This is a consultancy role to corporations that involves quantifying risk, risk management and assessing the impact on business. See Chapters 34 and 39.

● SOLICITOR

There are some top jobs working for specialist City law firms, but you could also consider working for one of the major consultants – for example, the professional services organisations, or in regulation. See Chapters 30, 35, 41.

● TELEVISION JOURNALISM

You will find a basic guide in Chapter 44.

● TRADING AND DEALING

Dealers buy and sell securities on behalf of the institution for which they work with the aim of making a profit. See Chapter 28.

● UNDERWRITER

The underwriter assesses a financial risk and recommends an appropriate premium for an insurance contract. See Chapter 39 and also Risk consulting, Chapter 34.

3
WORK EXPERIENCE: TEMPING, INTERNSHIPS AND SPONSORSHIP

There is no doubt that the best way to find out about an organisation is to work there on some sort of temporary basis. You might decide, for example, to apply for a formal internship where you work as a potential new recruit during your summer holiday before your final year at university. Some employers offer less formal holiday placements that last for just a few weeks. Both schemes are used by employers as a key recruiting source and are discussed below.

An alternative that seems to interest an increasing number of graduates is to spend two or three years post-graduation in temporary jobs, moving from one employer to another.

TEMPORARY WORK
Temporary work has many attractions. First and foremost, you don't have to commit yourself to a graduate training scheme with a major employer on the job-for-life basis that some City institutions still operate. If you want to travel you can fit your plans around some lucrative temporary contracts and maybe take on some extra IT training as well to boost your credentials.

The Recruitment & Employment Confederation (REC), the trade association for recruitment agencies, says that the growth of temporary and contract working is a phenomenon of the 1990s and that many graduates find sufficient work to fill their five-day week, 48-week year. The confederation includes some good advice on its website for those seeking the life of the temp, so do take a look (see Sources of information on page 25).

Temps need to be mobile and flexible. This is a two-way trade-off. If you can meet the employers' requirements you should be able to find the flexibility you need to fit your lifestyle. It's also important to remember that if you enter certain professions you can no longer expect an open-ended employment contract. 'Some people, for example in the IT or engineering sectors, consider working as a temporary or on a contract basis to be part of their career pattern,' the REC says.

SELECT THE RIGHT RECRUITMENT AGENCY
These first few years working on temporary contracts can be the most important in your career and should lead to new opportunities, new skills and a new future. Unless you have good contacts in high places in the City, as a temporary worker you rely heavily on your recruitment consultancy to highlight job opportunities for you. Treat the selection of your agency or agencies as though this were your first employer.

Look for a consultancy that is a member of the REC as this means the agency will work to a code of good recruitment practice. Apart from stringent membership criteria, the REC has a complaints and disciplinary procedure. Employers or job candidates who feel that they have not been treated properly have the right to ask the REC to investigate.

Once you have identified consultancies you would like to work with, contact them to discuss the type of work you are looking for. They are likely to ask you to make an appointment to visit one of their staff. When you go for an interview, take a CV, details of referees and your National Insurance (NI) number. Treat the interview just as you would any other. Don't make up your references – they will be checked. Also, expect some basic tests for numeracy, keyboard and IT skills, for example.

The REC stresses that you should explain honestly why you want to work as a temp and the type of companies you would like to work for. In return you should ask the consultant about availability of work and whether any training is offered.

REGISTERING AND PAYMENT

Make sure you know how the agency will pay you and remember to hand over your P45 (see page 24) and supply bank details before your first assignment. Different agencies have different payment systems, and you need to keep track of these if you register with more than one. Most will credit your bank account directly one week in arrears.

Some temporary jobs are on a contract basis and in this case the employer is likely to pay you directly and deduct your tax and National Insurance (see page 24). If this is the arrangement, the recruitment consultancy will tell you. Employers offering longer-term contracts may want to see you before confirming the job. If you work on a contract basis the assignment is likely to be for three months or longer, and you should be prepared to give your commitment for this period.

Once you are registered, the recruitment consultancy will start to search for suitable vacancies. Ask them to explain how they will put you forward for jobs. For example, you might want the agency to contact you before it sends your CV to a prospective employer in case there are certain organisations you want to avoid.

The REC stresses how important it is to keep in touch with your recruitment consultancy. 'Those candidates who appear most keen to work are understandably contacted first,' it says.

FIRST ASSIGNMENT

When the consultancy offers you an assignment, think about whether you can be available for its duration, for the hours required, and whether you can actually get there comfortably. The agency will confirm the rate of pay with you at this point. It should also tell you the name of your boss and cover house rules such as dress code, smoking policy and meal breaks. You will need to fill in a time sheet at the end of the week and ask your supervisor at the company to sign it to verify your hours of work.

ATTITUDE IS ALL!

Temporary workers are required to fit in rapidly and easily. You will develop flexibility and adaptability as you gain more temping or contracting experience. Try and keep a low profile and be enthusiastic and professional.

FOLLOW-UP

As a temp you should run yourself like any other business. Get feedback from employers on how you performed and make changes where necessary. This is all part of business survival and development.

INTERNSHIPS

If you are still at college and are happy to go direct to your first employer after you graduate, one of the best ways to find out about a financial institution before committing yourself to a full-time job is to apply for an internship (work experience) place.

The number of City employers offering internships is increasing. Their aim is to attract students in their penultimate year at university to identify and snap up the best of the bunch. Equally it is your chance to see what a company is like from the inside. The following example from Schroders' 2001 internship programme gives you an idea of what might be in store.

Each summer Schroders, a global investment manager, offers about 25 undergraduates in their penultimate year a ten-week internship. 'This provides you with the opportunity to see our business and work with our people first-hand,' Schroders explains. The minimum academic requirement is:

● 24 UCAS points (or overseas equivalent);
● Expected 2:1 degree, any discipline

Personal skills required include:

● Analytical skills
● Numeracy
● Team-working ability
● Communication and influencing skills
● Initiative
● Innate self-confidence
● Drive and tenacity
● Sound judgement

Schroders adds, 'To be considered for our intern programme, you must have a genuine interest in investment management – it is what we live and breathe here. Without that market curiosity, you would not benefit from the unique Schroders environment.'

Most internships start off with an on-line application in the January or February of your penultimate year. In Schroders' case, if you are successful at the initial screening stage the company contacts you for a brief telephone interview. Successful candidates are invited to Schroders' 'Intern Insight' event, usually held in March at the London offices. The programme includes a range of interviews, tests and social events. Always remember that the social events are an important part of the screening process.

If you clear the initial round of

interviews and testing for numeracy or other essential skills for the position, you are invited to stay for the remainder of the first day to take part in the assessment activities. These activities will depend on the business area for which you apply and may include a group exercise, a case study presentation, business interviews and a lunch with previous graduates. The company makes offers within one week of candidates attending the event.

THE INTERNSHIP PROGRAMME

The programme starts in early July with a three-day training course. You then move into your allocated department, where the work you undertake will be largely project-based. Schroders says, 'We will also introduce you to a "buddy" who can help you with everything from meeting people within the company to joining everyone for a Friday night drink.'

It seems to be a City tradition to offer you a chum. This is not a wild drinking partner. 'Be nice to your buddy,' says one successful graduate who went through an internship. 'The company will ask your buddy afterwards what he or she thought of you. Don't tell your buddy your life story or about all the things you didn't put on your application.'

TRAINING

This is intended to provide an introduction to investment manage-ment plus the technical skills and knowledge to prepare you for the type of work you would undertake as a permanent employee. The course is both practical and theoretical and aims to provide an overview of the following topics:

● The City and how it works
● How companies make their money
● Financial statements, accounting concepts and ratio analysis (for example, the price of shares compared with the company's earnings)
● How fund managers provide solutions for their clients
● Managing a portfolio asset allocation, where to invest
● Retail and institutional products
● Client management
● How to get the best out of the *Financial Times*
● An introduction to the company (the people and the business areas)

PROJECTS

Schroders designs projects that should give you a practical insight into the company's business, and at the same time allow you to demonstrate your skills and abilities. You are allocated a business supervisor who will ensure you get the most out of your project and help you determine the scope and objectives of your work. Examples of projects include:

FUND MANAGEMENT

● Preparation of a proposal on the Alternative Energy Investment Fund
● Analysis of the corporate governance polices of companies in which Schroders invests
● Evaluation of the real value of assets

RESEARCH
● Research into the investment potential in the emerging property sector
● Research into trends and prospects for companies with business-to-business e-commerce capabilities

CLIENT SERVICE
● Preparation of an index-tracker fund research paper
● Identification of clients interested in socially responsible (ethical) investment

MARKETING
● Designing a Schroders 'headline products' intranet site

IT
● Compilation and presentation of statistics for Schroders websites
● Incorporation of databases into current Web design
● Intranet development with Active Server Pages (ASPs)

FINANCE
● Financial analysis of competitor performance

BUSINESS AWARENESS
Weekly business lunches during your internship allow you to meet senior employees to raise your awareness of the company's business areas and highlight the opportunities it can offer. Irrespective of your project, you'll also be invited to attend a company meeting where you will see information exchanged first-hand.

SPONSORSHIP
Some employers offer financial sponsorship, which means that you get an extra allowance and holiday work. This can work very well if you are pretty sure of your career path. Alternatively, when you graduate and your choices are thin on the ground you could end up feeling like Faustus when the party is over. The moral of the story is to think first before you swap your soul for cash.

For this section we take a look at the Bank of England's sponsorship support schemes.

Undergraduate Scheme
First-degree students are sponsored for their final year and spend their second summer (six to eight weeks) on placement at the Bank. You are guaranteed an offer of a place following graduation if you complete your placement successfully, but you may also opt to apply directly for the postgraduate scheme.

Postgraduate Scheme 1 (PGS1)
Sponsorship is available for students to complete a one-year Masters in Economics or Finance prior to joining the Bank. This will consist of the payment of fees, plus a grant equal to one third of your starting salary. You will spend the preceding summer (six to eight weeks) on placement at the Bank.

Postgraduate Scheme 2 (PGS2)
Here you would enter via the usual graduate recruitment route, but with the assumption that you would be sponsored (on two-thirds of your

salary) to complete a Masters degree in Economics, Finance or Statistics after working for about two years, provided these years are completed successfully.

Postgraduate Scheme 3 (PGS3)
Further into your career, say after four or five years, the Bank can offer sponsorship support for nominated individuals for full-time study towards a Masters degree in Economics or Finance on a full-salary basis. This scheme cannot be applied for prior to joining the Bank.

INCOME TAX AND NATIONAL INSURANCE

If you earn or receive income over a certain amount in any given tax year (6 April – 5 April) you have to pay income tax. The more you earn the more you pay. If you work for a company or recruitment agency they are responsible for deducting the right amount and passing it on to the Inland Revenue. This is known as the pay as you earn (PAYE) system.

You also have to pay National Insurance Contributions (NICs) on earnings between a lower and upper threshold. The purists will howl at the oversimplification, but you can regard NI as just another form of taxation. In fact the days when NICs covered all the social security benefits are well past, so the distinction is rather academic.

The Department of Social Security (DSS) will send you your NI number when you reach the age of sixteen. It will look something like this: JX 34 25 16 B. You will need this number for an extraordinarily large number of things, so keep a note of it in your diary or tattoo it on your knuckles.

NI thresholds and tax rates change at the beginning of every new tax year.

WHAT IS TAXABLE?

The most common forms of taxable income are:

● Pay and other earnings from regular or part-time employment.

This includes:

● Tips, overtime and bonuses
● Profits from a business
● Interest from savings with a bank, building society and certain National Savings accounts (usually taxed at source unless you can prove you are a non-taxpayer)
● Dividends from shares in companies
● Unemployment benefit

WHERE IS MY TAX OFFICE?

Take a map of the UK and find the farthest point from where you live or go to college. That is where your tax office will be. However, the Inland Revenue has a Very Large Computer, which is supposed to be able to handle 64 million records, so if you need some information any tax office will be able to trace your details by checking under your NI number.

YOUR FIRST JOB

Your first employer will give you a PAYE code based on your personal allowance. If your earnings are less than this allowance you will not pay tax.

When you change jobs your employer will give you a P45 form which shows your PAYE code, your total earnings and how much tax you have paid since the start of the tax year. You must give this to your new employer or, if you are not going straight into another job, hand it in to your local Benefit Office. If you have claimed Job Seekers Allowance (JSA) in the past you will already have a P45 from the job centre.

At the end of each year your employer will give you a P60 form, which shows how much you have earned and how much tax you have paid. The Revenue also gets a copy and should check the figures. If you have overpaid tax you will get a refund. Underpayments are usually deducted from your earnings during the following tax year.

WHEN DO YOU PAY UP?

If you are subject to PAYE, most of your tax will be paid through your employer's deductions. However, there may be other sources of income that you need to declare and pay tax on, for example, any freelance earnings and income from savings and investments. You will need to enter these details on the annual self-assessment form, which you should receive in April.

STUDENTS AND TAX

Student loans are not taxable and you don't have to pay tax on part-time or vacation work provided you don't earn more than the single person's allowance (£4,385 in 2000/01 for under-65s). If you tell your employer you are a full-time student he or she will give you a P38(S) to complete.

Students on sandwich courses will be taxed on earnings during their year in industry and final-year students will start to pay tax as soon as they start work.

Make sure you claim back any tax paid for part-years in employment, for example, if your sandwich year straddles two tax years or if you work for only part of a year before starting a course or after finishing one.

SOURCES OF INFORMATION

● The Recruitment & Employment Confederation website is at www.rec.uk.com
● Schroders is at www.schroders.com
● The Bank of England website is at www.bankofengland.co.uk
● Everything you need to know about money (and films) is in *The Money Zone*, by Debbie Harrison, published by Financial Times Prentice Hall.
● Take a look at www.financialminds.com

4
TOP TIPS FOR GETTING IN AND GETTING ON

Employers, recent recruits and job agencies provided lots of tips for readers of this book. Here we summarise these pearls of wisdom and hope they will help you find your niche.

BEFORE YOU APPLY

Do the CV 'SWOT' test

The recruitment consultant Reed recommends 'SWOT' analysis for the best CV presentation. SWOT stands for Strengths, Weaknesses, Opportunities and Threats. This analysis is commonly used by businesses to assess their current position and future prospects. You can use it to judge your talents and skills.

List the positive and negative aspects of your character and situation under the SWOT headings. This is a valuable piece of self-analysis. Reed observes that, once in employment, many people know what they don't like about their job, but few take the time to assess what they are good at and enjoy. Honesty is important if you want to paint an accurate picture of where your future lies, so it is useful to get a close friend to help you complete this task. Of course, your close friend may not be quite so close after this brutally honest sharing experience.

On the positive side, under strengths, you might list qualities like dependability, loyalty and intelligence. OK, so you sound like a sheepdog so far, but add 'ability with numbers' and this pushes you into the primate zone. 'Opportunities' might include your contacts with people in the City who could help you with your career generally or even provide a job opportunity. It might also include access to further education – for example, the chance to do a higher degree or MBA.

On the negative side of the equation you might list weaknesses such as poor exam passes, laziness, bad communication skills. The 'threats' could include members of the family who rubbish your efforts or perhaps your tendency to take on too much. While it may be painful to identify these features, it could save you from accepting a job you can do in theory but in practice would be uncomfortable in because you do not fit the company's work ethic. Some of these features could be overcome – for example, if you are shy you might consider a course in making presentations, public speaking or even joining a drama class.

Knowledge is power

Before you start applying to City employers it is vital to have a good grasp of what goes on in the City as a whole. Part 2 provides a basic grounding in finance and details of some of the most historic and best-known institutions, including the Bank of England (see page 64), the Stock Exchange (see page 57), and Lloyd's of London (see page 70). You will also find a basic guide to the main City professions, such as law, accounting and investment banking.

Essential reading

It is very important to keep up to date with City events. A good basic week's reading would include the *Financial Times* (Monday to Saturday) and, for those who need to build up their knowledge on individual shares and companies, the *Investors Chronicle* (a weekly publication from the *FT* stable available from most newsagents). Check with the relevant professional body for your chosen career path (see Chapter 6) and subscribe to its publications. For example, aspiring lawyers should read the *Law Gazette*, while those planning a career as an actuary should read *The Actuary*. In Chapter 6 we list all the professional bodies and most of the specialist publications.

You also need a good grasp of financial statistics in the press. *The Financial Times Guide to Using the Financial Press* by Romesh Vaitilingham (Financial Times Prentice Hall) is a good bet, but you will find other similar guides in the business section of a large bookshop.

Keep files on companies

Keep press cuttings on City organisations and remember which ones are under financial pressure or making redundancies, for example. These cuttings will enable you to ask appropriate questions if you get an interview and help you to steer clear of companies that are in some sort of financial difficulty. For example, is the company the subject of takeover speculation? Has it recently been involved in a major flotation or legal case? Has there been any speculation about key personnel defecting to a rival?

YOUR TYPE OF COMPANY

Check who specialises in your chosen field

With the rise of the global consultancy it is easy to get the impression that every firm offers every service. This is not true, despite what these organisations say. If your particular interest is, say, IT consultancy, find out what proportion of the firm's overall work is dedicated to this line of business and examine the client list. This will give you a good idea of whether the firm is a serious player or a wannabe. Don't write off the wannabes but do make sure the company is putting enough resources into the new business area and not just offering the services as add-ons because they need to be seen to be a one-stop shop for global clients.

Big isn't necessarily best

Not everyone is suited to working for the big corporation. While it is true that the graduate training at some of the major professional services firms and investment banks is first-class and the money is about as good as it gets in the City, do not dismiss the smaller firms. They may be able to offer much more varied on-the-job training and a more relaxed atmosphere.

Timing

If you are starting your last year at university, make sure you understand the City's recruitment year. Many investment banks and large consultancies offer graduates jobs on an annual basis and close applications in December for jobs starting the following summer or autumn. Some will offer internships during the summer for students who have just finished their penultimate year (see Chapter 3). This is a chance to spend a few weeks during the summer working with the institution of your choice to find out if it would be a mutually satisfactory arrangement.

THE APPLICATION AND INTERVIEW

Interview training

If you want to improve your chances of success, get some training for interviews. Recruitment agencies that specialise in graduate placements should offer some help, or you could go to a specialist, like professional services firm Ernst & Young, which offers a two-day residential skills course. Minimum academic criteria: 22 UCAS points (excluding General Studies) and a predicted degree of 2:2 (any discipline). Phone the E&Y graduate recruitment team on 0800 289 208.

Recruitment consultancies

These can be particularly helpful if you are a graduate looking for your first job. What these consultants offer that you can't pick up from individual employers' websites is competitor analysis and a good explanation of the different career patterns.

Avoid multiple applications through agencies

Ask the recruitment consultancy to explain its policy on submitting your CV or details to a prospective employer. The Recruitment & Employment Confederation (REC) stresses that you should allow only the consultancy that first contacts you about a specific vacancy to act on your behalf. Multiple submissions by different agencies can confuse and irritate potential employers – they do not multiply your chances of success (particularly if you have told different stories to different agencies).

Zoology graduates may apply

Don't assume that you need a maths or economics degree to get a job in an investment bank or that you have to go to Oxford or Cambridge. Apart from instances where a specific mathematical bent is required, employers are more likely to be looking at the quality of your degree and your personality fit rather than the particular subject.

Don't waste time

Competition for top jobs is intense, so don't go chasing corporate finance careers that demand first-class degrees if you reckon you'll be lucky to scrape a 2:2. Upper seconds are about the minimum requirement for most of the investment banks and big consultancies. It is also useful if you have had a placement or internship with the organisation. If you are not going to make a 2:1, think about other companies that will accept your expected qualification and ask the recruitment agencies for advice. Remember, though, employers don't want to hear your views on being a late developer or about that little drugs problem that blighted your finals.

Understand the different job functions

As we stressed in the introduction, each organisation has its 'unique selling points'. You need to find out about these before you apply for a job, and certainly before you attend an interview. Browse the company's website and memorise what services or products the company offers that it believes set it apart from its competitors. Even where you are applying for a graduate trainee post, your prospective employer will expect you to have done your homework in order to be able to identify the different functions within the organisation, and to have thought about which jobs would best suit you and why. The more you know about the company at the interview, the better your chances.

Look at the people

Graduates often say that the training offered by top professional services firms and investment banks begins to look the same after you've seen two or three. If you are likely to get offered more than one place on a graduate training scheme, then take a really hard look at the business environment and culture. Think about whether you could see yourself being happy there. Look at the way they dress, how formal or relaxed they are, and how much of your valuable free time will be taken up with company events.

Networking

If you know people in the City, ask them for help. Some universities offer immediate access to an old boys' (and girls') network, but if you don't have a ready-made contact list, then use any existing contacts, even if they seem a bit tenuous. Be polite, respectful and clear about the help you are seeking and you will find that most people will be flattered you asked.

Social events during interview processes

Don't be fooled by the champagne and smiling faces – the social events are as important as the formal tests. In the City it's the people who make an institution fly, and your ability to fit in is critical to your success. This is particularly true if you are going to work at the sharp end, for example in corporate finance, where you will meet existing and prospective clients on a daily basis.

Try to remember names and faces and make an effort to get to know people. Most companies thrive on this type of networking, and this will always impress an employer if you are invited back to the second interview.

FURTHER INFORMATION

● For more on SWOT test analysis go to the Reed website at www.reed.co.uk

5
INTERVIEW TIPS AND DRESS CODE

When that interview for your ideal job comes along, don't treat it like a dress rehearsal. Take time to consider your interview technique and your dress code.

The following tips are drawn mainly from the Recruitment & Employment Confederation (REC) leaflet on interview techniques (see Sources on page 33 and also Chapter 4).

PREPARATION

● Research the subject matter using current press and website information.

● Ensure you have a good understanding of the company and the markets in which it operates. The company's website and latest annual report are essential reading.

● Think about possible questions you might be asked and your response to them.

● Prepare questions to ask the interviewer (see below).

● Think about your skills, qualifications and experience and make sure you can talk confidently about what is written on your CV.

● At the first interview it would be wise to restrict your questions to the details of the job and the organisation. Salary and benefit discussions are best left for a second interview or until a job offer is made.

● Plan your journey beforehand to ensure you arrive a few minutes early. Allow for possible travel delays (the Central Line is notorious – but any part of the Underground can grind to a halt at the drop of a hat). Just in case of a major hold-up, make sure you have your contact's telephone number so that you can call if you think you will be late.

TOP TIPS FOR INTERVIEWS

● Practise a strong, positive handshake and plan your greeting. Eye contact is important but don't overdo it or you'll scare the hell out of them.

● Remember to smile and be polite to all the staff you meet, including those at the recruitment consultancy, if applicable. They are an important link in the recruitment process and may influence a decision in your favour.

● Unless you feel particularly comfortable, do not accept tea or coffee at the interview as it can distract your train of thought – and get knocked over.

● If you are taking papers to the interview, carry them in a suitable case or folder.

● Try not to monopolise the meeting – let your interviewer talk.

● Be clear about your reasons for this choice of career.

● After the interview make sure you know exactly what the next steps will be, such as who will contact you to let you know if you have been successful and by when. You should also find out whether there will be second interviews and who will conduct them.

FREQUENTLY ASKED QUESTIONS

The interviewer will ask you if you have any questions. One of the best we came across was:

● How does the job contribute to the success, efficiency and profitability of the organisation?

Here are a few more drawn from Schroders' website.

● Who are your direct competitors?
● What can you offer me in terms of career progression?
● How soon can I gain real responsibility?
● Can I choose which business area I am allocated to?
● Is it possible to change between departments?
● What are the opportunities for travel?
● What is the starting salary and how quickly will it increase?
● Salary aside, what benefits does the company offer?

A–Z OF KEY SKILLS AND CHARACTERISTICS

Personal skills are extremely important for City employees, so it is helpful to know what employers are looking for and to understand that 'assertiveness', for example, is best demonstrated in a low-key manner

and should never be confused with abrasiveness. The following descriptions of important personal skills were drawn from the consultant Towers Perrin's website.

● **Assertiveness**
The ability to express yourself, your own wants, needs, concerns, feelings and opinions, in a direct, honest, appropriate way, and to stand up for yourself, your own rights and interests in ways that do not violate the rights and interests of others.

● **Business acumen**
The ability to apply understanding of business economics, the employer's client markets and lines of business to your own work.

● **Influence**
The ability to develop and use effective strategies to get others to take particular actions or to support your ideas.

● **Initiative**
Acting to ensure your goals are accomplished.

● **Integrity**
Being honest and trustworthy; acting to protect the rights and legitimate concerns of others.

● **Interpersonal awareness**
The ability to notice, interpret and anticipate others' concerns and feelings, and to communicate this awareness.

● **Learning orientation**
A tendency to seek out experiences, however difficult, tedious or uncomfortable, that will enhance skills and knowledge.

● **Listening**
The ability to focus full attention on a

speaker and to convey through your posture, tone and response that you have heard and appreciated both the content of the speaker's message and the speaker's associated feelings.

● **Openness to change**

A positive attitude towards new experiences, assignments and approaches; a willingness to move out of your comfort zone and try something new.

● **Oral communication**

The ability to express ideas clearly and convey information effectively when speaking to others.

● **Organising**

The ability to plan, schedule and co-ordinate work activities.

● **Persistence**

A willingness to keep trying to achieve a goal when a task is difficult, time-consuming or unpleasant.

● **Problem solving**

The ability to solve problems effectively, by:

→ Identifying the information needed to clarify the problem

→ Asking questions and gathering information

→ Analysing the information to diagnose the problem

→ Generating possible solutions, and

→ Comparing their merits in order to select one solution for implementation

● **Service orientation**

A concern for work that helps others or fulfils their business needs.

● **Teamwork**

The ability and desire to work co-operatively with others as part of a team and to contribute to the team's success.

Written communication

The ability to write clearly and concisely, using grammar and style appropriate for business letters and reports.

DRESSING UP AND DRESSING DOWN

Actually, we assume you know by now how to dress for an interview. Boys – best suit, dark everything except the shirt, and go for the most boring tie you can find. Girls – stick to suits with a knee-length skirt or possibly an inch or two above. Absolutely NO CLEAVAGE. Flattish shoes. Basically go for expensive but nun-like and you won't go wrong even if you are up against (no, we don't mean literally) some of the last bastions of male supremacy. Don't wear too much perfume and keep make-up, jewellery and nail polish simple.

Dressing down is far more problematic. The introduction of casual dress days for accountants and investment bankers has led to a huge increase in work for the style police. The practice was introduced when the economy was booming and the investment banks got nervous. For some reason they assumed that if they changed the dress code it would stop their bright young employees dashing off to the dot.com start-ups.

As the economy started to slow in 2000 the fashion police noticed that some employers were less enthusiastic about casual dress, although most that introduced the new code have stuck with it. Deutsche Bank has extended its dress down policy indefinitely but, as the *Financial Times* observed, 'It is, however, insisting that bankers tuck in their shirts – a worrying sign of things to come perhaps.' (*FT*, 30 December 2000).

The Vault.com website reported on a fashion show in New York put on by Saks Fifth Avenue and – wait for it – J. P. Morgan and Salomon Smith Barney, two of the biggest global investment banks. In front of about 150 of their colleagues, seven investment bankers and traders paraded up and down in Saks' version of business casual, wearing exquisitely cut sports jackets and $325 sweaters.

'Casual days in the office don't mean dressing down,' says Scott Omelianuk, the executive editor of *Esquire*. 'Dressing down is something you do when you clean the garage or work in the garden.' So, if you want to dress down for work, what you do is dress just a little less formally. Not sloppily and definitely not cheaply. For élite law firms and investment banks, the last industries in New York to adopt casual dress codes, Omelianuk says, 'You want to make sure the material of the clothing you're wearing is of the quality it was when you wore a suit. If you are a powerful man, you still want to suggest power and that means cashmere and flannel and all of those things.'

Judging by the Q&A sessions the style police have had with employees of major investment institutions, there's still a lot of confusion about the appropriateness of open-toed sandals and bright toenail polish for women, while men want to know if it's OK to wear loafers without socks.

Is all this important? you might ask.

Unfortunately, yes it is. Besides creating embarrassing situations, if you dress inappropriately it can be a career-stopper. While an underdressed man might run the risk of being labelled 'slovenly', for women it's far worse. Show too much cleavage, wear a short skirt or go for bright red nail polish and the label is likely to be 'cheap' or even 'available'.

'When somebody doesn't apply what is expected to be sensible judgement about how far they should go with dress, that affects senior management's perceptions of that person's overall judgement,' says Laurie Murphy, a Vault.com employee relations consultant.

And while most experts say it's better to overdress than underdress, don't show up your boss. If he's wearing an open-collared sports shirt to a meeting you might discreetly take off your tie – or just ask.

SOURCES FOR THIS CHAPTER
● Schroders is at www.schroders.com
● Towers Perrin: www.towers.com
● Recruitment & Employment Confederation (REC): www.rec.uk.com
● The Vault.com website is at www.vault.com

6
MEDIA, RECRUITMENT AND CITY WEBSITES

As you carry out your own research you will build up a list of useful contacts for your chosen career. This chapter is by no means comprehensive but contains the most useful websites we came across in the course of researching this book. Use the employer and recruitment agency websites in conjunction with sites for the relevant professional bodies. These provide a wealth of useful information for aspiring professionals.

READING MATTERS

We can't stress too strongly how important it is to keep up with financial events and news specific to the industry in which you wish to work. The *Financial Times* and the City pages of other quality nationals are a must. You might also read the *Wall Street Journal* and *The Economist* before your interviews. Check out the trade and professional bodies below and find out if they publish members' journals, and ask which other publications are relevant. Get sample copies and subscribe where necessary. It's a good idea to pay a visit once a week to a large public library to keep up with all the specialist press.

The financial press is also an important source of job information. Use a media directory like the Association of British Insurers' Media Contact Directory. For details, go to the ABI website at www.abi.org.uk. The advantage of the ABI guide is that it covers all the specialist press.

For the general press and access to newspapers' careers information, try the Media UK Internet Directory at www.mediauk.com/directory, which has links to all the main press, TV and broadcasting organisations.

Don't neglect current affairs. Interviewers are looking for people with well-rounded views. It's no good trying to impress an employer with your knowledge of currency derivatives if you haven't noticed the outbreak of World War III.

Here are just some of the websites you will find helpful.

NATIONALS
- Financial Times www.ft.com
- Daily Mail www.mail.co.uk
- Daily Telegraph www.telegraph.co.uk
- Evening Standard www.standard.co.uk
- Express www.expressnewspapers.co.uk
- Financial Mail on Sunday www.financialmail.co.uk
- Financial News www.financialnews.co.uk
- Guardian www.guardian.co.uk
- Independent www.independent.co.uk
- International Herald Tribune www.iht.com
- Mirror www.mirror.co.uk
- Money Observer www.moneyobserver.com
- Observer www.observer.co.uk

- Scotsman (City) www.scotsman.com
- Sunday Business
www.sundaybusiness.co.uk
- Sunday Express
www.expressnewspapers.co.uk
- Sunday Mirror
www.sundaymirror.co.uk
- Sunday Post (City)
www.sundaypost.com
- Sunday Telegraph
www.telegraph.co.uk
- Sunday Times
www.sunday-times.co.uk
- The Times www.the-times.co.uk
- Wall Street Journal www.wsj.com

TRADE/SPECIALIST TITLES

- The Actuary (no website but phone 020 7311 5075)
- Accountancy
www.accountancymag.co.uk
- Accountancy Age
www.accountancyage.com
- The Banker www.thebanker.com
- Banking Technology
www.bankingtech.com
- The Broker www.biba.org.uk
- The Economist
www.economist.com
- Employee Benefits
www.centaur.co.uk
- Euromoney www.euromoney.com
- Financial Adviser www.ftadviser.com
- Global Insurance Bulletin
www.rirg.com
- Insurance Age www.insuranceage.com
- Insurance Day
www.insuranceday.com
- Insurance Times
www.insurancetimes.co.uk
- Insurance Today
www.perspective-publishing.co.uk
- Investment Week www.invweek.co.uk

- The Lawyer www.the-lawyer.co.uk
- Lloyd's List www.llplimited.com
- Marketing Week www.mad.co.uk
- Money Marketing
www.moneymarketing.co.uk
- Pensions World
www.pensionsworld.co.uk
- Planned Savings
www.plannedsavings.com
- Professional Pensions
www.thepensionsite.co.uk

ON-LINE PUBLICATIONS/ INFORMATION SERVICES

- FT Your Money
www.ftyourmoney.com
- Bloomberg www.bloomberg.co.uk
- Dow Jones Newswires
www.dowjones.com
- Reuters www.reuters.com

CONSUMER PUBLICATIONS

- Bloomberg Money
www.bloomberg.co.uk
- Investors Chronicle
www.investorschronicle.co.uk
- Moneywise www.moneywise.co.uk
- What Mortgage
www.personalfinancenet.com
- Which www.which.net

TELEVISION AND RADIO

- BBC programmes www.bbc.co.uk
and www.bbc.co.uk/news
- Bloomberg Television
www.bloomberg.com
- Business World Tonight
www.newsdirect.co.uk
- Channel 4 News
www.channel4news.co.uk
- Channel 5 News www.channel5.co.uk
- The Money Channel
www.themoneychannel.co.uk

SPECIALIST GRADUATE RECRUITMENT

There are several organisations that focus on graduate careers. Three excellent services are offered by Prospects, GTI and the Higher Education Careers Services. If you are limited for time you need go no further than these.

Prospects Directory is an annual publication listing 1,900 graduate recruiting organisations with details of their websites. The address is www.prospects.csu.man.ac.uk. If you are at university, go to the graduate section of the websites for information about graduate trainee courses.

www.doctorjob.com is a first-class website run by GTI Specialist Publishers. GTI was set up in 1988 by three students from Reading University who spotted the gap in the graduate recruitment market. The company publishes a range of guides, including the best thing since sliced bread, *Target: City & Finance*, which you can order through the website.

A very helpful series of guides to graduate recruitment is produced by the Association of Graduate Careers Advisory Services (AGCAS) and published by the Higher Education Careers Services Unit. The guides are available through careers offices, but if you have trouble finding them contact CSU Ltd, Prospects House, Booth Street East, Manchester M13 9EP. **TEL** 0161 277 5240.

RECRUITMENT CONSULTANTS

Employer websites are a valuable source of information about a company and its graduate recruitment programme, but you should use them in conjunction with a recruitment agency that specialises in your area of knowledge or in City placements. A good agency will be able to explain what it is like on the inside of competing organisations – something you can't tell from the employer websites.

The Recruitment & Employment Confederation (REC) is the profess-ional association for this area and has 7,750 individual members and 6,000 corporate members. Its website provides useful information about CVs and job interviews, and also lets you search for agencies by location and specialisation. The REC is at www.rec.uk.com

There are hundreds of recruitment agencies in the UK, but the ones you want to find are those that specialise in City jobs. Read the nationals, the financial press and the specialist titles published by the trade and professional bodies (see above and below) to find out which agencies cover your area. The major agencies have very helpful websites with links to the sites of individual employers. Three tried and tested sites we liked in particular are:

● Michael Page City
www.michaelpage.net
● Reed www.reed.co.uk
● TMP Harrison Willis
www.monster.co.uk

TEMPORARY WORK

We cover temporary work in Chapter 3, but briefly it is worth remembering that this is not a second-class subculture but is used by many bright graduates as a way of finding out about the working environment in different organisations before signing up. The major City recruitment agencies will help you find suitable temporary or contract employment.

EMPLOYER WEBSITES

A word of warning: employers' websites vary considerably both in terms of the amount of information they provide and in the way the material is presented. Some of the best sites are provided by the investment banks, and you can access these through the Doctorjob and Prospects sites mentioned above. Insurance companies, by contrast, put up a pretty poor show, while some of the American law firms and management consultancies we examined were wordy and obtuse. All these sites are worth a visit, but you may have to sift through the pages to find out what you need to know.

If you are looking for a good guide to the financial markets and financial products then Reuters is well worth a visit (www.reuters.com). We also liked the financial glossary on UBS Warburg's site (www.ubswarburg.com).

WHINGE WEBSITES

If you get bored reading the same old 'good guys' stuff on employers' sites there are a couple of insider sites worth a glance. www.vault.com actually advertises a lot of good jobs and is pretty respectable as far as whinge sites go, and it does include message boards on just about every company you have ever heard of. The content is edited, but you can find out

who is saying what about whom and how much so-and-so got as a Christmas bonus. You can also ask questions and hope that a helpful or perhaps demoralised worker will come to your aid.

Less respectable is www. netslaves.com, which covers horror stories about working in technology. (Be warned – if, like us, you make the mistake of typing in 'slaves' without the prefix 'net', you will find yourself in a pornography site.)

We have no comment to make about www.fu**edcompany.com (our asterisks), but merely bring its presence on the Web to your attention ...

WOMEN IN THE CITY

'Opportunity Now' is the business-to-business campaign launched in 1991 to increase the participation of women in the City workforce. Visit www.opportunitynow.org.uk.

The following organisations are major City employers and also belong to the 'Women in investment banking' initiative – a group of employers who have joined forces to eradicate the less pleasant aspects of the traditionally male environment that still prevails in certain quarters.

- Barclays Capital www.barcap.com
- Chase Manhattan Bank www.chase.com
- Credit Suisse First Boston www.csfb.com
- Deutsche Bank www.db.com
- Dresdner Kleinwort Benson www.dresdnerkb.com
- Goldman Sachs International

www.gs.com
● HSBC Investment Bank
www.hsbc.com
● J.P. Morgan www.jpmorgan.com
● Lehman Brothers www.lehman.com
● London Business School
www.london.edu
● Merrill Lynch Europe www.ml.com
● Morgan Stanley Dean Witter
www.msdw.com
● N. M. Rothschild
www.nmrothschild.com
● Reuters Ltd www.reuters.com
● Schroder Salomon Smith Barney
www.smithbarney.com
● Schroders www.schroders.com
● UBS Warburg www.ubswarburg.com

Another useful site is:
● Women in Science and Engineering
at www.wisecampaign.org.uk

THE FINANCIAL REGULATORS

It is important to understand how the
City is regulated. Many jobs require
you to pass regulatory exams if you
give advice to individuals or
corporations. The Financial Services
Authority (FSA) is the main regulator
and most others either already fall
under its aegis or will do so in due
course (see Chapter 17).

● Financial Services Authority and
the Personal Investment Authority
(PIA) are at www.fsa.gov.uk
● Investment Managers Regulatory
Organisation (IMRO) www.imro.co.uk
● Securities and Futures Authority
(SFA) www.sfa.org.uk
● Securities Institute www.securities-
institute.org.uk

PROFESSIONAL BODIES AND TRADE ASSOCIATIONS

Apart from useful details about the
profession itself, many of these
organisations are the examiners for
their field and their websites provide
details of the financial qualifications
you may study for in your chosen
career.

● Association of British Insurers
www.abi.org.uk
● Association of Chartered Certified
Accountants www.acca.org.uk
● Association of Corporate Treasurers
www.corporate-treasurers.co.uk
● The Association of Insurance and
Risk Managers in Industry and
Commerce (AIRMIC)
www.airmic.co.uk
● Association of Investment Trust
Companies (AITC) www.aitc.co.uk
● Association of Private Client
Investment Managers and
Stockbrokers (APCIMS)
www.apcims.co.uk
● Association of MBAs
www.mba.org.uk
● Association of Taxation Technicians
www.tax.org.uk
● Association of Unit Trusts and
Investment Funds (AUTIF)
www.investmentfunds.org.uk
● British Bankers Association
www.bba.org.uk
● British Insurance Brokers
Association (BIBA) www.biba.org.uk
● Building Societies Association
www.bsa.org.uk
● Chartered Institute of Insurance
www.cii.co.uk
● Chartered Institute of Bankers
www.cib.org.uk

● Chartered Institute of Management Accountants www.cima.org.uk
● Chartered Institute of Public Finance Accountancy www.cipfa.org.uk
● Chartered Institute of Taxation www.tax.org.uk
● Consumers Association www.which.net
● Council of Mortgage Lenders www.cml.org.uk
● Faculty and Institute of Actuaries www.actuaries.org.uk
● Federation of Recruitment and Employment Services www.fres.co.uk
● Institute of Actuaries www.actuaries.org.uk
● Institute of Chartered Accountants in England and Wales www.icaew.co.uk
● Institute of Chartered Accountants in Ireland www.icai.ie
● Institute of Chartered Accountants of Scotland www.icas.org.uk
● Institute of Chartered Secretaries and Administrators www.icsa.org.uk
● Institute of Directors www.iod.co.uk
● Institute of Management Consultancy www.consult@imc.co.uk
● Institute of Investment Management and Research www.iimr.org.uk
● Institute of Personnel and Development www.ipd.co.uk
● Institute for Public Policy Research www.ippr.org.uk
● International Underwriting Association of London www.iua.co.uk
● Law Society www.lawsociety.org.uk
● London Bullion Market Association www.lbma.org.uk
● London Investment Banking Association www.liba.org.uk
● National Association of Pension Funds (NAPF) www.napf.co.uk
● Pensions Management Institute www.pensions-pmi.org.uk
● Royal Institution of Chartered Surveyors www.rics.org.uk
● UK Society of Investment Professionals www.uksip.org

THE MAIN CITY INSTITUTIONS

If you want to find out more about how the City ticks, visit these websites, some of which also have details about graduate training schemes.

● The Baltic Exchange www.balticexchange.com
● The Bank of England www.bankofengland.co.uk
● Corporation of London www.cityoflondon.gov.uk
● The International Petroleum Exchange www.ipe.uk.com
● London International Financial Futures Exchange www.liffe.com
● Lloyd's of London www.lloydsoflondon.co.uk
● London Clearing House www.lch.co.uk
● The London Metal Exchange www.lme.co.uk
● The London Stock Exchange www.londonstockex.co.uk
● London Securities and Derivatives Exchange www.omgroup.com
● London Underwriting Centre www.luc.co.uk

7
CITY SALARIES

So, you're after a big salary? Fine, but when you consider your pay packet it is important to look at salary *progression*, not just the starting point. The top-of-the-range packages tend to be offered to graduates who join major financial institutions in the areas of corporate finance, equities, fixed income, treasury and IT. Here you could be looking at a starting salary of anything up to £35,000 in very exceptional cases, although most organisations are likely to pay in the £25,000–£28,000 range. For more details on your prospective salary, look up the relevant job title in Part 3.

An increasing number of employers also offer a 'sign-on' or bonus for joining (often referred to as a golden hello). The bonuses vary from £3,000 to £10,000, and we found several in the £5,000–£6,500 zone. These are usually paid just before you start work or, as in the case of the £10,000 offered by Accenture in 2000, may be staggered over the first two years. Some employers do not pay a sign-on but may provide an interest-free loan to help you clear your student debt.

LOOK BEYOND THE HEADLINE FIGURES

While the opportunity to wipe the student debt slate clean is very attractive, clearly there is more to your first career step than the headline figures. An American investment banker has these words of advice to offer: 'Make sure you join an organisation that has the right business culture for your personality and offers good training and career progression. When it comes to money, it is important for graduates to consider the salary, annual bonus and benefits package as a whole rather than just the sign-on.'

So, make sure you receive a good benefits package in addition to the headline figures. As we explain below, the annual bonus, share scheme and pension plan could add another 30 per cent of base salary to your total remuneration. The value of these features increases with the number of years you work for and, in the case of the annual bonus, succeed for your employer.

WILL YOU GET A GOLDEN HELLO?

The US investment houses are the biggest recruiters of top graduates, and also tend to have the deepest pockets. Most of these organisations have had a sign-on policy for some time but have kept very quiet about it.

In 2000, however, the recruitment gloves came off and golden hellos became an important weapon in what one top investment banker described as 'an incredible war for talent'. Arguably it was Accenture, the information technology and management consultancy, that started the sign-on battle. In addition to a starting salary of £28,000, in 2000 Accenture's graduates were offered a £10,000 bonus: £6,000 on joining and £4,000 in their second year.

OVERTIME

Unusually, Accenture also pays overtime for hours worked in excess of the standard 7-hour day. Overtime for graduate trainees in City jobs is conservatively estimated at between 15 and 20 per cent of standard hours, so do take this into consideration.

A recruitment manager for a major consultancy comments, 'The salary should reflect the hours you work. Employees in some organisations work significantly less overtime than at other institutions. A good average to assume is ten to twelve per cent of the usual nine-to-five-thirty week.'

YOUR COMMITMENT

The high-value City benefits package may sound overly generous for an inexperienced 21-year-old, but these financial giants are pretty picky. A recruitment manager for an investment bank says, 'Despite the increasing number of graduates emerging from our universities there are very few who have the right qualifications, skills and attributes.'

We asked what these major employers are after. Typical comments were:

● 'We are looking for far more than just academic excellence.'
● 'We need graduates who have a hunger for learning and who are open to new concepts.'
● 'We don't just want people who have an urge to win – we want the actual winners.'

● 'Obviously they need to be highly numerate in every part of the business and have first-class analytical skills.'
● 'They should be confident in their ability while recognising that they still have everything to learn about our business.'
● 'We want graduates who are able to demonstrate an entrepreneurial flair which they can use within a global corporate environment.'

In other words, if you want a fantastic salary you've got to be a pretty fantastic person!

EMPLOYEE BENEFITS

Most jobs in the banking sector advertise 'banking benefits'. These are likely to comprise a core benefits package and a flexible benefits allowance equal to about 6.5 per cent of salary.

For example, at the Bank of England everyone has equal access to the same core benefits, irrespective of length of service, status or location. These are:

● Membership of the Bank of England Pension Fund
● 25 days' annual leave
● Life assurance of 2x annual salary
● Private medical insurance
● Interest-free season ticket loan

In addition you can take a combination of extra cash/benefits/days leave.

Investment banks also pay a discretionary annual performance-related bonus – typically 10–20 per cent of salary but in some cases a lot more.

In addition to the benefits quoted above you should also get:

● Income protection (which pays your salary if you are too ill to work)
● An employee stock purchase plan

Other benefits may include free use of the company gym and an employee support service (a confidential helpline). An increasing number of employers offer the option to buy other benefits at preferential rates – for example, dental insurance and additional medical cover for your family.

CHANGING JOBS

If you have already worked out your first year or two and are seeking a change, it is particularly important to pay attention to the non-cash benefits. It is easy to compare salaries, but after reading this chapter you will know that this is only part of the story. How are you going to feel if you find out too late that by moving on you have decimated the value of your pension or lost a lucrative stock option?

'The City in particular is totally cash-based and many people do not appreciate the monetary value of other forms of benefit,' says a recruitment consultant. Once you get into a senior position, stock options can be worth 50–100 per cent of your annual salary.

We asked a recruitment consultant which aspects of the package are negotiable if you are changing jobs. 'The share option scheme rules usually are set in stone but you may be able to negotiate entry terms and receive compensation for the embedded value

of the option in your existing scheme. As for the annual bonus, it may be possible to negotiate a guaranteed amount in your first year.'

EXPENSES

These days even the more flamboyant City organisations are run by professional managers keen to hone costs and keep business expenses under better control. Fat expense accounts are largely a thing of the past for two reasons. First, organisations recognise that they tend to damage the respect and integrity of senior management in the eyes of their workforce. Second, the Inland Revenue keeps a very watchful eye on the grey area between expenses, which are not taxed, and benefits in kind, the value of which may be liable to tax and/or national insurance.

As a result most large companies have a prescriptive and detailed policy on expenses. Behind the scenes they may permit their very senior and indispensable people to fly first class and stay in five-star hotels but, as one fund manager puts it, 'Sadly the days of lavish entertainment budgets are over.'

According to an adviser on pay and employment conditions at the Institute of Personnel and Development, 'Many City companies provide corporate credit cards, but usually only after you have completed your probationary period.' Where cards are issued, companies will police their use and have a policy for dealing with those who abuse the system, he adds. In most cases the card must be reserved for business use only, but some companies let you make private purchases and then send you the bill at a later date.

Although travel expenses wouldn't normally come up at interview, one recruitment consultant suggests that, if you expect to travel extensively in your job, you should find out the expenses policy operated by your prospective employer. 'The availability of business class, as opposed to economy, can make all the difference on those long flights, as does the standard of accommodation,' he says.

The other big factor to check is relocation expenses if your company is changing location or your new job entails a house move. The Inland Revenue allows you to receive up to £8,000 in removal expenses tax free, provided you meet certain criteria. This can be used towards the cost of buying and selling your home, moving your possessions, temporary travel and accommodation, and preliminary family visits to the new location.

If your job takes you overseas the expenses should be considered in more detail. You should, for example, find out if you qualify for 'rest and relaxation' benefits if you are sent to a dry state. A realistic and sympathetic employer will pay to transport you to a more relaxing environment at regular intervals so the heat and parched throat do not reduce your efficiency or force you to terminate the secondment.

GRADUATE SALARIES IN INVESTMENT BANKING

● Front office: £30,000–£35,000, possible sign-on and performance-related bonus.

Example position: corporate finance.
● Corporate banking: £30,000, possible sign-on and performance-related bonus.
● Finance: £25,000–£28,000 plus discretionary bonus. Training and study leave to become qualified. Example position: accountant.
● Operations and settlement: £25,000–£28,000 plus performance-related bonus. Example position: support functions, HR, IT (known as 'back office').
● Risk management: £25,000–£40,000 (PhD required at the top end for the more quantitative roles). Example position: analyst.

Note: Positions usually include a pension, life assurance and medical insurance plus other benefits.
Source: Michael Page
(www.michaelpage.net)

TOP TIPS FOR THE NEGOTIATING TABLE

● Check the contract terms. Many companies only offer a twelve-month rolling contract.
● Find out the £ value of the benefits offered. Straight cash is not always best.
● Is there a stock option?
● How is the annual bonus calculated? Check the level of discretionary bonuses in recent years. Can you get a guarantee for the first year?
● Does the job involve overseas assignments and if so will you be compensated in full for changes in the standard of living?

YOUR BENEFITS SHOPPING LIST

Essentials

● PENSION: A traditional scheme aims to provide a tax-free cash lump sum and up to two-thirds of final salary as a retirement income. A spouse's pension is also paid if you die. Employees tend to contribute about 5–6 per cent of salary, while employers contribute on your behalf a further 10–12 per cent. Your contributions benefit from full tax relief.

● LIFE ASSURANCE: This is a tax-free cash lump sum, which is paid to your dependants if you die. The maximum permitted by the Inland Revenue is four times annual salary. Most employers pay two or three times salary.

● DISABILITY INSURANCE: Aka permanent health insurance (PHI), this pays a replacement income for as long as necessary, even up to retirement if you are too ill to return to work. Two-thirds of salary is typical, index-linked. Alternatively the pension scheme may award you an ill-health pension.

● COMPANY CAR: The employer typically covers the purchase price, insurance, repairs and running costs. In some cases your employer might also pay for petrol for private use. The annual value might be anything from £10,000 to £20,000. Note, however, the car is not an automatic feature of City jobs where business use of a car is not a requirement.

The big extras

● ANNUAL BONUS: This can be anything from 15 to 20 per cent of salary, rising to 100 per cent for senior people in financial institutions.

● SHARE SCHEMES: There are several ways in which your employer can offer you the opportunity to buy shares in the company at lower than market value. You may be able to avoid income tax on what is effectively a benefit in kind (the difference between the reduced price and the market price is regarded as a type of payment from your employer) if the offer is part of an Inland Revenue-approved share option scheme.

● STOCK OPTIONS: This is a type of golden handcuff for the long-term dedicated senior manager and is a feature of dot.coms. The terms can be magnificent, but only if you are committed to staying put. Depending on market conditions and the company's progress, a three-year option is likely to add about 50–100 per cent to your annual salary – more for very senior people.

8
WORK-BASED QUALIFICATIONS FOR THE CITY

If you thought your exams were over after your finals, then think again. Almost without exception, jobs for graduates in the City are conditional on you continuing your studies and taking further exams.

The subjects you study and the exams you take will be dictated by the type of job you go for, but the exams will fall into two broad categories: regulatory requirements and continued professional development.

Regulation was mentioned briefly in Chapter 6 and is also the subject of Chapter 17. To work in many positions in the City – particularly where you are giving financial advice to individuals or corporate bodies and trustees – you will have to study for examinations set by the financial services regulator, the Financial Services Authority (FSA).

In most cases you will also be offered the opportunity – or be required – to study for professional qualifications, whether in the field of investment management, accountancy, the law or as an actuary. In some cases this professional study also meets the regulator's requirement.

Clearly, it is very important to establish at your interviews which exams are essential and which are options offered for your own professional development. Equally importantly, you should ask how much study time you will be given and what training your employer provides on the job. A good employer will cover most of your costs in terms of examination fees and external courses.

There are several City regulators – the Securities and Futures Authority (SFA), the Investment Management Regulatory Organisation (IMRO) and the Personal Investment Authority (PIA). As we explained in Chapter 6, these are all being drawn together under the Financial Services Authority (FSA). For the websites, see page 38.

Each of the professional bodies – for example, the Chartered Institute of Insurance (CII), the Chartered Institute of Accountants (CIA), the Chartered Institute of Bankers and the Law Society (see page 38–39) – runs its own examinations, so it is worth checking their websites for more details.

To give you a broad idea of the importance of these examinations, here we take a look at investment and accountancy.

INVESTMENT-RELATED EXAMINATIONS

This list is not exhaustive, but if you are planning to work in an investment bank or for a retail financial institution you may be required to sit one of the following:

● **The Securities and Futures Authority (SFA)** Registered Persons

Examination (RPE). This is administered by the Securities Institute and covers people within an SFA-registered firm who give investment advice or manage the investments.

● **The Investment Advice Certificate** (IAC) is recognised by IMRO and the PIA and is relevant if you will give investment advice direct to the public, as opposed to companies.

● **The Investment Administration Qualification (IAQ)** is aimed at those involved in settlement and administration – the so-called 'back office' jobs.

● **The Securities Institute Diploma** is a senior investment professional qualification for those in investment banking, stockbroking, fund management, accountancy and law firms, among others.

● **The Institute of Investment Management and Research (IIMR)** offers courses for those who wish to become associates of the Institute. This is particularly relevant for investment analysts and fund managers.

PROFESSIONAL SERVICES (ACCOUNTANCY) EXAMINATIONS

If you work for a professional services firm (or chartered accountant), you would probably study initially for the Association of Taxation Technicians (ATT) exams. The ATT course covers personal taxation, VAT and the principles of law and accounting.

Typically, graduate trainees follow the course full-time for ten weeks during the first year of employment. This allows you to concentrate fully on your studies and gain your qualifications within a year of joining the firm. You may then pursue your studies further, working towards the qualification of Associate of the Chartered Institute of Taxation (ATII). In addition, the major professional services firms would support and provide the funding to help you to study for a wide range of exams. Arthur Andersen provided the following details (for the association and institute websites see Chapter 6):

● **Certified Accountant (ACCA):** The objective of the Foundation in Accounting is to give you a grounding in accounting and related skills. The ACCA is one of the largest professional accountancy bodies in the world and its aim has always been to provide a qualification that is closely linked to the needs of the accountant in the modern business environment. Once you have completed the foundation papers you may elect to complete the qualification.

● **Certified Information Systems Auditor (CISA):** If you join the assurance, risk consulting and technology department at Arthur Andersen you will train for the CISA qualification, which is the globally recognised professional qualification for this field of work. The examination consists of 200 multiple-choice questions administered during a four-hour session, and is set once a year in June.

● **Certified Diploma in Accounting and Finance (CDipAF):** Graduates who join the people, strategy and human resource management team study for the CDipAF. This is a financial management qualification for leading professionals and managers to provide an essential grounding in the financial aspects of business management.

● **Chartered Accountancy qualification (ACA):** If you join assurance, risk consulting or corporate tax consulting, you will study for the ACA qualification. You may also choose to study for this if you join the human capital compensation and equity team. Arthur Andersen says, 'Becoming a chartered accountant is very hard work. You need to pass professional exams combined with relevant work experience. It takes three years to qualify.'

The company offers new graduates the choice of studying for the ACA qualification with either the Institute of Chartered Accountants in England and Wales (ICAEW) or the Institute of Chartered Accountants in Scotland (ICAS). The ICAEW qualification is a three-year programme with two levels, the professional stage and the advanced stage (including an advanced case study). ICAS runs a similar three-year programme. Its examinations comprise three levels: Test of Competence, Test of Professional Skills and Test of Professional Expertise. The latter is a multidisciplinary case study. Both exams provide you with essential knowledge and skills appropriate for work as a business adviser.

● **Financial Planning Certificate:** The Financial Planning Certificate (FPC) is a recognised qualification for financial advisers and requires both a broad general knowledge of financial products and a thorough grounding in regulatory aspects of the financial services industry. (There are other examinations and qualifications for advisers run by the Chartered Insurance Institute – see the website details on page 38.)

The FPC is split into three papers: financial services and their regulation; protection, savings and investment products; and identifying and satisfying client needs. Each paper requires between 40 and 80 hours of study, depending on career experience.

The FPC is accepted by various regulators as evidence of satisfying requirements under the Financial Services Act, and holders are entitled to use the letters FPC after their name. Holders of the FPC can subsequently study for the Advanced Financial Planning Certificate, which leads to professional membership of the Society of Financial Advisers (SOFA) and the designated letters MSFA.

● **MSc Human Resource Consultancy (MScHR):** Graduates in the people strategy and human resource management and the compensation and equity teams can choose to study for the MScHR. The course is run by Southbank University and involves two years of teaching one day a week and four months writing a dissertation. This qualification entitles you to graduate-level entry into the Chartered Institute of Personnel and Development (CIPD).

SOURCES OF INFORMATION

See Chapter 6 for the relevant websites. Arthur Andersen is at www.arthurandersen.com

PART 2
ESSENTIAL
INFORMATION

'Whenever we needed money, we'd rob the airport. To us, it was better than Citibank.'

Goodfellas, 1990

9
EQUITIES AND BONDS –
THE LIFE-BLOOD OF THE CITY

This chapter explains the characteristics of the chief asset classes that are used throughout the investment world. You do not need to know every buzzword in the City but you do need a basic understanding of how borrowing and investing work, whether you are acting on the part of a multimillion-pound global conglomerate or a private investor.

A good dictionary to have to hand is *Lamont's Glossary* (www.lamonts-glossary.co.uk or phone 020 7287 6771). Some investment banks – UBS Warburg, for example – provide a glossary of terms on their websites (www.ubswarburg.com). We include a jargon buster in the Appendix.

SECURITIES

Investment literature uses a lot of confusing jargon. Commonly used (and misused) terms include 'securities', 'stocks' and 'shares'.

Securities is the general name for all stocks and shares. What we call shares today were originally known as stocks because they represented part-ownership in the joint stock companies – the precursors to today's public limited companies or plcs. So to some extent the terms stocks and shares are interchangeable, and we still use the terms *stock* market and *stock*broker.

Broadly speaking, stocks are fixed-interest securities and shares are the rest. The four main types of securities listed and traded on the London Stock Exchange are:

● UK (domestic) equities: ordinary shares issued by over 1,500 UK companies
● Overseas equities: ordinary shares issued by non-UK companies
● Gilts: bonds issued by the UK government to raise money to fund any shortfall in public expenditure
● Bonds: fixed-interest stocks issued by companies and local authorities, among others

THE MARKETS

You will hear about a lot of different markets in the City, and it is important to understand the basic definitions. The main markets, in alphabetical order, are as follows.

● **Bond markets** are where medium- and long-term bonds are bought and sold.
● **Capital markets** usually refer to recognised and regulated markets where long-term capital is raised for industry and government from private and corporate investors.
● **Commodities markets** arrange for the sale and purchase of huge quantities of tangible assets, for example raw materials and foodstuffs.
● **Derivatives markets** trade

financial contracts based on underlying instruments such as securities and contracts to buy and sell commodities, currencies and indices.

● **Foreign exchange (FX) markets** are where the currencies of different countries are bought and sold.

● **Money markets** refers primarily to the wholesale market for short-term debt – for example, Treasury bills – which is usually repayable in three months.

● **Primary markets** are where a product is first traded or where a company first raises capital, for example by 'going public' (see page 51) and launching on one of the FTSE exchanges.

● **Secondary markets** trade in the products launched on the primary markets. For example, once shares and bonds are launched by companies they can be bought and sold on the Stock Exchange.

● **Stock markets** are where shares are bought and sold.

THE FTSE INDICES

When a company goes public its shares are quoted on the Stock Exchange under a range of different indices. As a broad rule of thumb, the smaller the company the higher the investment risk. Smaller companies often do perform well, but they tend to be isolated stars rather than representative of the sector as a whole.

With the exception of the Fledgling, all the indices are reviewed every quarter (March, June, September and December) and the constituent companies will change. The Fledgling is reviewed annually in December.

The FTSE indices are arithmetically weighted by market capitalisation so that the larger the company the greater the effect its share price movement will have on the relevant index. Market capitalisation is the stock market valuation of the company. This is calculated by multiplying the number of shares in issue by their market price.

By June 2001 all the FTSE indices will reflect the new 'free float' system where the index constituent weightings are adjusted to reflect the companies' share capital that is freely available for trading rather than the total capital, some of which might be retained by directors, for example. This is a welcome development that will improve transparency in the markets. FTSE was the first major global index provider to address this issue.

The total market capitalisation of the FTSE-monitored indices – that is all 1,500 or so stocks in the UK – was £1,797 billion at the end of 2000.

The main indices as at 31 December 2000 are as follows:

● **The FTSE All-Share** is the most comprehensive index. It consists of just over 770 companies (down from 800 in 1999 due to mergers and takeovers) with a total market capitalisation of about £1,720 billion. The All-Share is regarded as the professional investor's yardstick for the level of the UK equity market as a whole, and represents about 98 per cent of UK stock market capitalisation. Within the All-Share, companies are allocated to 39 industrial sectors.

● **The FTSE 100 index** consists of the 100 largest companies by market capitalisation. Together they represent about 78 per cent of the total UK stock market capitalisation (not just the All-Share).

● **The FTSE 250 index** consists of the next 250 companies below the FTSE 100 and may include or exclude investment trusts. There are no fixed parameters for market capitalisation, but the companies currently in this index are capitalised at between £350m and £3bn. Together these 250 companies represent about 13 per cent of the UK stock market capitalisation (including investment trusts).

● **The FTSE SmallCap index** does not have a fixed number of constituent companies as it comprises all the remaining companies in the All-Share that are too small to qualify for the top 350. Together they account for about 4.4 per cent of the total market capitalisation.

● **The Fledgling** index covers about 680 companies that are too small for the All-Share. Together the SmallCap and Fledgling are known as the All-Small index.

● **The Alternative Investments Market** is the market for young and growing companies, which are likely to be higher risk than companies admitted to the London Stock Exchange's Official List. There are just over 500 companies in AIM.

THE MAIN ASSET CLASSES

UK equities
An important function of the investment banks is to help companies raise finance. If a company wants to raise money – for expansion, for example – it has two main options. It can sell part of the ownership of the company by issuing ordinary shares (equities) or it can borrow money by issuing bonds, which behave like a sophisticated IOU. Shares and bonds are bought and sold on the stock market.

Equities are the quoted shares of companies in the UK and tend to dominate most private investors' portfolios, whether they are held directly or are pooled through collective funds such as unit and investment trusts. The average pension fund will hold over half its assets in UK equities.

Historically, the return achieved by UK equities, when measured over the long term, has exceeded both price and earnings inflation, so this is considered the best asset class to hold for long-term growth. The investment manager's aim is to select companies that will achieve a good return in exchange for an acceptable level of risk.

Companies 'go public' when they are quoted on the Stock Exchange (or a minority exchange such as the Alternative Investment Market, for example). In this way a company can raise the money it needs for expansion by issuing shares.

A share or equity literally entitles the owner to a specified share in the profits of the company and, if the company is wound up, to a specified share of its assets.

The owner of shares is entitled to dividends, the six-monthly distribution to shareholders of part of the company's profits. The 'dividend yield' on equities is the dividend paid by a company divided by that company's share price.

In contrast to a bond, there is no set redemption date for an equity when the company is obliged to return your original investment. If, as a shareholder, you want to convert your investment into cash ('to realise its value') you must sell. The price you get will depend on supply and demand and will vary from day to day, so the timing of the purchase and sale of shares is critical.

Market makers are members of the Stock Exchange who buy and sell the securities which the firms are registered to sell. The market maker sells at the 'offer' price and buys at the 'bid' price. The spread or profit is the difference between these two.

'Bull' investors buy because they believe that the price will rise and therefore that they can sell at a later date and make a profit. 'Bear' investors sell because they believe the price will fall; they hope to buy back the shares at a lower price at a later date.

SHARE CLASSES

There are different classes of shares.
● Most investors buy **ordinary shares**, which give the holder the right to vote on the constitution of the company's board of directors. Since this is the most common type of share, the term 'ordinary' is usually dropped unless it is intended to distinguish the shares from a different category.
● **Preference shares** carry no voting rights but have a fixed dividend payment, so can be attractive to those seeking a regular income. These

shares confer 'preference' over ordinary shareholders if the company is wound up, hence the name.

CONVERTIBLES AND WARRANTS

There are several subclasses of equities or equity-related investments. Convertibles and warrants are special types of shares with characteristics that make them attractive in certain circumstances.
● **Convertibles** are more akin to bonds (see below), in that they pay a regular income and have a fixed redemption date. However, a convertible confers the right to *convert* to an ordinary share or preference share at a future date. This can be a good opportunity if the price is attractive on the convertible date.
● **Warrants** confer a right but not an obligation on the holder to convert to a specific share at a predetermined price and date. The value of the warrant, which is itself traded on the stock market, is determined by the difference or premium of the share price over the conversion price of the warrant.

DERIVATIVES

Derivatives, as the name suggests, *derive* their value from the price of an underlying security. This is the generic term given to futures contracts and options, both of which can be used to reduce risk in an institutional fund or, in the case of options, even in a large private portfolio.

A futures contract binds two parties to a sale or purchase at a specified future date. The price is fixed at the time the contract is taken out. These futures contracts can be used by institutional funds to control risk because they allow the manager to quickly increase or reduce the fund's exposure to an existing asset class. Futures have also proved popular as a cost-cutting mechanism, particularly in index tracking funds and other funds where there are rapid changes of large asset allocations.

Options allow you, for a down payment, to have the right but not the obligation to buy or sell something at an agreed price on a specific date. Some private investors use options as a type of insurance policy to protect their portfolio against a fall in the market.

OVERSEAS EQUITIES

These are similar in principle to UK equities but there are differences in shareholder rights. Investment overseas provides exposure to the growth in foreign markets, including younger, fast-growing economies. However, these shares also expose you to currency fluctuations. This can be both good and bad, of course, but the point is that it adds an extra layer of risk.

The taxation of foreign shares can be less favourable than in the case of UK equities. In particular, some or all of the withholding tax on dividends deducted by the foreign country may not be recoverable.

As a rule of thumb, exposure to the major developed economies, for example the European Union countries, the US and Canada, is considered medium risk while exposure to the emerging economies is high risk.

BONDS AND GILTS

UK bonds are issued by borrowers, for example the government (these bonds are known as gilt-edged securities or just 'gilts') and companies (corporate bonds). Bonds are also issued by local authorities, overseas governments and overseas companies. You will also come across Treasury bills, which are used for short-term borrowing by the government.

In return for the loan, the borrower agrees to pay a fixed rate of interest (known as the coupon) for the agreed period and to repay your original capital sum on a specified date, known as the maturity or redemption date.

UK domestic bonds are either secured on the company's underlying assets – for example, its property – or they are unsecured, in which case there is no physical asset backing the bond's guarantee to pay interest and to repay the capital at maturity.

Secured bonds are known as debentures and unsecured bonds are known as loan stocks. Since the security offered by debentures is greater than for loan stocks, the former tend to pay a lower rate of interest.

The point to remember about fixed-interest securities is that the investment return is determined more by the level of interest rates than the issuing company's profitability. Provided the issuer remains sufficiently secure to honour the future coupon payments (the regular interest) and redemption payment (the return of the original capital), you know exactly what your return will be, *provided* you hold the bond to maturity.

Gilts offer the highest degree of security because they are issued by the UK government – specifically by the UK Debt Management Office (DMO), an executive agency of the Treasury.

TRADED BONDS

If a fund manager sells a bond before its maturity date, then the value of the future coupon and redemption payments will depend on the prevailing interest rates at the time of sale.

So, if interest rates are rising, then the value of the fixed-interest security will fall. This is because, for the same amount of capital invested, you could get a better return elsewhere.

Conversely, if interest rates are falling, then the value of the fixed-interest security will be higher because it provides a greater stream of income than you could get from alternative sources.

This volatile pattern of behaviour is more apparent with fixed-interest securities that have a long period to run to maturity since they are more likely to be traded before the redemption date.

To summarise, as a general rule equities are considered more risky and volatile than bonds because they behave in an unpredictable way whereas, provided the company or government backing a bond is watertight, the return on a bond *held to maturity* is predictable. However, it is not predictable if you decide to sell before maturity.

EUROBONDS

UK companies can raise money outside the UK market by issuing 'Eurosterling' bonds – that is, bonds denominated in sterling but issued on the Eurobond market. Despite what the name suggests, the Euromarkets are not confined to Europe but are international markets where borrowers and lenders are matched.

The main advantage of Eurosterling bonds, from the borrower's point of view, is that they can reach a much wider range of potential lenders. This is an institutional rather than a private investor market.

INDEX-LINKED GILTS

Index-linked gilts are issued by the UK government and are guaranteed to provide interest payments (the coupon) and a redemption value which increase in line with annual inflation. For this reason they are one of the lowest-risk assets for income-seekers. Having said that, in practice they have not proved particularly attractive compared with other income-generating alternatives.

The return on index-linked gilts in excess of the Retail Price Index varies, but usually it is possible to buy these securities in the marketplace at a price that guarantees a real rate of return to the holder, assuming that the stock is held to maturity.

CASH

Cash does not refer to stacks of £20 notes stuffed under the mattress but usually means a deposit account. Deposits have the advantage that the value in monetary terms is known and is certain at all times. What is unknown is the interest that will be received, and by how much this will fall short of the rate of inflation.

PROPERTY

In investment terms, 'property' usually refers to the ownership of land and buildings that are used by a business or other organisation. The owner of the property receives income from the rent charged to the tenant and, over time, this rent is expected broadly to keep pace with inflation. The dominant factor in the value of a property is the desirability or otherwise of its location.

There are several problems with property that make it a specialist area of investment. First, it is often sold in large blocks that cannot be easily split for investment purposes. As a result, only the larger institutional funds can afford to own property directly. Second, property is a very illiquid asset and it can take several years for the right selling conditions to arise. Moreover, unless you invest via a collective fund, private investors cannot dispose of their investment piecemeal to make best use of their annual capital gains tax exemption and could be landed with a whopping CGT bill.

INFLATION

It is important to keep in mind the relationship between inflation and returns. Inflation is a key benchmark against which returns are measured. If retail price inflation is 4 per cent and your fund returns 7 per cent, then you have made a 'real' or inflation-adjusted return of 3 per cent. In the 1980s, when inflation was high, you could get double-digit returns on a building

society account but the 'real' or inflation-adjusted return was still very low, although these accounts remain the safest home for your short-term capital. Stock markets may not be prepared for an inflation 'shock' (a sudden and unexpected change in the rate of inflation) but they adjust over time and provide a long-term hedge against price rises. Gilts and cash are not generally considered suitable inflation hedges.

PERIOD OF INVESTMENT

Clearly, returns on equities, gilts and cash should be viewed with some caution, and certainly should not be treated as a guide to the long-term future. While history indicates that equities should provide a better return than bonds over the *medium to long term*, there is an important caveat.

'Medium to long term' means a minimum of five years. If private investors go into the stock markets for shorter periods they are in danger of getting their fingers burned, either because the markets take a tumble just before they want to get out or because the fixed costs associated with setting up the portfolio undermine the return over the short term.

DIFFERENT STYLES OF INSTITUTIONAL FUND MANAGEMENT

Active managers

Active investment managers aim to increase a fund's value by deviating from a specific benchmark – for example, a stock market index. There are two basic techniques used in active

information

stock selection.

The starting point for active managers who adopt a 'bottom up' approach is the company in which the manager may invest. He or she will look at in-house and external research on the company's history and potential future prospects. This will include an examination of the strength of the balance sheet, the company's trading history, the management's business strategy, and the price/earnings ratio (the market price of a share divided by the company's earnings/profits per share in its latest twelve-month trading period).

From the company analysis the manager will proceed to look at the general performance and prospects for that sector (for example, construction and building materials, chemicals, general retailers, and so on), and then take into consideration national and international economic factors.

The 'top down' manager works in reverse, looking first at the international and national economic factors that might affect economic growth in a country, geographic area (for example, the 'tiger' economies of South-East Asia) or economic category (emerging markets, for example) and gradually working down to the individual companies.

Among private investors, the 'fundamental' analyst focuses almost exclusively on individual companies and tends to disregard the economic climate and market conditions. The 'technical' analyst, also known as a 'chartist', concentrates on historical price movements.

Passive managers

Passive managers aim to track or replicate a benchmark. This style is also known as index tracking. It may sound simple but in practice this is a complex process based on emulating the performance of a particular stock market index by buying all, or a wide sample of, the constituent shares.

The passive manager does not consider the merits of each stock, of different sectors and economic cycles. If it is in the index then it must be represented in the fund. To date, index tracking funds have done very well compared with actively managed funds, largely because the passive manager's charges are very low compared to the active manager's.

Passive management becomes very complex when the process tries to outstrip the index returns by deviating in a specific way. This is known as quantitative management.

FURTHER INFORMATION

If you are interested in finding out about gilts, visit the Debt Management Office website at www.dmo.gov.uk The site includes an on-line version of the informative 'Private Investors Guide'.

10
THE STOCK MARKETS AND THE LONDON STOCK EXCHANGE

If you are going to work in the City you need to understand the rudiments of the functions it performs. This chapter explains the workings of the London Stock Exchange (LSE) and describes briefly the role of the other important exchanges.

A market is a place where buyers and sellers come together for mutual benefit and gain. The LSE is no exception. Here companies can raise finance for expansion, while private and institutional investors can lend spare capital and in return share in the growth of their chosen companies.

London is one of the top three stock markets in the world. The other two you will hear about most frequently are New York and Tokyo. The LSE is also the world's leading international exchange. More international companies are listed, and more international equities are traded, in London than on any other exchange.

For the history buffs there are many books dedicated to the origins and development of the LSE, including those available from the Exchange itself.

This chapter covers the essential details and helps to explain the context in which the Exchange works. Do remember that, for all its fancy jargon, it is, after all, just a marketplace.

Career opportunities exist within a wide spectrum of organisations ranging from multinational banks to small stockbroking firms. In order to work in the stock market – as a trader, for example – you will need to be able to explain clearly why you want to do this particular job. The LSE itself doesn't employ stockbrokers or traders. Its business is to provide an efficient and attractive marketplace for users.

A (VERY) BRIEF HISTORY LESSON

The origins of the stock market go back to the coffee houses of the seventeenth century, where people who wanted to raise money met with those who wanted to invest in the original 'joint stock' companies – the forerunners of today's public limited companies (plcs). Joint stock, in this context, refers to a company where partners pooled their stock, or ownership, with that of outsiders. Therefore the company was jointly owned by both the original owners and private investors.

As the volume of trade in joint stock companies grew, the number of dealers expanded. The original traders were the brokers, who bought and sold the shares on behalf of clients, and jobbers, through whom the brokers made their transactions. In 1986 the jobbers were replaced by market makers (see below).

The early market was a far cry from

the elegant, pin-stripe-suited gentleman's club it later became. Some of the original traders were so unruly that in 1760 a group was kicked out of the Royal Exchange, which had largely replaced the coffee houses as a central marketplace.

About 150 of these financial hooligans formed a club at Jonathan's Coffee House to carry on the business of buying and selling shares. In 1773 the members voted to change the name of their meeting-house to The Stock Exchange.

Following a tremendous boom in trade and accompanying scandals, most notably the South Sea Bubble (in which a trading company went bust following a period of speculation and inflated share prices), the members of the Stock Exchange agreed on a set of rules and tighter controls. This resulted in the 1812 Deed of Settlement, which formed the basis of the rules for the operation of the markets today.

BIG BANG

We now skip a century and a half and move to the 1970s, when London's pre-eminent position in international markets was under threat. In particular, in 1979 the abolition of foreign exchange controls made it easier for UK savings institutions to invest money overseas in non-UK securities. As a result, London Stock Exchange member firms were exposed to competition from overseas brokers who were also contending for UK and international company shares.

As if this weren't bad enough, in the early 1980s the government took the

Exchange to court, claiming that some of the principles on which its rules were based restricted trade. Under the terms of an out-of-court settlement, the Exchange agreed to abolish its system of minimum commissions by the end of 1986 in order to encourage greater competition. This in turn was expected to bring down commission rates and the overall cost of share transactions.

Big Bang took place on 27 October 1986. The important changes were as follows:

● Ownership of member firms by an outside corporation was allowed, enabling member firms to build larger capital bases to compete with overseas competition. Many firms were bought by UK and foreign banks, and by major overseas securities firms.

● The separation of member firms into brokers and jobbers ended. All firms became broker/dealers able to operate in a dual capacity – either buying securities from or selling them to clients without having to go through a third party.

● Minimum scales of commission were abolished, opening the way for much greater competition on charges and services.

● Voting rights at the Exchange were transferred from individual members to member firms.

● Trading moved from the Exchange floor, where it was carried out face to face in a single hall, to separate dealing rooms, where transactions were performed using telephones and computers.

● Two computer-based systems were introduced: SEAQ (Stock Exchange Automated Quotations) and SEAQ International. These enabled investment managers to see share price information from anywhere in the UK. In 1993 SEATS (the Stock Exchange Alternative Trading System) was introduced for less liquid securities.

TROUBLESOME TIMES

During 2000 the LSE hit the headlines on a regular basis as it steered through a series of spectacular failures to merge or be acquired. In March 2000 members voted to turn the 200-year-old institution into a company. On 5 April – the end of the tax year and one of the busiest days in the financial year – a systems breakdown halted trade for more than eight hours.

The breakdown occurred as the Exchange was in merger talks with Deutsche Borse. The merger talks fell through. Then, on 29 August, OM Group, an aggressive Swedish technology company, launched a hostile bid to acquire the LSE – a bid that failed, but not before Gavin Casey had resigned as chief executive.

It will be interesting to see what happens in 2001 and 2002.

THREE KEY FUNCTIONS OF THE STOCK EXCHANGE

The Stock Exchange has three key functions, namely:

● To raise capital
● To trade services
● To regulate the stock markets

RAISING CAPITAL

The Stock Exchange provides a range of markets that allow UK and international companies, governments and other entities to raise capital and to gain wide access to investors and borrowers.

There are three main ways in which investors can buy shares. Different institutions are involved at each stage, but the investment banks dominate the whole process.

1) The primary market for initial public offerings. This is when a company first offers shares on the stock market – a process known as flotation. Investors may be able to buy direct or, in the case of institutional investors, they may buy through the investment banks. In some cases shares may be allocated to the major institutions, particularly where the company for sale is not very well known.

Mutual institutions such as building societies and life offices (life assurance organisations) go public by demutualising. In this case the institution's members are likely to be given 'windfall' shares in exchange for giving up their right to a share in the mutual's ownership.

2) Further issues. Companies often need to raise more money at a later stage to fund large projects. In this case a company can launch a 'rights issue', where existing investors have the opportunity to subscribe for the new shares at less than the current market price.

3) Secondary or trading market. The most common way of investing in a company's shares is in the secondary or trading market, where investors buy shares through a stockbroker from existing investors who wish to sell.

THE ROLE OF THE PRIMARY MARKET

So, how do companies 'come to the market' and trade their shares? Many UK and international companies come to London to raise new capital or to have their shares more widely marketed and traded. They can raise capital via the main market (known as the 'Official List') or the Alternative Investment Market (AIM), which is more suitable for smaller, newer companies. For descriptions of the indices, see page 50.

Companies can raise capital both at the time of going public and, subsequently, by issuing securities for cash. Access to equity or debt finance gives companies greater flexibility to fund expansion and development programmes or to reduce borrowings.

During a typical year, UK companies might raise over £50 billion, while a further £44 billion might be raised by government securities (gilts – see page 53).

THE MAIN MARKET (OFFICIAL LIST)

Companies on the main market come from all sectors of business and range from those with a £1 million market capitalisation ('market cap') to those capitalised at £90 billion. The market capitalisation is calculated by multiplying the current share price by the number of shares in issue.

Remember that one. It will keep on cropping up.

A company that applies for a listing has to supply the Stock Exchange with a great many details about its trading history, financial records, management, business prospects, information on the securities to be listed, plus the terms of any fund-raising.

This information is included in the company's 'listing particulars' or prospectus, a document which provides prospective investors with most of the information they need to decide whether to proceed. Clearly an independent assessment is also important.

The company must appoint a sponsor approved by the Exchange to handle its application to join. This can be a member firm, a bank, an investment manager or a firm of solicitors or accountants, among other advisers. There are about 150 approved sponsors.

Trading on the Exchange is carried out through SEAQ for UK companies, SEAQ International for international companies, and SEATS PLUS for smaller companies.

The companies on the main markets are divided into various categories or sectors so that performance can be related to that of competitors in the appropriate peer group. The companies are also divided into different indices, based on market capitalisation. It's worth learning the names of the sectors and indices. If you read the *Financial Times* each day – including the Companies and Markets section – you will quickly become familiar with the different

Current Share Price ✗ No. of Shares = Market Cap

sectors and the type of corporate activity that makes money for City institutions, such as raising finance and mergers and acquisitions.

REGULATION: THE FINANCIAL SERVICES ACT (1986)

The regulatory system designed to protect investors was completely overhauled with the introduction of the Financial Services Act (FSA) 1986. The Exchange had always been responsible for regulating member firms, but the Act added a new statutory dimension so that it became illegal for anyone except for those authorised or exempted under the Act to carry on investment business.

Under the Act, the Stock Exchange regulates both capital-raising and trading markets. Its activities include:

● To assess the credentials of companies which apply to join the main market (the Official List)
● To monitor listed companies' compliance with the rules
● To deal with any breaches of the rules
● To supervise the conduct of the 300 member firms which deal on its markets

OTHER EXCHANGES

There are a number of important exchanges in the City, some of which we describe below. Opportunities to work directly in the exchanges are limited, but it is worth checking their websites to find out what they do and to see if there are any vacancies.

THE BALTIC EXCHANGE

The Baltic Exchange is the world's only self-regulated shipbroking market, where members arrange transportation of a wide range of bulk commodities, from Brazilian iron ore to Australian coal, and from American grains to Chinese steel. The Baltic broker's job is to match cargoes and ships. To do this they need to know the availability of ships and cargoes and their locations. They must also be up to date with the world's political conditions, because these will affect the viability of certain shipping routes.

The Baltic Exchange is also the world's foremost market for the sale and purchase of ships – or 'tonnage', as it is called. Over half the world's tonnage is bought and sold through the exchange.

It was the Baltic Exchange which enshrined that most famous of City phrases in its motto 'Our word is our bond'.

LONDON INTERNATIONAL FINANCIAL FUTURES EXCHANGE (LIFFE)

Liffe opened in 1982 and provides a wide range of financial, equity and commodity-based derivative products. You don't have to understand all the contracts Liffe trades, but it is helpful to understand the two basics – futures and options (see page 52).

The primary function of a futures market is to manage or 'hedge' price risk so that those responsible for selling and buying huge quantities of raw materials, for example, can be sure of a future price for the goods.

The secondary function is to enable

a market of buyers and sellers to trade the contracts in the hope of making a profit. Hedgers use futures contracts to protect themselves against adverse price changes over a specific period of time during which they are exposed to price fluctuations as buyers or sellers of the underlying shares or commodity. Conversely, investors are interested in taking on a price risk in the anticipation of making a profit from price changes over the specified period.

In very broad terms, using a futures contract to hedge risk is considered a prudent measure and is used, for example, by most UK pension funds. The more speculative side of investing in derivative contracts as an asset class is considered a high-risk strategy.

Exchange-traded equity options first became available in London in April 1978 when the London Stock Exchange listed call options on the shares of ten leading companies. It is now possible to trade options on over 80 major UK stocks and also on the FTSE 100 index.

Only traders registered to Liffe member firms can trade directly on the exchange.

LONDON METAL EXCHANGE

The LME is the world's premier non-ferrous metals market with an annual turnover value of US$2,000 billion. Its origins date back to the sixteenth century, but the exchange was formally launched in 1877 as a direct result of the Industrial Revolution, which led to a massive increase in the UK's consumption of metal. This in turn required the import of enormous tonnages from abroad. Merchant

venturers investing in this activity were exposed to great risk, partly because the voyages themselves were hazardous and partly because the cargoes could lose value if there was a fall in price during the time it took for the metal to reach Britain.

Merchants began meeting in coffee houses, where they traded with each other in order to protect themselves against the fall in value of a cargo by selling the cargoes as 'forward contracts'. The LME was founded to bring order to this activity. As mentioned earlier, the use of futures contracts to protect against price risk is known as hedging.

The three activities of the exchange are to hedge, to provide reference prices relating to non-ferrous metals, and to facilitate delivery by providing for storage facilities to enable market participants to make or take physical delivery of the metals traded.

The high-grade metals traded are aluminium, aluminium alloy, copper, zinc, nickel, lead, tin and silver.

THE INTERNATIONAL PETROLEUM EXCHANGE

The IPE is Europe's leading energy futures and options exchange, where industry participants such as the oil producers, refiners and distributors are able to use derivative contracts to minimise price risks. Over $1 billion in underlying value is traded every day.

The exchange was founded in 1980 following the dramatic oil price shocks of the 1970s. Previously the price of oil had been comparatively stable, but from the 1970s onwards it became very volatile.

Oil futures and options are still traded in pits on the market floor using the open outcry system, where all orders are shouted in public. However, the exchange is moving towards a fully automated energy trading system (ETS) located within customers' offices, and already uses an ETS for natural gas futures. In due course the exchange may add contracts for non-oil products such as electricity.

FURTHER INFORMATION
The London Stock Exchange publishes many useful information leaflets and books.
● For details contact: The Public Information Department, London Stock Exchange, London EC2N 1HP.
TEL 020 7797 1372.
FAX 020 7410 6861.

WEBSITES
● The Stock Exchange
www.londonstockexchange.com
● The Baltic Exchange
www.balticexchange.com
● London International Financial Futures Exchange www.liffe.com
● The London Metal Exchange
www.lme.co.uk
● The International Petroleum Exchange www.ipe.uk.com
● London Clearing House
www.lch.co.uk
● London Securities and Derivatives Exchange www.omgroup.com
● London Underwriting Centre
www.luc.co.uk
● Tradepoint www.tradepoint.co.uk

11
THE BANK OF ENGLAND

The Bank of England bears little resemblance to a high-street branch of Barclays or Lloyds TSB. Situated in the heart of the City in Threadneedle Street, this is the government's bank and the banks' bank. It also holds accounts for the central banks of other countries that conduct business in the UK.

As the central bank of the UK, it is independent from the government but closely allied with government monetary policy. The Old Lady of Threadneedle Street, as the bank used to be known, prints banknotes for England and Wales. Coins are produced by the Royal Mint. The Bank used to issue government debt, known as gilt-edged securities (or just 'gilts'). These are now issued by the UK Debt Management Office (DMO), an executive agency of the Treasury.

The Bank has a high profile in the media, particularly when it makes a decision on interest rates, which have a knock-on effect on the rates charged by retail banks for lending and the interest rates offered to savers.

But there's much more to the Bank's work than this. It has three core purposes, which are:

● To maintain the integrity and value of the currency – largely by controlling interest rates and the amount of money in circulation
● To maintain the integrity of the domestic and international financial system – for example, through its influence on foreign exchange rates
● To promote the efficiency and effectiveness of the UK's financial services through its regulatory role

The Bank's principal activities fall broadly into the following categories:

● Monetary analysis and statistics
● Financial stability
● Financial market operations
● Europe
● Central services

Under the Banking Acts of 1979 and 1987, the Bank of England has the power to authorise and regulate all deposit-taking institutions – for example, the retail banks. This includes checking that the banks are solvent and well run. The Bank also operates a compensation scheme for depositors if the worst should happen and a bank goes bust.

FURTHER INFORMATION
● Good sources of information about the Bank's different areas of operation are the Bank's Annual Report & Accounts and its website, which is at www.bankofengland.co.uk

12
THE INVESTMENT BANKS

It is important to understand the basic functions of the different types of bank, although some of the major banks, like Barclays, for example, may cover all three functions through different operations. Well, you didn't expect it to be simple, did you?

● **Investment banking**, also known as corporate finance, is the biggest sector in terms of salaries and the deals you work on. This is the stuff headline news is made of – the global mergers and acquisitions, the hostile bids, the cross-border deals that change the shape of a country's financial services sector.

● **Corporate banking** is banking to medium-sized companies, typically defined as those that might need to raise £10–£15 million and which also require a host of other banking facilities. The big corporate banks also tend to offer **custodial services** on a global basis – a huge business in its own right.

● **Retail banking**, also known as high-street banking, is banking to individuals and small partnerships and companies that do not need a fancier service.

In this book we focus primarily on investment banking, although we also cover corporate banking.

YOU'VE GOT IT MADE
If you are looking for money, prestige and power, you need look no farther than investment banking. Working in this sector is also about as stressful as it gets. Investment banks make and break companies, literally. They take a new company to the market to raise finance and they break up older companies through sell-offs and demergers.

Corporate finance is one of the most sparkling careers in the City, and if you don't want to stay put all your life then a few years with a good bank can lead to some pretty amazing jobs in management consultancy, because if anyone knows what makes a business tick it's investment bankers. They also know a lot about champagne and cocaine, but we won't worry about that for now.

If you are going to make it in this business you have to be thick-skinned and play the corporate game, until you get poached by a rival bank and take the entire department with you. You need to be that loyal.

Investment banks are the bankers to major companies and to multi-million-pound institutions such as local authorities and pension funds. They do not deal directly with individuals, with the exception of the pheno-menally rich, for whom they make time through the private client services (PCS) department. PCS used to be known as stockbroking and frankly still is in most circles, despite brave attempts by the industry to change the image of the pin-striped, old-boys'-network brigade.

CORPORATE ACTIVITY

The investment banks are the biggest movers and shakers in the City and behind all the important corporate activity you will read about in the *Financial Times* and elsewhere – for example, mergers and acquisitions (M&As), flotations and privatisations. Long before these deals go public the investment banks concerned have carried out an investigation into the financial position of the companies involved, priced the various options for their clients, and extrapolated detailed business projections to see how, for example, raising funds through debt or equity will affect the business, assuming various future changes to interest rates.

The top ten global M&A advisers in 2000, according to Computasoft Research/CommScan, were:

- Morgan Stanley
- Goldman Sachs
- Credit Suisse First Boston
- Salomon Smith Barney
- Merrill Lynch
- Chase Manhattan
- UBS Warburg
- J.P. Morgan
- Lazard
- Lehman Brothers

Where the objective is to raise finance – for example, by issuing shares – the investment bank leading the project is likely to underwrite the package. This means that it agrees to purchase any remaining shares if subscriptions are insufficient. If this is a really big corporate deal the lead bank will put together a syndicate of other banks to spread the risk.

As an investment banker, the finance or corporate restructuring deal you work on may prove to be a one-off, but in most cases you will retain the client and advise on further details in the future. In fact the banks are not just passive advisers who wait for a client to come up with a good wheeze. These institutions are at their best when they are proactive. If you work for an investment bank, eventually you will become so familiar with the sector in which you specialise that you will be able to spot business opportunities on behalf of your clients and take proposals to their boards.

Over the past decade the City has witnessed frenzied corporate activity among the banks themselves. Many of the old names have gone following takeover by a foreign owner – for example, Merrill Lynch, which took over Mercury Asset Management. More and more US banks are coming to London with the intention of using it as their springboard into European markets.

This trend towards the global investment bank is important from the career point of view. You may decide you want to work for a truly international operation, but then again you might prefer to take your chance with one of the dwindling number of blue-blooded UK investment banks (also known as merchant banks). To survive in a cut-throat market, these smaller operations tend to specialise – for example, in corporate finance.

CAREERS

There is no doubt that the global investment banks are the biggest

Underwriting

recruiters of top-quality graduates in the City. They are also the highest payers (see Chapter 7). Graduate opportunities are on the increase, especially in the area of fund management, which is undergoing a huge expansion with the growth of private pension funds in both the retail and corporate markets.

Apart from serving the big institutional clients, most of the investment banks package their fund management expertise and offer it in the form of pooled or collective investments to individual savers. This allows small savers to buy units (in the case of unit trusts, for example) or shares (in the case of investment trusts) at a competitive price in a fund that offers a wide diversification of assets and stocks.

Traditionally this was a very male-dominated environment, but some organisations do practise what they preach about equal opportunities. 'Opportunity Now' and the 'Women in investment banking' initiatives demonstrate which companies are really making efforts to change the male-dominated culture. For a list of the banks that support the Women in investment banking initiative, see page 37.

Unlike their predecessors the merchant banks, which tended to restrict business to a national market, the major investment banks are international in outlook, location and career prospects. As a result, there are a number of key career paths within different departments that you can follow, including:

- Fund manager
- Investment analyst
- Venture capitalist
- Corporate finance
- Property management
- Debt trading
- Money markets
- Administration/operations
- Client relations manager
- Marketing
- IT

As with other City careers, you don't necessarily have to have a relevant degree. A first in sports science or sociology is just as likely to get you on to some of the graduate training courses as a degree in economics. Unless the job demands specific skills – like law, economics or mathematics – then what employers are looking for is enthusiasm and commitment.

Despite the slow trend towards 'family friendly' policies – where your employer actually recognises that you *have* a family and that you might want to see it once or twice a month – generally investment banking is a slog. Working hours often extend to ten or eleven a day on top of the commuting.

Despite the many similarities, each bank has clear characteristics and areas of expertise, both in terms of classes of business and in the geographical areas in which it operates. They also differ in their internal structures. Some of the older City institutions still maintain a fairly traditional hierarchy and pecking order. Others – in particular the American banks – tend to have a flatter reporting structure and try to create an atmosphere where everyone feels equal. The idea behind this modern approach to management is to allow each individual to fulfil his or her potential. Of course, equality does not stretch as far as the pay packet.

A good way to get a feel for the opportunities offered by this sector is to take a look inside one or two of the biggest players (see the list of members of the Women in investment banking initiative on page 37).

CORPORATE AND RETAIL BANKING

The corporate banks provide banking services to organisations and play an important role in the raising of loans and Treasury instruments for small- to medium-sized companies. Some of the major corporate banks also offer global custody services, where they safeguard the assets of trusts – for example, for pension funds and unit trusts.

The roles of the retail bank and building society have blurred in recent years. Banks offer mortgages; building societies offer cheque-book accounts. Both offer insurance and investment services, and in some cases estate agency as well. As a result there is considerable demand for graduate managers within these organisations.

Retail banks and building societies are more likely to offer you a career outside the City. We do not cover these roles in detail in this book but would recommend interested readers to look at the websites of the leading retail banks and building societies for information about careers at A level and beyond. You might also consider the newcomers – such as Prudential's Egg and the Co-operative's Smile –

both of which bypass the high-street branch altogether and offer Internet-only services.

With the growth of on-line banking there is considerable scope for IT jobs, while graduates with economics degrees are always in demand. What the banks are looking for is good management potential, skills in IT and the imagination to design new products for this very competitive marketplace.

In addition to the basic banking skills – customer liaison, assessing credit worthiness for loans – you will also need to become conversant with all aspects of financial services. As margins on lending and borrowing shrink, so banks and building societies are developing their range of savings and insurance products to boost profits. Here you will be in competition with the traditional insurance companies and also the newcomers – Virgin and Marks & Spencer, for example – which are building financial products from scratch on the back of their trustworthy brand images.

THE BUILDING SOCIETIES

In the past the building societies were limited in the amount of commercial banking they could undertake, but these days the differences between the societies and the retail banks can be hard to spot. Originally building societies (and life assurers) were mutuals, which means they were set up and owned by their members. Mutuality has become less popular in recent years as these institutions have recognised the need for expansion and the cash backing of shareholders.

Many of the big societies and life offices have demutualised – that is, they have converted from member-owned status to public companies owned by shareholders. In some cases this change of status has been forced through by carpetbaggers – members who want the windfall shares and cash usually handed out on demutualisation. Recently legislation was introduced to prevent carpet-baggers influencing the future of an institution purely for personal gain, although some would argue that this is only mirroring the behaviour of shareholders.

The point is that if you have strong views about member-owned financial institutions you might prefer to look at the smaller building societies or friendly societies (similar to building societies although more restricted in their range of products). The majority of these operate outside London and tend to be very provincial in nature. If you want a City career at the forefront of banking technology, then stick to the more innovative major players.

FURTHER INFORMATION

The investment banks run websites and most of these provide details of graduate recruitment.
● For access to the banks' websites go to one of the major recruitment agencies, including the specialists www.prospects.csu.man.ac.uk and www.doctorjob.com

13
LLOYD'S OF LONDON

Good coffee and reliable shipping news were the foundation for one of London's most venerable financial institutions. Lloyd's (don't forget the apostrophe -- that's what distinguishes it from the Lloyds TSB bank) retains many of the entrepreneurial and idiosyncratic characteristics associated with its early days, when the business was run from an eighteenth-century coffee house.

The Lloyd's building – a fine example of quirky modern architecture designed by Sir Richard Rogers – is worth a visit. It is widely considered to be one of the City's most prestigious buildings – if you like your central heating pipes on the outside, that is.

Like the Stock Exchange, Lloyd's is a marketplace, but in this case it is risk that is bought and sold. If you have something unusual to insure, you take it to a Lloyd's broker. Today you can insure virtually anything at Lloyd's, but historically the chief market was shipping. Wealthy individuals would underwrite the risk of a ship losing its cargo or the loss of the ship itself. If the ship went down these individuals would pay up. If the ship reached its destination the underwriters could pocket the insurance premium.

As Chapter 14 explains, the aim of an insurance policy is to cover the cost if something goes wrong. The middleman between the underwriter and the person or company that wants to insure the risk is the broker, who aims to secure the right level of cover at the best price – and, of course, to make a profit.

The underwriters are effectively the buyers of risks. Their assessment of a proposal is based on past experience, research into the specific risk involved, and what they already have on their books. The peculiar thing about Lloyd's is that it is not a single company. About 120 different businesses operate under the Lloyd's banner and conform to the stringent regulatory requirements of the institution. Lloyd's brokers negotiate insurance programmes or packages with these expert underwriters. About two-thirds of the business comes from overseas, most notably the US. Clients range from individuals to blue-chip international corporations.

INNOVATION
Innovation is what makes Lloyd's so exciting. If insurance is your thing, then this is the cutting edge. Lloyd's was the first underwriter to insure a motor vehicle when, in 1901, it adapted a marine policy for the purpose, because at that time motor policies did not exist. It insured the first commercial aircraft and the first flight across the Atlantic. More recently, Lloyd's underwriters developed the first policy to protect financial organisations against 'rogue trading' (the cost of putting right the mayhem caused by traders who are either corrupt or mad – usually both)

and arranged the underwriting for the successful attempt on the land speed record by the British-built Thrust supersonic car.

Most of Lloyd's business is transacted in the underwriting room, known simply as 'the Room' by those who work there. Trading takes place on the ground floor and in galleries where underwriters sit at 'boxes' or desks and negotiate with brokers who bring business into the market.

Typically, for each proposal a broker negotiates with several underwriters who specialise in the relevant class of business – for example, shipping, airlines, personal health, and so on. Each underwriter represents a syndicate of individuals or corporate members of Lloyd's. Syndicates range in size from a single corporate member to several hundred.

There are about 3,300 individual members, known as 'Names', who trade with unlimited liability. A further 2,400 individuals have converted to limited liability membership. This means that in the event of a real disaster, when the time comes to pay up they would not lose everything (including their homes) as can happen where liability is unlimited. The issue of unlimited liability has been a major problem for Lloyd's following a period when Names' losses were substantial.

The syndicates, agents and business conducted at Lloyd's are all regulated by the Council of Lloyd's, a body established by the Lloyd's Act 1982. The Council consists of elected representatives from the Lloyd's community as well as nominated members approved by the Governor of the Bank of England. However, from 1998 the Financial Services Authority (FSA) has also played an important role in the overall regulation of the market.

Lloyd's List was launched in 1734 and is London's oldest newspaper; it provides daily information about the movements of some 20,000 merchant ships. Take a look at a copy if you want to get an idea of this specialist world. The Green Book – the name given to Lloyd's Register of Shipping – provides detailed information on the construction and characteristics of individual ships, rather as racecourse booklets provide information about horses' form.

You can go on guided tours of Lloyd's, which are an ideal way to get a feel for the atmosphere. You also get to see the famous Lutine Bell, two tolls of which used to bring the good news that a ship had come in; one toll meant a ship had gone down.

If you are interested in specialist insurance you should investigate the International Underwriting Association of London (IUA) – a group of companies that underwrite maritime and aviation risk, among others.

FURTHER INFORMATION

● Lloyd's of London is at One Lime Street, London EC3. www.lloydsoflondon.co.uk

● The International Underwriting Association of London (IUA) is at 3 Minster Court, Mincing Lane, London EC3. www.iua.co.uk

14
INSURANCE

The insurance industry is one of the biggest employers in the City. Here we are talking about the major risks insured through Lloyd's and the International Underwriting Association of London (IUA). The City is also home to the major risk consulting services, which advise corporations on a wide range of business risks and the potential financial impact of different scenarios.

What most people think of as insurance embraces companies that sell individual lines like motor and home policies. Most of these also underwrite huge business risks. This type of 'general' insurance company represents one of the largest service organisations in Britain. Most of them are located outside the City.

WHAT IS INSURANCE?

At its most basic, insurance involves two parties. Take motor insurance, for example. If you drive a car, there is a risk that you might have an accident. The cost could be significant if you are at fault and the accident involves more than one vehicle and serious injury. The underwriter or insurer – assesses the likelihood of your having an accident by considering various factors – for example, your age and occupation, how long you have been driving, where you live, and the type of car you drive.

The underwriter looks at the insurance company's past experience as well to determine the risk it is

taking if it insures you. For obvious reasons, an 18-year-old student with a sports car who lives in London is going to be a worse risk than a 60-year-old schoolteacher who runs a Fiat Punto, lives in the country and has been driving for 40 years.

This same approach can be applied to virtually any risk. Standard risks like motor and home insurance are sold by a huge number of companies, so brokers or intermediaries often act as middlemen to 'broke' the market and get you the best price. If the risk is unusual – for example, if you have a very old listed property or you run a vintage car – you would need to find a specialist broker who can track down an insurer that will underwrite this type of risk, taking into account the higher costs of repair, among other factors.

In addition to the specialist Lloyd's market, which is discussed in Chapter 13, there are several distinct components of the insurance market, and these are outlined briefly below.

LIFE AND PENSIONS

Life assurance companies, or 'life offices', as they are known, sell a wide range of long-term savings and investments. Originally these would have included a substantial element of life assurance, but these days the life cover is often minimal.

Endowment policies, for example, are a combination of life assurance and an investment plan. In the past these were a popular method of repaying a mortgage, because if you died before you saved enough to repay the capital, the life assurance policy would cover the debt. Today advisers generally recommend separate life assurance and investment plans, as these are usually more efficient and flexible than an endowment.

One of the biggest markets for life offices is individual pension plans and small company schemes. Pension plans also provide a minimal level of life assurance, but their main purpose is to build up a fund while you are working which can be used at retirement to purchase an annuity from an insurance company. In return for the lump sum the annuity provides a regular income for life.

GENERAL INSURANCE

As mentioned above, this covers the big risks such as aviation and shipping but also the more mundane house, motor and protection insurances. Protection insurance has become an important market and has grown in response to the reduced levels of benefits available from the state welfare system. It includes private medical insurance (PMI); life assurance, which provides a lump sum when you die; income protection, which pays a regular income if you are too ill to work; and critical illness insurance, which pays a lump sum if you are diagnosed with a serious condition.

REINSURANCE

Sometimes the underwriting risks are too great for one insurer to take on. In this case the insurer either seeks partners to share the risk or reinsures part of the risk. In this sense reinsurance can be described as insurance for insurers.

Say, for example, an insurance company takes on a big risk such as a large ocean liner. The insurer does not want to bear the full cost if the liner joins the *Titanic*, so it pays a reinsurance company a premium to reinsure the cost above £10 million. If the liner sinks, the insurance company pays the first £10 million on the claim and the reinsurer pays the rest.

There are about 45 reinsurance companies in the UK, most of which have offices in the City. Many of these are subsidiaries of major international operations that have their head-quarters in Europe (in particular Germany and Switzerland) or in the US.

LOSS ASSESSORS AND LOSS ADJUSTERS

These are the specialists who investigate claims to check they are valid and then calculate a fair payout. They cover everything from car accidents and house break-ins to flood damage and fires. This type of work can require engineering, scientific and forensic skills.

WEBSITES

Most of the insurance companies run websites and some of these provide details of graduate recruitment.

● For access to these, try the employers direct or go to one of the major recruitment agencies, including the specialists:
www.prospects.csu.man.ac.uk and
www.doctorjob.com

15
THE LAW

The legal profession is divided into two broad camps:

● Barristers (or advocates, as they are called in Scotland) provide specialist services as advocates or advisers in law. They have 'rights of audience' in all courts. They usually work from 'chambers' and are hired by solicitors to represent clients. As William Brown put it in the 'Just William' stories, they also eat a lot of dinners in temples.

● Solicitors can be regarded as the general practitioners in law, although these days they do have increasing powers of advocacy (that is, the right to speak in court). Most work in firms that may also employ assistant solicitors.

Most barristers and solicitors tend to work in private practices, but big financial institutions like the professional services firms have their own legal departments, as do the financial services regulators. However, these organisations are unlikely to offer training facilities.

In recent years medium-sized firms of solicitors have tended to merge to provide a wide range of specialist knowledge. US law firms continue to develop their presence in London either directly or through affiliations. In terms of salaries, the US firms are generally among the top payers.

SPECIALIST CITY FIRMS

The City law firms tend to be quite different from the high-street operations in that their clients are companies rather than individuals. Some of the law firms in the City specialise – for example, in pensions law, which is a massive subject in its own right and has huge implications for Britain's multimillion-pound pension schemes as well as for the national and global employers who set up these schemes and the investment managers who run them.

The following points, from the AGCAS 'Legal Profession' graduate careers information booklet, outline the scope of law firms in the City:

● City firms tend to cater for businesses rather than individuals. They concentrate on large-scale commercial work, such as mergers and acquisitions, joint ventures, management buy-outs, loan documentation, bond issues, tax work, corporate insolvency and major civil litigation.
● Specialist 'niche' practices are known for their expertise in a particular area of law, such as shipping, insurance, entertainment, environment, intellectual property, planning, construction or medical negligence. Such firms can be especially attractive if you wish to use your specialist interest.
● International work is increasingly important for the larger commercial

firms. They will advise on issues as diverse as cross-border mergers, sovereign debts and their restructuring, and the regulation of financial institutions overseas, among other subjects. Some firms will have their own offices in other countries, providing opportunities for qualified solicitors and sometimes trainees to spend time abroad. Other firms may be members of international law groups, with links with law firms overseas. In all these environments language skills are seen as increasingly valuable.

In some large organisations, the legal department will resemble a small or medium-sized firm of solicitors and will carry out all the legal work for the organisation. However, this type of department is declining. What is more likely is for in-house lawyers to concentrate on compliance and negotiation and to advise senior management on important trans-actions. This is seen very much as preventative work, so that as important corporate deals go through, for example, there are no major loopholes that opponents can use to scupper the deal.

There are other opportunities for solicitors and barristers in the City. Some who work as in-house legal staff eventually move away from purely legal work to become company secretaries or to enter general management.

This book does not cover the training or qualifying procedures necessary to become a solicitor or barrister, only the types of firm and the variety of work you may find in this field. Training and qualifying remains a tough business, while the lack of financial support continues to present problems for most graduates.

FURTHER INFORMATION
● General Council of the Bar www.barcouncil.org.uk
● Law Society www.lawsociety.org.uk
● For further details about AGCAS publications, contact CSU Ltd, Prospects House, Booth Street East, Manchester M13 9EP.
TEL 0161 277 5240.
FAX 0161 277 5250.

16
ACCOUNTANCY/PROFESSIONAL SERVICES FIRMS

The term 'accountancy' is no longer used by the major firms that have grown through mega-mergers to become today's big five 'professional services' organisation.

The likes of Arthur Andersen, Deloitte and Touche, Ernst & Young, KPMG and PricewaterhouseCoopers (PWC) are full-blown consultancy firms offering services including investment and actuarial as well as the traditional tax and auditing roles.

If you are interested in the traditional services offered by chartered accountants, read the AGCAS leaflet *Accountancy, Taxation and Financial Management*, which provides a brief description of the different types of professional accountant, as follows:

CHARTERED ACCOUNTANT
Chartered accountants provide a wide range of fee-earning advisory and management services to a variety of clients, mostly in the industrial, commercial and charitable sectors. They train mainly in private practice and belong to one of three professional bodies, depending on their geographic location:

● The Institute of Chartered Accountants in England and Wales (ICAEW)
● The Institute of Chartered Accountants of Scotland (ICAS)
● The Institute of Chartered Accountants in Ireland (ICAI)

CERTIFIED ACCOUNTANTS
These provide both financial and management accounting information and can train in commerce, industry, local and central government, or in private practice. Certified accountants often work alongside chartered accountants in private practice and management accountants in industry. They may move sector both during and after qualification. The relevant professional body is the Association of Chartered Certified Accountants (ACCA).

Management accountants
Management accountants provide the financial information required to plan and run a business. They train mostly in manufacturing industry and commerce and belong to the Chartered Institute of Management Accountants (CIMA).

Accountants in public services
These provide both management accounting and financial accounting information and train in government departments, local authorities, the health service and public service industries. Some also work in private practice or move between the two sectors after qualification. This type of accountant belongs to the Chartered Institute of Public Finance and Accountancy (CIPFA).

WHICH QUALIFICATION?

The following questions posed by AGCAS may help you decide the appropriate qualification to pursue for your career:

● Do you look forward to advising clients on the financial aspects of their business? (Look at ACCA and ACAEW.)
● Would you prefer to carry responsibility and manage a business? (Look at ACCA and CIMA.)
● Is public service and value for money of interest to you? (Consider CIPFA.)
● If tax planning seems attractive, consider the ATII qualification or, if this is only part of your interest, look at ICAEW or ACCA.

AGCAS also recommends that you read the job adverts in *Accountancy Age* to get a feel for the type of job you can apply for with your qualifications and experience.

As well as the professional services firms, banks and insurance companies are big employers of accountants.

Academic background

Graduates in any degree subject can qualify as a tax adviser by finding a position as a tax trainee and taking the Association of Tax Technicians (ATT) exam, which leads to the qualification of Taxation Technician. All ATT students are required to have two years' relevant work experience in UK taxation in addition to passing the exams in order to obtain membership. The next step is to take the Institute's ATII examination. Alternatively, you

can first qualify as an accountant or solicitor and then specialise in taxation, in which case you are eligible to proceed straight to the Institute's examination. To become an Associate of the Institute you must have completed three years' professional experience. Details of the career opportunities are set out in Part 3 of this book.

Tax services

Arthur Andersen describes itself as a 'professional services organisation' that offers 'risk management, tax, consulting and corporate finance strategies to national and global clients'. Briefly, if you work in taxation for one of the mega-firms you can expect to train and specialise in one of the following areas:

● Corporate tax consulting
● Indirect tax
● Private client services
● Tax depreciation
● Technology solutions
● Transfer pricing

These are described in Chapter 30.

SOURCE MATERIAL

For further details about AGCAS publications, contact CSU Ltd, Prospects House, Booth Street East, Manchester M13 9EP.
TEL 0161 277 5240.
FAX 0161 277 5250.

USEFUL WEBSITES

● Association of Chartered Certified Accountants www.acca.co.uk
● Association of International

Accountants www.a-i-a.org.uk
● Association of Taxation Technicians
www.att.co.uk
● Chartered Institute of Public
Finance and Accountancy
www.cipfa.org.uk
● Chartered Institute of Taxation
www.tax.org.uk
● Chartered Institute of Management
Accountants www.cima.org.uk
● Institute of Chartered Accountants
in England and Wales
www.icaew.co.uk
● Institute of Financial Accountants
www.ifa.org.uk

17
FINANCIAL SERVICES REGULATION

The financial services market is self-regulated, which means that the organisations responsible for selling and buying are also responsible for policing their activities. This system has been widely criticised for being too slow to act and too soft on the bad guys. As a cynical observer put it, the golden rule of self-regulation is 'He who has the gold makes the rules.'

Whatever your views, you need to understand how the City is regulated if you want to work there. The chances are you will be required to take regulatory exams in order to carry out your job if it involves advising individual or corporate clients or running investments on behalf of others.

FINANCIAL SERVICES AUTHORITY (FSA)

There are three main investment watchdogs, which are currently being combined under the Financial Services Authority (FSA). The FSA is the designated agency to which Parliament has delegated many of the powers under the Financial Services Act 1986. The FSA reports directly to the government (HM Treasury) and has statutory powers to enforce its requirements and decisions.

The Financial Services Act makes it a criminal offence to undertake investment business without being either authorised to do so or exempt

under the Act. Authorisation is normally obtained from one of the three front-line regulators (IMRO, SFA and PIA). The main exception is professional firms whose business inevitably includes some investment business – for instance, accountants or solicitors. In this case authorisation is provided by their professional body (see page 38).

Each watchdog is responsible for regulating different types of investment business.

● Investment Management Regulatory Organisation (IMRO) regulates those managing investments; acting as a manager or trustee of authorised unit trust schemes; managing or operating other collective investment schemes; giving investment advice to institutional investors.
● The Securities and Futures Authority (SFA) regulates stockbrokers dealing in shares, options and financial and commodities futures.
● The Personal Investment Authority (PIA) regulates firms that advise, market and sell investments to private investors.

In May 1997 the government announced its intention to create a single financial services regulator, replacing the present framework of statutory and self-regulation established by the Financial Services Act. In June 1998, responsibility for the financial regulation of banks was transferred from the Bank of England to the FSA, and the majority of IMRO and other self-regulatory organisation staff transferred to FSA contracts of employment.

THE PROCESS OF AUTHORISATION

To be authorised, organisations must demonstrate that they are, and will remain, fit and proper to undertake investment business of the kind proposed. The 'fit and proper' test encompasses:

● The honesty and integrity of the organisation, its directors, managers, staff and any controlling shareholders
● The experience, qualifications and competence of its management
● The adequacy of its financial resources
● Its ability to conduct investment business of the kind proposed honestly, fairly and competently
● Its ability to comply with the regulator's rules

The organisation must establish systems to ensure that all the rules are followed, to report key facts to the regulator, and to report regularly on its financial welfare. It must be ready to co-operate with any request for information or any investigation. Finally, it must accept that it is subject to the disciplinary system of the regulator and must pay its share of the regulation costs.

WEBSITES

● Financial Services Authority (FSA) and also the Personal Investment Authority (PIA) www.fsa.gov.uk
● Investment Managers Regulatory Organisation (IMRO) www.imro.co.uk
● Securities and Futures Authority (SFA) www.sfa.org.uk
● Securities Institute www.securities-institute.org.uk

PART 3
YOUR GUIDE TO CAREERS IN THE CITY

'It's not a question of enough, pal.
It's a zero-sum game – somebody
wins, somebody loses. Money
itself isn't lost or made, it's simply
transferred from one perception to
another.'

Wall Street,1987

a) Banking and Investment

18
THE JARGON

- **AAA** A top credit rating. The credit rating of a company or financial institution indicates its ability to service any bonds it issues and to repay the capital when a bond matures. As a rule, the lower the credit rating the higher the yield (interest rate) but also the higher the risk of the company defaulting.
- **Beauty parade** This is the final interview process for a major fund management appointment. The investment consultant puts together a short list and the investment managers are called on in turn to make a presentation to the trustees of the pension or charity fund.
- **Broker/dealer** In the broad sense a broker is an intermediary who sells financial products to consumers on behalf of the institutions. A dealer (or broker-dealer) is involved in the marketing and the buying and selling of securities.
- **Cash management** Balancing the day-to-day cash flow and making the most of money on short-term deposit.
- **Chinese walls** These are invisible information barriers that separate two different parts of a bank to avoid conflicts of interests and regulatory problems.
- **Collective/pooled fund** Investors buy units in a collective fund such as a unit trust or open-ended investment company (Oeic) in order to gain access to a wider range of assets than they could otherwise afford through direct investment. In this way, pooled funds spread risk. They also reduce the dealing transaction costs.
- **Convertible** This is a type of equity that is more akin to a bond in that it pays a regular income and has a fixed redemption date. The owner can convert it to an ordinary or preference share at a future date.
- **Corporate banking** Banking to medium-sized companies, cash and currency management, custodial services.
- **Corporate finance** A simile for **investment banking**.
- **Credit rating/risk** If you are a bank lending money to businesses you need to assess the likelihood of a borrower not being able to service the loan (the regular interest payments) or repay the capital at the end of the loan period. A borrower's credit rating will dictate the terms of the loan, including the cost.
- **Custody** The safe-keeping of assets. The biggest custodians offer global custody to the multimillion-pound pension funds.
- **DCMs** The debt capital markets are where big companies issue bonds to raise finance.
- **Investment banking** Advising companies on major changes to their corporate structures through loans and issuing shares, supervising the financing of mergers and acquisitions.

Aka corporate finance.

● **Fixed-rate bonds** Bonds that pay a fixed rate of interest (the coupon) for a predetermined period.

● **Floating rate notes** An FRN is a Eurobond that has its interest rate linked to a base rate (for example, the London Interbank Offered Rate or Libor). FRNs usually have a maturity of between seven and fifteen years.

● **Insider information** Market-sensitive knowledge that is not available outside the company or its advisers. To invest on the basis of this knowledge is illegal.

● **Market maker** This is an institution that acts as a principal in the securities markets, creating two-way prices for the sale and purchase of blocks of securities.

● **Operations/support** Used to be known as the 'back office' function where all the settlement and risk management takes place.

● **Over the counter (OTC)** In the UK this refers to a security that is not listed on a recognised exchange. In the US the OTC market is for smaller companies that do not qualify for a full listing on the main markets like the New York Stock Exchange (NYSE).

● **Pitch** The investment banking term for a proposal you put to a client regarding undertaking a corporate development – for example, acquiring a rival company that you happen to know is going cheap.

● **Real time** means, er, real time, as in now. Real-time trading means you are buying and selling at the current price rather than at yesterday's closing price, for example.

● **Retail banking**, also known as high-street banking, is banking (loans, current and deposit accounts) to individuals and small partnerships and companies that do not need a fancier service.

● **Securitisation** This is the process whereby financial contracts – mortgages, for example – are bundled together so they can be bought and sold.

● **TMT** The technology, media and telecoms sector.

● **Treasury** services cover a wide range of currency and interest rate exposures for corporations that have overseas markets and operations.

● **Underwriting** In insurance terms this means agreeing to cover the costs if things go wrong. In banking terms, in cases where the bank has advised on a share or bond issue it usually refers to the agreement that the bank will buy any remaining securities that are not bought through public subscription. Where the issue is very large the lead bank may organise a syndicate of banks to underwrite the public offering, and so spread the risk.

19
THE BANK OF ENGLAND

k MONEY: Starting salary for an A-level entrant in 2000 was just under £14,500, while the figure for graduates was £22,000–£23,000.

h HOURS: Standard 9–5.30, although the starting time may vary from department to department. For a big institution there's a surprising amount of flexibility in the hours you work, which means you can sometimes balance intensive periods of work with quieter times by taking a longer lunch or leaving early.

PRESSURE RATING: 6/10. Working for the Bank is considered less pressured than investment banking, where you would have to deal with commercial clients who are paying you vast sums to get it right. However, you still have to work to demanding deadlines.

C GLAMOUR RATING: 7/10. Not as glam as investment banking but, as economics graduate Jamie points out, 'For economists the Bank of England really is *the* place to be, especially in the field of monetary analysis.'

l TRAVEL RATING: 4/10. You may get the chance to travel if your job involves contact with foreign central banks and foreign monetary policy, but you don't have the chance to visit the rich global corporations associated with investment banking.

SUMMARY

The Bank of England is a bit of an ivory tower in the City. Working there is heaven for economics boffins.

However, remember that this is a different career from, say, working for the investment banks, which are very commercial operations. The Bank of England has more of a regulatory and supervisory role in the City and in the economy as a whole. If you are interested in mergers and acquisitions or in asset management, then look at the chapters on investment banking and fund management.

An analyst at the Bank, for example, would focus on public policy and money markets rather than UK or foreign companies. An A-level entrant could become a research or records management assistant, secretary, local area network supervisor in IT, settlements clerk, or provide support for one of the operational areas.

The Bank's structure reflects its key objectives of supporting monetary and financial stability while maintaining the efficiency and competitiveness of the markets. Its principal activities fall broadly into the following areas:

- Monetary analysis and statistics
- Financial stability
- Financial market operations
- European financial markets

THE BANK OF ENGLAND

WHO CAN APPLY?

Like many major institutions, the Bank has a trainee course for graduates and, unusually, for A-level candidates as well. This means that your first jobs will take you into different departments until you get a feel for where you want to specialise – for example, supervision, capital markets, economic analysis, or administration.

If you are a keen academic, take a look at the wide range of sponsorship programmes the Bank offers for first degree and postgraduate research. See the website for details.

The Bank is very open about its pay and benefits package, so do visit the website. In addition to the starting salaries mentioned above, in some jobs – for example, if you join as an IT graduate – you get overtime and occasional shift supplements.

The training looks good and could set you up nicely for jobs elsewhere in the City if the Bank itself can't fulfil your long-term needs. 'Our strong commitment to training reflects a highly supportive learning culture which encourages mobility and progression within the Bank. If you perform well in your role and demonstrate plenty of enthusiasm and potential, we'll provide you with support to study for professional qualifications.'

You are likely to join at the same time as about 25 other graduates of your own age with whom you will undergo your training. Workers at the Bank say they often make good friends among this group of colleagues.

A-LEVEL ENTRY

For A-level entrants there is an induction programme that leads to a structured series of training events, each designed to help develop your skills. Your first job with the Bank will probably be within a team responsible for processing day-to-day administrative work. You should expect a bit of repetition here but, having said that, there's no point applying for the job unless you can demonstrate your ability to work accurately and methodically. This period in your training also helps you understand the way in which the Bank operates on a day-to-day basis.

The Bank makes no promises about your subsequent progress, and there's no set career pattern. However, the more motivation you display and the more qualities you develop, the quicker you'll be able to apply for other jobs within the Bank – all of which are advertised internally. Any promotion you earn and responsibility you shoulder will be a reflection of your own efforts.

Once you've established yourself, the Bank will help you by providing support (in terms of both finance and time) to study on a part-time basis towards higher academic and professional or vocational qualifications in fields such as securities, settlements and personnel.

On-the-job tuition is backed up by a series of short, interactive training modules, as well as a 'menu' of development opportunities including project work, coaching, distance learning and study.

Jeanette joined the Bank of

England in 1986 after completing her A levels. She now works in the Bank's regional agency network. 'I've always been interested in the world of finance and applied to all the high-street banks. However, the Bank of England stood head and shoulders above the rest.

'When I first joined, I found myself tackling a wide range of jobs, from account and customer maintenance through to cheque clearing and note sorting. Today, much of this work takes place in London. Having moved on from a role in the clearing, notes and accounts sections, I now work in the Birmingham Agency. Our brief is to visit a wide range of companies throughout our region to find out how the economy is affecting them in the fields of supply, demand, costs, prices, wages, employment and exports. This information is then passed on in the form of a monthly report to the Monetary Policy Committee, who use it to help set interest rates. My part in this process is to provide administrative support to the Agent and his deputy, conduct research on new contacts and maintain information databases.'

Jeanette rates the training she has received highly. 'Recently, I've attended courses that have introduced me to techniques on supervision, analysis, assertiveness and confident speaking. As I meet a lot of chief executives and finance directors in the course of my job, I've found the last of these programmes particularly helpful. I've also had the chance to learn all about the various software packages used throughout the Bank on courses held either externally or at the head office in London. At the same time, the Bank is supporting me to study part time for an HNC in Business and Finance at a local college.'

One of Jeanette's best experiences was when she was seconded to the City head office to help develop a computer program for accounts management. 'Originally this was only for a three-month period, but I ended up staying for nine. The project involved liaising with customers regarding changes to their accounts, conducting trials of the new system, and I co-ordinated these with all the Bank's regional offices. Working in the City really helped my development and boosted my confidence, and one of the most pleasing aspects is that the system is still used now, four and a half years later.'

GRADUATE RECRUITMENT

Recruitment takes place in several key financial areas.

ECONOMISTS

The Bank is working towards becoming a broad-based centre of excellence for monetary policy research and analysis. At the same time, it is enhancing its surveillance of financial stability conditions and outlook. This includes the on-going analysis of relevant developments in financial markets, statistics and emerging market economies. In addition, the Bank is in the process of reorganising its banking and market services to provide more cost-effective and efficient banking services to its customers.

The Bank's Analyst Career Training (ACT) starts the development process and includes the following elements:

● Induction: split into two parts, this gives you a clear insight into the Bank's structure, how it operates and where it stands in the context of the City, Europe and the rest of the world.
● Mentor scheme: as a new graduate entrant, you will be assigned a mentor – typically someone a few years ahead of you in his or her career. They are there to provide you with informal advice and support as and when you need it.

Apart from the on-the-job training, you also take part in development workshops – interactive training courses that build your skills in analysis, problem-solving, time management, personal presentation, communication and team-building. Longer term, the economics and finance training can lead to sponsored part-time or even full-time post-graduate study. You'll get the opportunity to listen to visiting speakers from the academic and business worlds to keep you informed on the latest developments in economics and the financial sector. Where necessary you can also expect area-specific technical and language training.

The ACT programme lasts for three to four years. After eighteen months you will attend a professional development workshop, which identifies the areas that you need to develop in order to move into the next grade in the Bank.

IT GRADUATES

The Bank does not expect its graduate trainees to be experts in IT. 'But we do need individuals who are familiar with the application of IT in a range of environments,' a spokesperson says.

If you join as an IT graduate, initially you will spend some time on an induction course to find out how the Bank operates and to mix with other non-IT graduates.

David joined the Bank in 2000 with a history degree from Cambridge University, after a year out working for the Bank of Nova Scotia and attending a language school in France. 'The variety and high profile of the work certainly appealed to me, as did the friendly and supportive working atmosphere. These factors helped me to choose the Bank despite a job offer from a corporate finance organisation.

'At present I work in regulatory policy, which examines the financial stability implications of major regulatory developments. My role initially involved analysing reports and writing notes from meetings and briefing documents. Over the last four months, however, I've been writing a high-profile article on current developments in accountancy for a Bank publication called the *Financial Stability Review*.'

David likes the fact that the Bank of England's decisions have an impact at a national and international level. 'The work is more policy-based than in other banks, and involves looking at the bigger picture rather than focusing purely on operational matters. Probably the most satisfying aspect about my job is the high level of intellectual stimulation and challenge. I'd very much like to stay with the Bank – it provides you with a uniquely broad understanding of the financial system. I hope to embark on the Masters programme with the Bank in three or four years' time.'

Jonathan has a degree in economics from Bristol University and was sponsored by the Bank in his final year. He deferred entry by a year to pursue lighting and sound work for theatre and production companies and eventually joined in 1999. 'I'd picked up a brochure about the Bank at a university careers fair, and applied for a summer place. Its worldwide reputation appealed to me straight away, but once I was there I could see the variety of work undertaken as well as the opportunities that existed for training and development.

'I'm a Note Policy Analyst in the Issue Office. It's a new role, in which I analyse factors such as how many notes should be printed, and it involves a good deal of policy work with retail banks. It also involves advising people at senior levels, which was daunting at first.'

Tanveer, who has a degree in Government and Economics from the London School of Economics, works in the Financial Markets Operations section within the Gilt-Edged and Money Markets division, which implements monetary policy, as well as providing market data and intelligence. 'At the moment, I'm particularly involved in a project to enable paperless trading of money market instruments. Much of my time is spent preparing for meetings and writing papers, which demands plenty of background reading. There's always something landing on my desk that needs urgent attention, so time management is absolutely vital. I also have the chance to interact with lots of other parts of the Bank, especially the Financial Stability side, as well as the external Stock Exchange, HM Treasury and market practitioners.'

Rain studied Politics, Philosophy and Economics at Oxford University, then took a Masters in economics at the London School of Economics, sponsored by the Bank. Rain joined in early 2000 and is an economist in the Monetary Analysis department. 'My team briefs the Monetary Policy Committee (MPC) on developments within the UK corporate sector. Assessing the impact of structural changes in the economy involves in-depth research on topics such as the effect of the Internet on firms' behaviour. We are also responsible for interpreting and forecasting aggregate investment in the economy and explaining developments to the MPC and to our colleagues.'

QUALIFICATIONS AND SKILLS

For A-level entry you will need a minimum of five GCSEs at grade C or above, including maths and English. You'll also have already passed (or expect to obtain) at least two – and preferably three – A levels in academically oriented subjects. Economics, business studies and IT will be particularly relevant.

As the work can be repetitive, an eye for detail is essential. You can see the qualities the Bank will be looking for on the 'Interested in Applying?' page on its website. Remember, the Bank receives a large number of applications every year, so it does not consider applicants who do not fulfil the minimum criteria.

As far as personal qualities are concerned, you must combine the capacity to learn new skills quickly with the ability to use your initiative, set your own targets, and use sound reasoning and clear objectives to make decisions. Flexibility and the communication skills to work well as a member of a closely knit team are other important qualities.

Economists and IT graduates need a numerate degree (minimum 2:1). IT graduates need a degree course with substantial exposure to IT (such as science, engineering, economics, statistics or mathematics). You must be able to demonstrate an analytical approach to problem-solving.

TIPS

Remember, a job at the Bank of England will be more academic in nature than working for the investment banks. If you want to develop your commercial acumen in the fast lane, see Chapters 21–28.

Keep in mind the Bank's recruitment timetable. You should submit your application by the end of March. Interviews usually take place in April and May. New entrants normally start between June and September. All positions are located in the City.

SOURCES OF INFORMATION ON CAREER
● Applications are made on-line. Go to www.bankofengland.co.uk

20
THE STOCK EXCHANGE

k **MONEY:** £22,000–£28,000. Benefits include a discretionary bonus linked to company-wide performance.

h **HOURS:** A 7 a.m. start is necessary for some jobs, while for others it's a standard 9–5.30.

PRESSURE RATING: 5–8/10 depending on the department. Some parts of the Exchange are very technical but one step removed from the pressured, deadline-driven work.

C **GLAMOUR RATING:** 8/10. As one of the graduate entrants says, 'You are working for one of the key players in the market – you're certainly always at the forefront of what's going on.'

1 **TRAVEL RATING:** 9/10 if you are in the right department. The business development team, for example, has to make presentations to overseas companies that are considering a launch on the Stock Exchange.

SUMMARY

London is one of the top three stock markets in the world. The other two you will hear about most frequently are New York and Tokyo. The LSE is also the world's leading international exchange. More international companies are listed, and more international equities are traded, in London than on any other exchange.

Graduates at the LSE get involved in a range of business areas including:

● Trading and information
● Business development
● IT
● Regulation

The Exchange also recruits individuals for other departments, for example:

● Finance
● Personnel
● Audit
● Legal
● Property

WHERE WILL YOU WORK?

Trading and information

The Exchange distributes a wide range of high-quality, up-to-date market and securities information. The London Market Information Link is its datafeed for information services. Through this it provides information such as order, quote and trade data, regulatory company news and other reference information to over 85,000 terminals around the world. Its teams are responsible for identifying new opportunities for its markets and for the information demanded by the market.

Business development

The Exchange needs to ensure that it attracts new business to list on its markets and consistently nurtures relationships with member firms to ensure that products and services match the demands of its customers. Its teams actively manage these relationships, promoting its markets across the globe and developing new business opportunities. To do this the Exchange needs excellent knowledge of its markets, so there's also a dedicated team which analyses and monitors market trends.

IT

Technology is vital to the smooth and efficient operation of the markets. IT teams manage a variety of projects, developing and enhancing the trading systems and internal desktop applications to ensure that the Exchange remains at the forefront of technology. The IT department has close relationships with third-party suppliers, so the Exchange isn't necessarily looking for individuals with a highly technical background. Mainly, it is seeking to recruit business analysts and project managers.

Regulation

Under the UK's financial services regulatory system, as a Recognised Investment Exchange the Stock Exchange has to regulate against abuse. To do this it constantly monitors and supervises the market in real time. This ensures that adequate information is available to market participants and that the appropriate degree of transparency is maintained. Where necessary the Exchange investigates market activity if suspected abuse has occurred. To do

this it employs a highly sophisticated system that roots out trades and quotes that deviate from the norm.

The regulation team endeavours to develop the rules that govern market makers and brokers, ensuring that they remain up to date and reflect the rapid developments that are taking place.

TELL IT HOW IT IS

Bikita is a business analyst in the Service Development Department. 'I graduated in 1995 with an economics degree from the University of Stellenbosch. Since joining the Exchange in October 1999 I've gained a fantastic insight into how the financial markets operate. And working for one of the key players in the market, you're certainly always at the forefront of what's going on.

'I'm involved in project work, generally with an IT emphasis. Working with teams from different business areas and liaising with external development consultants, I make sure that the systems delivered to the Exchange fulfil initial business requirement. It's hard work, but extremely enjoyable.'

Satnam is head of the Stock Monitoring Unit in the Market Supervision Department. 'I joined the graduate scheme in October 1999 after graduating in Politics, Philosophy and Economics from Oxford University. What attracted me was the opportunity of a real job with responsibilities from the start – the graduate training is there more as a support.

'I head a unit of six people, monitoring market activity to ensure that price-sensitive information is released in a timely manner to the market. My day starts at seven a.m., when I review the newspapers to ensure issues covered in the press have been announced correctly. I get a lot of contact with senior people in large firms, which can be quite daunting, so influencing and persuasion skills really are essential.'

Vanessa is a personnel manager. 'I think everyone has their own view of the Exchange, but I've discovered a dynamic, modern environment, with professional, well-trained and, above all, friendly staff. When I first joined in June 1999, I had to learn about the complexities of Exchange activities and the financial markets, but I received a lot of support from staff across the business.

'I'm one of three personnel managers – we each have responsibility for different business areas. Mine include Business Development, Property and Strategy, so I get involved in everything from running courses to advising managers on management issues, recruitment and policy.'

Anne is an executive in the Business Development Department. 'I joined the graduate training programme in August 1998 after completing a degree in Business Administration and an MA in Export Marketing. As a graduate, you're given a "real" job right from the beginning. I had responsibilities placed on me and was given objectives to deliver, while the graduate training gave me the support I needed to enhance my performance.

'Initially I was involved in identifying European companies seeking to float and then attracting them to list in London or undertake a dual listing. I had to research the companies and the markets, making direct contact with potential companies and giving presentations. This gave me an excellent understanding of the Exchange and the financial markets themselves. Now, I attract new member firms to trade on the markets – this involves making overseas trips to visit the firms in person.'

Stock Exchange benefits include a non-contributory pension scheme, a season ticket to cover travel within a 60-mile radius of London, a lunch allowance, private healthcare, life assurance, and 25 days' annual holiday.

QUALIFICATIONS AND SKILLS

The Exchange recruits a number of graduates and MBAs each year. To meet the entrance criteria you will need a minimum 2:1 qualification in a degree discipline such as finance, accountancy, economics, mathematics, marketing or business studies. Ideally you will have at least six months' relevant work experience in an environment where you have taken on direct responsibility. Work experience or industrial placement schemes are not offered.

The Exchange says it aims to recruit 'dynamic, innovative individuals with drive and enthusiasm'. You should be able to demonstrate an ambition to work in the financial markets and to offer practical evidence to support this.

Like many City organisations, the Exchange recruits first among internal applicants when opportunities become available, after which it will advertise externally in the national and regional press and specialist publications.

TIPS

The number of graduates employed each year varies, so phone or check the website to find out whether there are any vacancies likely to fit in with when you graduate. Even if you join direct from university, you are likely to start a proper job straight away rather than spend several months in training.

If you want to apply, just click on the job search page link on the website. Even if there are no vacancies that match your skills and experience at the time you apply, the Exchange will keep your details on its database and contact you if a suitable opportunity arises.

SOURCES OF INFORMATION ON CAREER

The London Stock Exchange (LSE) and other important exchanges are described in Chapter 10. If you are interested in working for an exchange, visit the websites listed on page 39. If you can't find the information you are looking for, e-mail your query to: personnel@londonstockexchange.com.

21
INVESTMENT BANKING – CLIENT MANAGER, CORPORATE FINANCE

k **MONEY:** £27,000+ together with possible sign-on bonus of £3,000–£10,000, plus banking benefits.

h **HOURS:** Don't ask! If you raise this point at your interview you won't be considered. This isn't so much a job for life as a job instead of a life.

PRESSURE RATING: 9/10. Most people in corporate finance who are on the front line live on adrenaline, caffeine and alcohol. You will probably go to the gym three times a week, but only because looking good is part of the job and it's expected of you.

C **GLAMOUR RATING:** 10/10. This is definitely sexy provided you've got the stamina to look good through twelve-hour days. The big firms put on socials from time to time to make sure you can still do the small-talk thing – but frankly these are not occasions where you can let down your hair (assuming you have any left).

l **TRAVEL RATING:** 7–10/10. Travel is a big part of the job if you are on the front line. Destinations will depend on client locations, but the big firms will deal with global companies, so it could be anywhere.

SUMMARY
Corporate finance involves making and breaking companies – mergers and acquisitions (M&As), takeovers and management buy-outs, for example. It also involves raising finance through debt (issuing bonds or taking out an institutional loan) and equity (issuing shares in the company). M&A activity is experiencing a boom at present, and underlying these structural changes are massive transfers of capital, debt instruments and shares between the different parties.

Your job as client relations manager will be more immediate – to smooth the way for a successful transition for the businesses themselves and for the investors (the shareholders). Share prices fluctuate dramatically when a corporate restructure or a takeover is in the offing, particularly in the case of a hostile bid.

CORPORATE ACTIVITY
If you want to work in investment banking you need to be passionate about money and business. Read the Companies and Markets section of the *Financial Times* to get a feel for the different types of corporate activity, and examine how the market reacts. Consider why an imminent takeover can send the shares of the company to be acquired through the roof but may pull down the share price of the

acquiring company. The latter is probably going to have to buy the target company's shares at a premium (higher than the market reckons they are really worth) and is taking on a big financial risk, which may take several years to pay off.

Whatever the corporate activity, it is the investment bank which will take charge of the operation, using accountants to achieve a correct valuation for the deal, lawyers to ensure that it is shipshape and not open to challenge by competitors, and a marketing or advertising agency to promote the sale of shares, where applicable, or simply to announce the development in a positive light to the public.

TELL IT HOW IT IS

Corporate finance is classed as a 'front office' career. Jonathan joined Credit Suisse First Boston (CSFB) in 1996 after graduating from Pembroke College, Cambridge, with a degree in history. He is now Vice-President, Pan European Equity Sales. 'I've had the opportunity to be directly involved in a string of high-profile transactions that have attracted widespread media interest and proved to be significant market events. These include the flotation of Freeserve in the UK and the US$2.5 billion offering of STMicroelectronics, the largest technology follow-on public share offering in history.

'It was also extremely gratifying to be given as much responsibility as I could handle from an early stage. Now, after less than three years in the industry, my clients include a number of extremely influential fund managers, some of whom have decades of experience but clearly value my opinion.'

Bear in mind that many deals cross international borders and so require very specific expertise – for example, the purchase of a company abroad or the issue of corporate bonds on behalf of a client on the debt capital markets (DCMs) requires a detailed knowledge of that country's stock exchange regulations, legal structure, competition policy, taxation and labour relations, among other issues. For this reason you will specialise in certain business sectors or geographical areas. Business sectors are likely to mirror FTSE index industrial categories, for example oil and gas, software and computer services, and food producers and processors. Geographical areas include Europe, Japan and emerging markets. As you come to understand the markets in which you specialise, you will be able to put forward a proposal (known as a pitch) when you spot an opportunity for one of your clients.

This part of the business also involves raising finance for client companies by issuing shares – or even floating a private company on the Stock Exchange. Alternatively, companies may restructure existing debt to get better terms. For example, if interest rates have changed dramatically since a loan was arranged your client may benefit from paying off that loan and negotiating a new one with a different lender.

As a trainee you are likely to be involved in the research behind a client proposal (pitch), so you need to be good at processing lots of information and presenting it in a lucid format. You also need first-class people skills – you are likely to be meeting some of the people who run the economy before too long.

TRAINING

Global corporate finance training covers technical, operational, financial, industry and management skills. As one investment bank puts it, 'This is a not an environment for the faint-hearted. You need stamina, determination, tact, entrepreneurial flair and the ability not to be fazed by anything that our business throws at you.'

CLIENT RELATIONS MANAGER

Job titles in corporate finance vary but a common one is 'client relations manager' – you might also come across 'account manager'. This role provides a link between the investment bank and the client. Your aim is to understand a roster of clients' businesses and the personalities involved to make sure the bank is targeting the right services. Effectively you are the point of contact with what otherwise would be a huge faceless institution.

You might also become a specialist in certain types of client – for example, those with a geographical or business sector in common – and build up relationships with potential clients, learning about what makes that particular sector tick. In terms of the geographical sectors you are likely to need to be fluent in at least one

language other than English. Your overall aim is to understand your clients so well that you can recommend future strategy rather than wait for a business idea to arise.

Behind the high-profile corporate activity lies a host of painstaking details, so attention to detail is an essential requirement – there is simply no room for mistakes.

Your job is likely to involve the following functions:

● Client reporting – regular and *ad hoc* responses to client requests for information on their investments
● Day-to-day account management and client liaison
● Producing and analysing key performance indicators for senior management
● Client communication to report on their investment objectives
● Preparing presentations for clients
● Making recommendations and implementing asset allocation to meet clients' investment objectives

'Client service is about communication,' says one manager. 'To succeed, you need a broad understanding of investment management. It is that knowledge that gives you the confidence to handle any topic from corporate governance to asset allocation.'

As an account manager you have to be able to explain how your company has performed for a client at meetings. You also have to write papers, provide accurate quarterly reviews, take the lead in new business presentations, and occasionally deal with some difficult clients. Some but not all account managers have fund management experience.

Rebecca, a graduate at a major bank, says, 'I chose client service because of the client contact. After all, clients are what this business is about. From day one you are part of the team. The work is varied; no two days are ever the same. You need to be up to speed on what the markets are doing, what's happening globally, and how the company is performing within that context, because the phone will ring and you never know what the next query is going to be. "What's your view on the US equity market deal?" Or "Can you comment on developments in the technology sector?"

'I work for six account managers who between them have over one hundred clients, ranging in size from a million pounds up to a billion. I write market reports for clients and put together client presentations, which means pulling together market information gathered from people throughout the business – the Economics team, the Investment Strategy Unit, the US equity desk, the Fixed Income team, Property and Unit Trusts.

'You get wide exposure to every part of the business. However, be prepared for the unexpected. I went along to a client meeting for a presentation I had prepared. Suddenly I heard the account manager say, "... and now Rebecca will talk about the reorganisation of your fund." I took a deep breath and ...'

QUALIFICATIONS AND SKILLS

A 2:1 degree is the minimum, and you may need a first for the top investment banks. To give you an idea of the competition, Credit Suisse First Boston received 10,000 applications for 100 jobs in 2000.

You need really strong inter-personal skills and passion for finance. Good presentation skills and languages are also very important.

TIPS

Internships are the best way to see what a bank is like on the inside (see page 21). Make sure you are aware of the application dates for the banks, particularly if you want to apply for an internship. You really need to start thinking about this at the beginning of your second year at university.

SOURCES OF INFORMATION

To help with this chapter we looked at the sites for
- Credit Suisse First Boston, www.csfb.com, and
- Schroders, www.schroders.com.
- We list the members of the Women in investment banking initiative on page 37.
- For access to the banks' websites, try the employers direct or go to one of the major recruitment agencies, including the specialists: www.prospects.csu.man.ac.uk and www.doctorjob.com.

22
FUND MANAGER

Money: £27,000–£35,000 plus possible sign-on bonus of £3,000–£6,000.

Hours: 7 a.m. start with a ten- or eleven-hour day is common. You need to be at your desk early to meet with the analysts and to find out the state of play as other markets are opening and closing. Remember, what represents a sociable hour in New York or Tokyo is anything but in London.

Pressure rating: 8–10/10. Star fund managers tend to quit the business early – and not always voluntarily. Expect a very high burn-out factor.

Glamour rating: 10/10. This is it. It doesn't get any more glamorous – from the outside, at least. As one fund manager says, 'When you get it right and you outwit the market, it's euphoric.' Get it wrong and at best you end up out of a job, at worst you end up in prison or a psychiatric ward – possibly both.

Travel rating: 5–10/10. Much depends on your area of specialisation. If it's emerging markets, be prepared for exotic climes – and jet-lag.

SUMMARY

Fund managers (aka investment managers and asset managers) run money (other people's, not their own, which is safe in the building society). They invest money on behalf of individuals, insurance companies, pension funds, charities, governments and local authorities, among others. Their job is to invest the money in the best possible way in accordance with the aims specified by the client. So, while part of your job is to spot the companies that will outperform their peers or the market benchmark, you will always have to act in accordance with the 'statement of investment principles' and the trust deed or rules. Otherwise you get sacked.

A unit trust emerging markets fund might specify maximum capital growth, never mind the risks, while a charity fund may require a very low-risk strategy that produces the regular income the charity needs to pay wages and support its benevolent activities. In the former situation you can go out on a limb because investors will expect considerable volatility in returns with a clearly identified high-risk fund. In the case of the charity, you would be very wrong to invest in stocks that fall outside the investment brief, even if you think they are a safe bet. Fund managers are sacked for straying from their brief, even though the performance of the fund looks good.

SO, WHAT'S IT LIKE TO BE A FUND MANAGER?

This has to be one of the most glamorous jobs in the City. Certainly, if you make it to the top the rewards are phenomenal and you will learn to yawn with indifference every time you are headhunted by a rival company with even deeper pockets than your present employer.

There's a price to pay, of course. As in Hollywood, few actually make it to the top, and those who do, live life in the fast lane. Investment companies that deliberately create high-profile star managers will make you pay for your celebrity status. You will be watched by everyone in the industry, and when it comes to big decisions it is not just your neck on the block but just about every other precious bit of your anatomy as well.

There are three basic types of investment management service:

● Segregated institutional clients
● Pooled retail funds
● Wealthy private individuals

INSTITUTIONAL CLIENTS

Institutional clients such as pension funds and the larger charities will have their own segregated portfolios. This means they hold all their investments directly and set their own investment aims. In practice the pension and major charity funds will appoint a professional investment adviser, who decides the asset allocation – that is, how the fund should be divided between the main asset classes. Although the pension fund trustees are legally responsible for making the final decisions, the adviser recommends a short list of investment managers to run each of the mandates. The final selection process, in which the managers are invited to make presentations to the trustee board, is known as a beauty parade. These advisers tend to work for either an actuarial or a professional services firm, although for smaller segregated funds the investment manager will do this job (see Chapter 32).

Some of the very large pension funds have their own in-house investment team, while the insurance companies, unit trust groups and investment trusts are also major employers of asset managers for the pooled funds they offer pension funds and individual investors.

Investing money on behalf of others is definitely one of the most interesting jobs in the City. However, you are unlikely to be let loose with a billion-pound pension fund as your first job.

Schroders outlined the following job profile for a graduate entrant into fund management:

● Preparation of monthly and quarterly UK and world equity market commentaries for clients
● Assisting fund managers in stock buying/selling transactions
● Participating in fund management meetings
● Assisting fund managers with portfolio restructuring
● Liaising with the researchers and analysts to understand their market perspective

TELL IT HOW IT IS

Lucy is a fund manager with Schroders; she joined the organisation in 1993 with a history degree from Cambridge. She started as an analyst in the UK research department covering property and utilities (gas, water, electricity). In 1994 she switched to analysing US consumer goods and then took a secondment to New York for a year. She returned as a fund manager and joined the US small companies group. Today she is the head of the US desk in the UK and is responsible for all US equity investment.

'Our job is to invest our clients' money to produce the best returns. This could be in equities, bonds, cash or property. What I like is the immediacy of the job. Every day the markets open there's news – something is going on which changes the way you look at companies or the economy. It's a very dynamic process as you're the one taking decisions and formulating opinions.

'You're meeting clients and company managers, reading, research-ing, discussing ideas with analysts, economists, strategists, anybody who has a view. Decisions are always considered. However there are bad days and you will make mistakes. Schroders people want to win. When you get it wrong, it can be hard to take. That's when you value the supportive culture. But when you get it right and you outwit the market, it's euphoric.'

Even the most enthusiastic fund managers acknowledge that this can be a really tough job and is certainly not one for the faint-hearted or thin-skinned. 'A sense of humour, self-confidence and above all a sense of proportion are essential to survival as a fund manager,' Lucy says.

Simon is 25 and has been with Schroders for two years. He has an Economics and History degree from Durham. Simon started on the UK equities desk, working closely with five fund managers. After a year he moved to the growing fixed income group, which has given him the opportunity to develop his knowledge of gilts and bonds.

'You are part analyst, looking at companies and what they do, part economist, looking at the bigger picture and what world markets are doing, and part psychologist, trying to second-guess what other investors will do and what drives share prices. It's the combination of these three factors that makes this a fascinating area of work.

'As a new graduate you are learning from experienced fund managers while helping with dealing, restructuring portfolios and reporting back to clients. You become involved in external meetings with companies and brokers, and right from day one you are questioning and challenging senior management. You'll work closely with analysts and fund managers to decide which stocks to invest in. You are expected to contribute and your views and your opinions will be sought.

'In your second year you will probably concentrate on an industry sector and if, like me, you are on the small companies desk, then you could find yourself the only person attending company meetings, which might also involve European travel.'

SMALLER COMPANIES CAN BE FUN

Fund managers work closely with the company's analysts, who undertake the detailed research for the markets. Your job can be made much easier if the analysts do a thorough job, but some investment managers like the challenge of the under-researched sector. David is a fund manager with a major investment bank. He has a degree in economics from Durham; after working on the UK equities desk for two years, he moved to smaller companies.

'Think carefully about the area in which you specialise. It can be very difficult to make a really inspired decision in an area like the FTSE 100 or even the 250 companies. Everybody seems to know everything about these companies. I prefer working with the smaller companies towards the bottom of the All-Share. Here you can spot winners and losers much more easily and get to know companies in a way that knocks the spots off the competition.

'People think that smaller companies all follow the same trends and are all in favour or out of favour at the same time. This is simply not true. When you hear in the press that smaller companies are doing well it is usually a result of a massive outperformance by a few stars. My job is to find those stars and avoid all the dross.'

It is usually up to the analysts to do the company visits. Your job as fund manager is to make the asset allocation decisions and to buy and sell based on information provided by the analysts and other sources of research, plus your own intuition. You will probably be expected to meet the clients from time to time. Some investment banks put forward specially trained people to handle client relations (see Chapter 21) so that the fund managers can stick to doing

what they are good at – managing money. However, if your company is making a big pitch to a pension fund, for example, you will probably be invited to make a presentation to the trustees.

COLLECTIVE FUNDS

If you work for a unit trust group you will focus on pooled or collective funds. Investors buy units in a collective fund in order to gain access to a wider range of assets than they could otherwise afford. In this way, pooled funds spread risk. They also reduce the dealing transaction costs.

If you want to find out more about unit and investment trusts, contact the trade bodies mentioned on page 38. Unit trusts are divided into different categories so that consumers get a rough idea what they are buying. For example, a retired investor might want a fairly moderate risk fund that produces a regular income to supplement his or her pension. A higher-income equity fund might be appropriate or, where the investor feels it is essential to protect the capital, he or she might choose a corporate bond fund.

PRIVATE CLIENT SERVICES

The third category of investor – the wealthy individual – tends to be catered for by the private client services departments of the investment banks as well as by the individual firms of private wealth managers or stockbrokers. This topic is covered in Chapter 27.

FURTHER INFORMATION

See page 97.

23
RESEARCH ANALYST

k MONEY: £27,000–£35,000 plus possible sign-on bonus of £3,000–£6,000.

h HOURS: Your day is likely to start at about 6.30 so you can pick up on the close of markets in Japan. However, you may be able to knock off earlier than the nine-to-fivers – and leave at about 4 p.m. with the opening of business in the States.

PRESSURE RATING: 8/10. Not quite so frenzied as the dealers and traders but still very much driven by deadlines.

c GLAMOUR RATING: 9/10. This job is regarded as the brains behind the fund management operation. It is a tremendously powerful position. What you say will have a fundamental impact on the companies in which your bank and its clients invest.

1 TRAVEL RATING: 6–10/10. There are likely to be good prospects but they depend on the sector in which you specialise. For example, you could be researching companies and markets in remote locations for the emerging markets desk, but if you opt for UK smaller companies you could end up with a free rail pass and that's it.

SUMMARY

Analysts are at the heart of the investment banking business and provide the essential information without which fund managers could not make successful investment decisions. You will have to specialise, but there are plenty of opportunities to move into different sectors and markets.

At the crack of dawn each morning you will sift through what has happened in the foreign markets overnight – particularly in the US and Hong Kong. You need to interpret this information and suggest the likely impact on securities held by your bank's fund managers or by institutional clients.

INFORMATION OVERLOAD!

As an analyst you will have a huge range of resources, including Reuters, news services and information from the companies themselves. It is your job to interpret all this in an easily digestible form so that the fund managers know whether to buy, sell or hold.

According to Schroders, if you are appointed to act as a researcher and analyst for a specific market you will:

● Develop a thorough understanding of the dynamics and trends in your sector
● Forecast industry changes and how these will affect the companies in your sector

● Maintain financial models and valuation analysis on key companies in your sector

● Attend company meetings, results announcements and press launches with management

● Communicate best stock ideas to fund managers

● Assign stocks under analysis an investment grading and inform fund managers

Jess is a UK equities analyst with Schroders. She is 25 and joined the company in 1997 with a degree in history from Bristol University. Jess specialises in UK utilities and property and recently joined the financials team.

'As we're a major player in the marketplace, many companies come in to talk to us, but there is no substitute for seeing them on their own turf. With your research you will build valuation models on companies and provide feedback to fund managers. We meet many of the high-flying industry moguls who dominate the press headlines.'

Jess outlines some of the key skills required to be a successful analyst. 'You need to be persuasive, articulate and a skilled presenter. In this business we suffer from information overload. Time is at a premium. At most you'll have twenty seconds to catch someone's attention. So it's got to make an impact and you have to have something interesting to say. In the London office we have around thirty-two analysts working in an open-plan office where we work in teams. You have to be creative and constantly

come up with ideas and find ways to outwit the market. Yes, it is exciting!'

Alan joined Schroders to become a fund manager and started on the UK equities desk. He then moved to the small companies group to focus on high-growth technology companies just at the time when many new companies, like Lastminute.com, were floating their businesses. He met many of the key players and helped Schroders make their investment decisions. Alan has now decided to move into research.

'Analysts are the eyes, ears and information-gatherers of the business, providing the detailed company analysis on which fund managers' decisions are made. We specialise in either industry sectors or geographical regions and provide an in-depth knowledge of individual companies. We visit companies, meet and question company management, attend presentations and lunches.'

You have to learn to put up with the lows as well as the highs, Alan warns. 'The hardest thing is when your sector is out of favour. Even if you are making all the right calls, telling people to sell, it can be very demoralising. But when it is in favour it's fantastic. As an analyst you have to be able to argue your case and stand your ground. Asset management attracts intellectual thinkers with sharp minds. If you have a view people are always willing to listen. The more you learn about a company the more you understand how small things can affect its performance. You see how it is evolving, changing and making money. That's what makes this business exciting.'

To give you a taste of what is involved, Schroders describes below the research required for a range of different issues.

THE ABILITY TO ASSESS COMPANIES IN WHICH YOU INVEST

Schroders says: 'We consider our company research and analysis to be one of our core competitive advantages.' A range of factors are used to form an investment opinion on companies. These can include:

- Financial modelling.
- Forecasting of industry dynamics
- Future market sizes
- A strategic analysis of the positioning of a company
- The quality of the management team

ANALYSING COMPANY STRATEGY AND ACCOUNTS

Business never stands still, and nor does the competition. As an investor, you need to be confident that the companies you invest in can offer a solid financial performance and a competitive advantage that will maintain their success. The strategies and structures that company management employ are vital in determining the future value of the company. Schroders looks for the following factors:

- A clear vision to guide the business
- The ability to expand when necessary, and be flexible in tough times

- A good-quality management team directing future business growth
- A good understanding of what makes them better than the competition
- Strategies for developing competitive advantage over rivals
- A motivated workforce
- A customer-oriented culture

REGULAR RESULTS MEETINGS

In the UK an investment house will typically meet most large companies at least twice a year. 'These meetings are a chance for management to highlight key developments over the period, and for us to question the company on their latest results and current strategic positioning,' Schroders says.

If you are researching a company you will need to meet the chief executive and finance director, as these roles are central to the financial and strategic health of a business. However, management can only disclose information that is already in the public domain otherwise you would be gaining inside information. Consequently, a large amount of time goes into preparing the questions that will draw out the most revealing answers from company management. For example:

- Is pricing pressure likely to increase or decrease over the next two years?
- How are you seeking to build and retain intellectual working capital (key employees)?
- At what level do you expect gross

and operating margins to plateau and over what timescale?

● Can you break the growth in revenue down into repeat business and revenue from new customers?

● How do you intend to utilise the Internet and e-commerce to your advantage?

MAJOR ANNOUNCEMENTS

When a major announcement is made to the markets, company management will often visit financial institutions to explain the impact of the news. Major announcements may include a merger or acquisition, profits warning, substantial new product launch, or the raising of new finance through the debt or equity markets. Here you should focus on the impact of the major event and how it is likely to affect future business. The questions you might ask at this point include:

● What is the rationale behind the merger?

● What savings do you think are achievable through synergy/duplication?

● Why are gross margins declining so much? Is this due to lower overall sales or the higher cost of sales?

● How are you going to change your business model in view of the current crisis?

● How much will your debt have to rise to fund the new factory?

● Will the current dividend level be retained in light of this year's problems?

INITIAL PUBLIC OFFERINGS

Most companies that float on a stock exchange have a 'financial roadshow' to promote their business. Often they will have a relatively low profile as a private company. Consequently, these presentations tend to focus on explaining the products or services and the competitive position of the company within the industry, as well as their plans for utilising the proceeds from the public offering. Typical questions you would be expected to ask include:

● What market share do you have and how does this compare with your major competitors?

● Who are your largest customers and what percentage of revenues do they each account for?

● What is your policy on acquisitions?

● What is your competitive advantage over other industry players?

● What are the opportunities/threats for international expansion?

FURTHER INFORMATION

See page 97.

24
MANAGEMENT ACCOUNTANT

k **MONEY:** £25,000–£28,000 plus possible sign-on bonus and banking benefits.

h **HOURS:** 9–5.30 plus a significant chunk of (unpaid) overtime.

PRESSURE RATING: 6/10. Not as stressful as client relations but does involve dealing direct with clients.

C **GLAMOUR RATING:** 6/10. Investment banking itself gets a high score but this is not the most glamorous area.

1 **TRAVEL RATING:** 5/10. Opportunities may arise to travel to the company's overseas locations and, occasionally, to visit clients, but these will be rare.

SUMMARY

As far as investment banking goes this is not the sexy end but it is a well-paid and highly skilled job for the mathematically minded. The job function will vary but it is likely to involve:

● Preparation of various management accounting reports such as the Group Quarterly Review and the Invested Capital Reporting
● Liaising with other offices regarding cash flow requirements
● Preparation of Group Forecast & Budget packs, analysed by business area
● Payment of retail client and distributor rebates on a quarterly basis
● Benchmarking financial performance and organisational structure against industry peers
● Preparation of a summary of costs for the monthly Business Area Profitability Report

TELL IT HOW IT IS

Hayley joined Schroders in October 1998 with a Statistics with German degree from Exeter University. After working with the financial director on a number of EMU projects she moved to the profitability analysis team, where she has gradually taken on responsibility for the European management accounts and for building relationships with the company's European offices.

'It is the exposure to the breadth of the business and its strategic position that makes Financial Control in Schroders so interesting. We see our graduates as our future managers, we expect a lot of them, and provide them with the opportunities to succeed and develop.

'It's all hands-on involvement in the day-to-day running of the business. Increasingly the focus of our work is to provide information support for the business, and we work closely with the business managers and IT. The business is changing, and nowhere is this felt more than in Financial Control. We have a young team, with a strong team ethic. People are very professional. Graduates can study for either CIMA or ACCA qualifications (see page 38), for which full support is given.'

As another graduate says, 'If you want a City career plus management accounting then this is the perfect solution. The variety of opportunities is amazing, and your long-term future doesn't necessarily need to be in the financial arena. There's choice and wide experience. You just never know where your career will take you next with a global company, that could be abroad. I've been here less than two years and I'm already visiting locations in Europe.'

FURTHER INFORMATION
See page 97.

25
MARKETING

SUMMARY

For this job you need to be tailored to swooning point. It's a front-line job where your role is to promote the products, services and reputation of the fund manager you represent. The role will vary but it is likely to involve:

● Preparing for new business opportunities
● Maintaining the company's profile in the marketplace
● Putting on your own seminars and speaking on investment banking at high-profile conferences
● Building relationships with clients
● Originating promotion material

TELL IT HOW IT IS

Jeff is a marketing manager with a major investment bank. He joined four years ago with a degree in economics. 'My job is to create awareness of the company and our products. This means preparing documents and presentations for new business proposals, talking to prospective clients and the press. We get to know a lot of journalists and from time to time I am asked to write for specialist publications on investment issues. This has a far greater impact than advertising.'

The marketing director of a new asset management company in London says, 'We are here to do something quite different from the traditional institutional management services offered by UK banks. My job is to create name awareness and to build our reputation. It can take time to gain acceptance in the investment community, particularly with the investment consultants that dominate the pension fund appointments.'

A major bank explains, 'Graduates join as generalists and must be prepared to undertake responsibility right from the start. We will train and support you, but it's learning by doing, and what you will be doing will depend on what comes through the door – it could be a client with a billion-pound or even a five-billion-pound opportunity. As you progress, you will begin to specialise in one area. This could be in charities, UK pension funds, international clients, product development – the choice is yours.'

Angela joined a City bank two years ago and has enjoyed developing the marketing department. 'Marketing in the City is a new and growing area. This is what attracted me to the department. I was told to learn as much as I could when I first joined, and that meant getting involved in a wide range of activities. I have to prepare marketing materials for clients and our consultants. Then there are lots of conferences where we attend as delegates or perhaps as speakers. This is a great place to meet prospective clients but it does mean organising lots of dinners and being a host at various functions.'

FURTHER INFORMATION
See page 97.

26
CORPORATE BANKING

k **MONEY:** £22,000–£30,000 plus possible sign-on bonus and banking benefits.

h **HOURS:** Standard 9.30–5.30 plus overtime.

PRESSURE RATING: 6/10. This job requires a steady head and a risk-averse nature. Safety first is the aim of the treasury and custodial departments. The same goes for cash management and credit. A good City job for those who value their stomach linings.

C **GLAMOUR RATING:** 6/10. Not as racy as investment banking but still carries clout.

l **TRAVEL RATING:** 5–9/10. It depends on the department, but if you join a big international bank you should get a chance to visit or go on secondment to overseas offices.

SUMMARY

Corporate banking (aka institutional banking and relationship banking) covers the huge middle ground between the investment banks and the retail banks. Some of the big custodial banks, like Standard Chartered, for example, also offer corporate banking and are a good bet if you want to travel.

With corporate banking you are looking at companies that need the full range of cash management and treasury services. Many of your clients are also going to be looking for business development services, including finance packages typically in the £10–£15 million bracket. The range of services you will offer includes:

● Cash management – accounts, payment and collection for local and cross-border transactions, liquidity management
● Treasury services – exchange and interest rate exposure management
● Trade services
● Lending – loan structure and syndicates, provision of working capital
● Custody – safe-keeping of assets globally

WHAT'S INVOLVED?

With modern cash management services, for example, corporate clients can manage their company's total financial position from a desktop computer. Standard Chartered says it aims to help its corporate clients:

● Manage the availability of their funds efficiently
● Monitor and control the movement of funds
● Settle payments to suppliers in a timely and cost-effective way
● Capture every investment opportunity to increase income

A strong international presence enables a corporate bank to help businesses develop their customer bases overseas. Standard Chartered has a presence in 40 countries and is focused on the established and emerging markets of Asia, Africa, the Middle East, the subcontinent and Latin America.

The Royal Bank of Scotland is another leading corporate bank. Its Financial Markets division focuses on providing financing, risk management and investment solutions to customers' problems. This includes:

● Products and services designed for a range of businesses – from the largest financial institutions to the owner-managed operation
● Treasury business
● Foreign exchange
● Financial futures
● Interest rate derivatives
● Money markets

RBS offers financing alternatives for borrowers, such as sterling Eurobonds, private placements, tax-driven or asset-backed financing, and synthetic risk transfer through credit derivatives and financial insurance. 'We also offer for our institutional investor base fixed-rate bonds up to thirty years across the risk spectrum from AAA to high-yield government bonds, floating rate notes, asset swaps, structured medium-term notes, interest rate and credit derivatives for floating rate investors.'

The bank is a market leader in securitisation and debt derivatives. 'We deliver tailored debt origination, structuring and distribution solutions for companies, governments and institutions around the world.' The Royal Bank of Scotland is the first

major UK bank to offer customers the ability to outsource their treasury requirements.

TELL IT HOW IT IS

Dawn works for Standard Chartered in Singapore but she is here in London on a special project. 'I started work with Standard Chartered in January 1998, at the Singapore Treasury Office. I was attached to different desks in the dealing room for one month, where I learned many skills from the other traders.

'Then I attended a two-month training and induction programme where I met other graduates from Hong Kong, India, Africa, Malaysia, Taiwan and Indonesia.' Dawn was seconded overseas to an assignment at the bank's UK Treasury office, where she is involved in a joint project between Treasury and IT.

Mark travels overseas several times a year in his job as relationship manager in Standard Chartered's institutional banking arm. 'We provide the international network of services within Standard Chartered to other banks. The product and geographical coverage involve the whole group, so it is important for me to be aware of the disciplines employed.' Mark says he was attracted to Standard Chartered by the people, whom he describes as 'approachable and friendly while maintaining professionalism'. He also liked the opportunities for travel. 'So far I have undertaken a short secondment and several trips to our Asian offices.'

Jane works for another major institutional bank as an analyst. 'My job is to look at the requests for credit and assess whether the client is a good risk. We need to be confident the client can service the loan and will be able to repay the capital at the agreed date. It involves a lot of research – we use a wide range of methods to check the client's current financial health and to project the outcome of its business plans. Basically, it's down to me to say whether we should do business with a prospective or existing client and to advise the terms on which we proceed. All this type of work is overseen by the bank in order to manage our overall exposure to different levels of risk and to different sectors.'

TREASURY PRODUCTS

The Treasury Products section at UBS Warburg offers a full range of currency and exchange-rate-driven financing solutions. The company outlines the type of graduate applicant it is seeking. 'In Treasury Products we need spirited self-starters – it's not a soft environment. It's a flat-structure, no-nonsense place: the people who run the business are just two seconds away from where you sit. You'll be expected to come up with ideas and contribute to the development of the organisation. There's a growing cross-product culture between Treasury Products, Fixed Income and Equities – you certainly won't be pigeon-holed.'

UBS Warburg divides Treasury Products into two main areas:

● Foreign exchange/precious metals and
● Cash and collateral trading

The systems are highly sophisticated. Take foreign exchange, for instance. The company has FX teams in fourteen cities. 'We deliver financial expertise and technology direct from the dealing floor with our floor traders and specialist teams providing valuable, client-focused content long before anyone else. That knowledge allows our clients to maximise their usage of our transactional platform.'

QUALIFICATIONS AND SKILLS

Corporate banks, like the investment banks, will offer places to graduates in any discipline but prefer a strong academic subject. Top banks will expect a 2:1. You will probably get the opportunity to study for Association of Corporate Treasurers (ACT) exams.

Good people skills are again a must. You also need to demonstrate clear logical thinking, total trustworthiness and the ability to be methodical.

TIPS

As with the investment banks, a good way to see life on the inside is through a vacation job or a formal internship (see Chapter 3).

FURTHER INFORMATION

● Try the websites of the employers direct or via the employment agencies.
● Don't forget the specialists www.prospects.csu.man.ac.uk and www.doctorjob.com
● Standard Chartered www.standardchartered.com
● Royal Bank of Scotland www.rbsmarkets.com
● UBS Warburg www.ubswarburg.com

27
PRIVATE CLIENT SERVICES/STOCKBROKER

k **MONEY:** £22,000–£27,000.

h **HOURS:** 8.30–6 quite common but there can be lighter days and later starts.

PRESSURE RATING: 6–8/10. Ideally you need to know as much about the markets as the fund managers themselves. Clients can be very demanding of your time and attention.

C **GLAMOUR RATING:** 9/10. This has to be the quintessential City job, although very much at the gentlemanly end of the market compared with the Porsche-driving, champagne-swilling image of the trader and investment banker.

1 **TRAVEL RATING:** 5/10. Your clients are likely to be wealthy UK citizens, although you may get the chance to travel if your company is a large investment bank with operations overseas.

SUMMARY

The old-fashioned term for this job is stockbroking, but private client services (PCS, aka private wealth management) are the modern face of the old bowler hat and pin-striped suit brigade. In this job you look after a range of individual clients who have sufficient wealth to warrant personal attention and an individual portfolio of shares. You may still use pooled funds to create exposure in some markets – smaller companies or emerging markets, for example – but generally speaking these clients want direct ownership and are willing to pay for the personal touch.

At its best PCS is all about good client relations and trust. You need to get to know your client well and to understand his or her financial position in relation to work and family. You will almost certainly know far more about your client's money than his or her spouse.

'THE FIRM'

Who you work for is important because it will dictate the training you get, the technology at your fingertips and your likely client base. When the stock market was deregulated in 1986 (see page 58) many of the independent stockbrokers were taken over by UK and foreign investment banks. However, even where a stockbroker has a major financial institution for a parent, it is likely to operate quite separately from the main organisation.

There are also some independent firms of stockbrokers in London, as well as in other major cities. These tend to focus on wealthy private clients who need advice on investments and other aspects of financial planning.

Large firms of stockbrokers employ

their own analysts – usually just for UK companies, although occasionally for foreign markets as well. Stockbrokers also employ sales people and dealers.

If you join the PCS department of an investment bank your training will probably be similar to that of other graduates who enter mainstream banking as fund managers or client relations managers, for example. Refer to the previous chapters for an overview of what it is like working for a large City institution.

TELL IT HOW IT IS

Jenny works for the PCS department of a major investment bank. 'My job is similar in many ways to my institutional counterpart. I make an early start to see what's been happening in the markets and apply this knowledge to my clients' portfolios. I look after individuals with millions invested in the stock market. It's not all direct equities, though. Even with this amount of money I still use pooled funds to gain exposure to some of the high-risk and very specialist markets.'

Robert works for one of the few independent firms of private client stockbrokers. He says, 'The thing I love about this job is the variety of clients. With institutions you tend to see more grey suits than real individuals, but the people who have personal wealth may be titled "gentry" who have been lucky enough to inherit their money, or it could just as easily be a pop star or film star, or an entrepreneur who has sold off his company and at fifty intends to live off

his investments while he does charity work. The most difficult clients are the lottery winners. They haven't got a clue how to deal with the money and are excited and terrified at the same time. You have to be prepared to act as a personal counsellor some of the time.'

PCS firms are currently regulated by the Securities Institute (now part of the Financial Services Authority), which has a register of members who are qualified to deal with the public. To qualify you must have passed the Registered Representative exam. The Securities Institute runs a range of voluntary exams, and it is in your interests to pursue these, as investors who are seeking a financial adviser are often told to look for those who have passed the Securities Industry Diploma, which covers private client investment advice.

The Association of Private Client Investment Managers (APCIMS) represents well over 90 per cent of private client stockbrokers as well as an increasing number of other investment managers. Members have direct access to the stock market for buying and selling shares.

STOCKBROKER SERVICES

You don't need to know everything about investing to work in PCS but you should be able to demonstrate a basic knowledge of the job and a keen interest in investment. In theory there are three types of stockbroker service, although in practice the boundaries between advisory and discretionary are blurred and many investors require a combination of the two. The following definitions, therefore, are intended only as a guide:

DEALING OR 'EXECUTION ONLY'

This service is designed for investors who do not require advice but who need a stockbroker to buy and sell shares for them. Some stockbrokers specialise in this low-cost, no-frills service, and offer competitive rates and a rapid service. This type of firm will almost certainly offer on-line dealing to speed up the process and give greater control to clients. Good IT skills and an ability to understand investment procedures are probably more important with this type of firm that the desire to give investment advice face to face.

ADVISORY

With an advisory service, the client usually makes the buying and selling decisions based on a combination of his or her own ideas, possibly with your advice thrown in. In practice there are different types of advisory service. Some simply advise on the sale and purchase of clients' shares. Others offer a more comprehensive service to include advice on capital gains tax and to provide regular valuations of client portfolios.

The main point to remember is that an advisory manager does not take any investment decisions without the client's authority, although you might give an opinion if appropriate. It's up to you and your client to decide whether you should make contact at regular intervals or phone with tips.

DISCRETIONARY OR PORTFOLIO MANAGEMENT

This is the most interesting of the services, as here you are trusted to make all the decisions for your clients. This does not mean the client has no say. You and your clients will have regular meetings to discuss their current financial circumstances and any changes to their investment aims. At these meetings you will update the client's plan and your investment guidelines.

COMPREHENSIVE FINANCIAL PLANNING

Increasingly, private client services are extending to cover all aspects of personal financial planning, so you may be called on to advise clients on how their investments fit in with the rest of their financial plans. Important topics to integrate with investment planning are:

- Cash and deposits
- Protection insurances
- Tax mitigation strategies
- School fees
- Pension planning
- Estate or inheritance tax (IHT) planning

HOW TO CHOOSE YOUR FIRM

In the past the dominance of the old-boy network meant that firms were not so open as they are today about their resources and their performance. This made it difficult to judge whether one firm was better than another. It can still be difficult to penetrate the wall of secrecy that guards the portals to these traditional City firms. A useful benchmark, however, is to examine the firm's resources and the quality of the research on which the client relationship managers base their decisions to buy, sell and hold.

Ask about the internal research carried out by the firm's analysts. Firms that are not linked to an investment bank may claim to operate in a niche market, but if they do not employ full-time analysts you need to consider carefully how they overcome this potential shortfall in information.

PCS firms also get research from the market makers, based on which they buy and sell shares. As a general rule the market makers do not make an explicit charge for the research they provide to stockbrokers but regard it as something of a quid pro quo in return for a firm's business. However, regulatory rules forbid any tied arrangements, since the stockbroker's priority is to find the best dealing price, not the market maker that offers the best 'free' research.

The level of research provided depends on how valuable a stockbroker is regarded as a client. Market makers may provide the smaller firms of stockbrokers and financial advisers with weekly reports on companies and sectors and on unit and investment trusts. They might also provide the bigger stockbrokers with daily commentary and, for the favoured few, they will provide an on-line information service updated throughout the day.

Frank works for a big investment bank in the PCS department. 'A lot of people assume we just mirror the decisions made by our top fund managers, but this is far from the case. We treat all the research we get from our own analysts and from the market makers as raw data that we must interpret for our clients. The tips that may be worth acting on for a large pension fund may be wholly inappropriate for the private investor. For example, a small movement in a share price might trigger a decision to buy or sell for a large fund where the economies of scale would make it worthwhile. For the private investor the small price change would not be worth chasing.'

You are unlikely to see jobs advertised for most firms of stockbrokers, and if you are keen on this type of work your best bet is to apply direct to suitable firms, although check first that the parent does not cover this area of recruitment.

There are advantages to joining the private client services arm of a big investment bank. For a start you will get access to all the firm's research, its analysts, traders and investment bankers. Equally important, though, is the training. The big banks often rotate trainee private clients services people around the different functions so they get a feel for what is really going on in the specialised product and trading areas within the firm.

QUALIFICATIONS AND SKILLS

You'll need a good degree in any discipline and must be able to demonstrate a genuine interest in money and investment. Also vital is your ability to build relationships with clients, so you should be presentable and have good people skills. You will need strong analytical skills, an effective sales manner and the ability to take measured risks. The firm should provide on-site training and appoint a mentor who you shadow for the first few months.

TIPS

The APCIMS directory of members provides a brief guide to the services offered by its member firms and is a good place to find out more about the firms you might target for a job.

Frankly, if you know someone who knows someone in PCS, then make use of the contact. Don't believe it when City people say the old-boys' network is a thing of the past.

SOURCES OF INFORMATION

● The Association of Private Client Investment Managers is at www.apcims.co.uk
● *Investors Chronicle* publishes an annual guide to PCS firms. *IC* is available from large newsagents and runs a website at www.investorschronicle.co.uk. You can buy back issues by phoning FT Business on 020 7896 2000.

28
TRADERS AND DEALERS

k **MONEY:** £25,000–£35,000 plus potential big bonuses.

h **HOURS:** A very early start – typically 6.30 – in order to catch the markets as they close in Japan. However, you should be able to knock off at about 4 p.m. with the opening of business in the States.

PRESSURE RATING: 10/10. This job requires you to think on your feet even if you are sitting at a terminal or three. Drinking around the clock has led more than one trader to an early grave.

C **GLAMOUR RATING:** 10/10. Regarded as sexy but also the rough end of the business.

1 **TRAVEL RATING:** 5–10/10. Travel is a prominent feature of this job, as you need to see the companies and markets on which you work. Where you go depends on your area of specialisation. Funnily enough, emerging markets like South America and the Far East are popular with young analysts.

SUMMARY
This is the really pointy end of investment banking and fund management. The dealers and market makers buy and sell securities and other financial products on behalf of the organisations for which they work or for their bank's clients.

The job starts early when you pick up on what's been happening overnight in the US and Hong Kong. If you are a proprietary trader your job is to increase the value of your bank's capital by making trades. You could make just a few trades or dozens each day, depending on market conditions and your area of specialisation.

You may also provide market information to clients and buy and sell on their behalf. Your institutional clients will be corporations, governments, pension and hedge funds, among others. You will be trading in millions, often billions, of dollars. Inter-dealer brokers are the people who provide a dealing service to market makers and match deals (bargains) between them.

TELL IT HOW IT IS
Bear Stearns says its sales and trading team has 'daunting stamina' and 'thrives on chaos'. And this is the polite company view. The descriptions of an average day from those who possess this daunting stamina and who apparently thrive on chaos are unprintable.

Why so daunting? Well, your job is to buy and sell blocks of stocks very quickly, committing capital and making markets. In the process you will be working with a wide variety of equities and debt securities in the debt capital markets (DCMs), as well as with currencies and derivatives.

'Whether or not you are trading for

a client or for Bear Stearns itself, measured risk is at the heart of what we do. In sales and trading your primary responsibility is to make money for your clients,' the company says.

For mathematicians with the trader's mentality, the derivatives markets is the place to be. KBC Financial Products specialises in convertibles and equity derivatives. A company spokesman says, 'The markets in which we operate are highly competitive. Consequently, working at KBC Financial Products can be demanding of time, energy and thought. Working here can also be incredibly rewarding and can place new hires in an unusually open work environment.

'From our founding we have placed a premium on work practices that respect productivity: a casual dress code, open access to Internet resources, and an intentionally flat management structure.'

For this sort of dealing you need to combine brains with quick thinking. You also need the right sort of trousers. Casual dress does not mean old jeans and cheap T-shirts (see page 32 for 'dressing down' rules). What else? Oh yes, you must be able to cope with extremely high pressure, just like Terry, one of KBC's derivatives sales staff. His job involves marketing structured and 'vanilla' over-the-counter (OTC) equity derivative products to North American financial institutions. ('Vanilla' usually means simple or straightforward when it is used to describe a financial product, so it's something of a contradiction in terms used in this context.)

Before joining KBC, Terry did a long stint in a leading securities house. He was also a medallist at the 1984 Olympic Games, and headed a high-school mathematics department after graduating from MIT with first and second degrees in applied biology and genetic toxicology.

Robert is a convertibles trader at KBC. When asked to describe his job, he explains that he 'facilitates institutional order flow in over-the-counter convertible securities, and identifies potential mispricings for customer information'. Robert spent five years trading equities and convertible securities at a major US investment bank after studying economics and industrial management at Carnegie-Mellon University. Since joining the financial products team in 1998, he has played a significant role in establishing the firm as one of the pre-eminent providers of liquidity in US convertible securities.

As you've probably gathered, trading is as stressful as it gets. At least it's gentler on the eardrums these days, unless you work in one of the commodities markets, where you may still have to use the old outcry system. Most traders sit at a desk in a huge dealing room with screens flashing left, right and centre. You need to be sharp, fantastically numerate, and have the patience of a skilled poker player. Seconds matter in this game, so if you can't take the heat, don't go anywhere near this particular fire.

Joe is a proprietary dealer and so invests money on behalf of his bank. He says, 'If you have a really good appetite for risk you could opt to cover the emerging markets, for example, which are less well researched than the main markets and require a considerable amount of intuition as you sift through the rumours to detect the real potential for a deal. You start the day by checking what's happened overnight and the current state of play, then, when the markets open, it's a case of thinking on your feet – even if you are sitting down at a desk full of terminals!'

Job security can be poor. After all, you are only as good as your last deal. But the rewards can be great, as many dealers work on a basic salary and earn commissions for the deals they package together. If you're the techie sort, you might also get involved at the forefront of new product development – financial instruments that require a high level of mathematical ability.

One step removed from the trading rooms are the brokers who buy and sell on behalf of major financial institutions – for example, the pension funds and insurance companies. Here you will act only on orders from your clients, and the deal will be discussed in detail by the fund managers beforehand. Timing is still critical, but the decision on what to buy and sell is made for you.

QUALIFICATIONS AND SKILLS

The more the merrier, but above all you need to be a fast thinker. A technical degree is a must for some jobs. Personality-wise you need lots of confidence and then some. Plus a thick skin, energy in abundance and a strong constitution so you can take the adrenaline flows and panics without losing your stomach lining. If you don't do mornings, don't bother to apply.

TIPS

● Use the website links through www.prospects.csu.man.ac.uk and www.doctorjob.com to find the specialist traders and dealers and find out if you might fit in.
● Approach companies directly and ask questions. The more confidence you can exude the better – although don't slip into arrogance. Nobody likes arrogance.

SOURCES

KBC Financial Products asked us not to reveal the identities of its staff, so the names used are fictitious.
● The company's website offers an excellent insight into this field: www.kbcfp.com

b) Professional Services/Consultancy

29
THE JARGON

One of the most widely used and misunderstood titles in recruitment adverts is 'consultant'. Like 'engineer', it can mean pretty well whatever you want it to.

The Institute of Management Consultants points out that it wasn't until 1972 that the compilers of the *Oxford English Dictionary* widened the definition of consultant from 'a person who consults oracles' to include 'a person qualified to give professional advice or service'. In the City the term 'consultant' is usually interpreted as indicating a specialist agency of professionals. Unlike their Greek counterparts, they do not consult oracles or read chicken entrails.

These days companies are encouraged to focus on their core businesses, and from time to time may need to outsource a one-off project or a specific function for which they do not have the necessary resources in-house. So, for example, IT consultants may be called in to build a new system, or they may be required to run the administration of, say, a pension scheme.

In the investment world, property is regarded as a highly specialist asset class and as such tends to be dealt with by property consultants. Management and actuarial consultants are also important functions in the City.

Consultant can also mean 'company doctor' – the troubleshooter a company brings in to sort out big problems, often of a nasty nature. It may be that the director reckons the company needs to cut its payroll and focus on the core business, but he might bring in a consultant to restructure the business and recommend a 'downsizing' plan. Downsizing is a wonderful euphemism for making redundancies.

SYNONYMS

The terms 'management' and 'strategy' consultant may be interchanged indiscriminately, but there is a difference. For strategy consultant think in terms of the strategic long-term view and the big picture. It may be that a company has a serious problem with its target market or its business plan which requires some radical rethinking. In this field you might be called in to do some dirty work – for example, to decide which tier of management can be eliminated if the solution for the company is to go for a much flatter management structure, or which subsidiaries should be sold off.

Management consultants tend to be brought in to solve a specific problem – for example, to design the new IT system mentioned above or to help launch a new range of products. The management consultant may even be involved with implementing a plan that the strategy consultant has recommended.

There are other sorts of consultants. As we mentioned in the 'How to use this book' section, the old firms of chartered accountants have been busy merging (and paying partners vast amounts of money in the process). The result is half a dozen or so huge 'professional services firms' that do everything (see Chapter 16). Not to be outdone, the actuarial and employee benefits consultants have been merging to form global firms. They do everything too.

This is all very helpful to the global client, no doubt, but to the graduate jobseeker it's pretty confusing. If you are particularly keen on a career in, say, chartered accountancy or actuarial work, look at the firm's history to find out what its areas of specialisation were before it became all things to all men. You should also look at its client list and its annual sources of revenue. This information will highlight where the firm's real strengths lie.

PROFESSIONAL AND CONSULTANCY BUZZWORDS

● **AKM** stands for Applied Knowledge Management.
● **ALM** Investment consultants carry out an asset/liability modelling exercise to ensure that a pension fund is invested in the right sort of assets to match the scheme's liabilities in terms of benefit payments.
● **CRM** stands for Customer Relationship Management.
● **High-net-worth clients** Very rich clients indeed.

● **Intangibles** This refers to assets that have no physical form – for example, royalties and patents (aka intellectual property).
● **Operations/support/back office** These terms cover a range of jobs that relate to the administration and settlement of the functions of an investment bank, for example.
● **Pro bono** A legal phrase that describes work done for the public good.
● **SIP** Statement of investment principles – the document that sets out the socially responsible (ethical) investment principles, among other features, for a pension fund.
● **Tax depreciation** is a form of tax relief on expenditure such as buying properties, constructing or refurbishing buildings, or leasing fixtures or equipment.
● **Transfer pricing** involves transferring goods or intellectual property, for example, between subsidiaries of the same company.

30
ACCOUNTANCY/ PROFESSIONAL SERVICES

k **Money:** £22,000–£28,000 with benefits, plus possible sign-on bonus or interest-free loan.

h **Hours:** Depending on position, expect a significant chunk of overtime on top of the standard 9.30–5.30. One or two companies pay overtime but this is not the norm. Expect to work hard for exams in your free time.

Pressure rating: 5–8/10. Varies depending on the department. Higher rating for those on the front line dealing with corporate clients. You will learn to dread the months before the end of the tax year on 5 April, when overtime soars.

C **Glamour rating:** 5/10. Well, you know what they say about accountants … But if you get into one of the big professional services firms you can still cut a dash in certain circles.

1 **Travel rating:** 0–8/10. You could end up crunching numbers in the same office for a lifetime or you could get in some serious travelling if you are on the front line working for international clients.

SUMMARY

Professional services organisations offer a full range of consultancy, including risk management, tax and corporate finance strategies to national and global clients.

Corporate finance teams deal with investment banks and provide merger and acquisition and capital market transaction leadership, plus advisory services to corporate and financial groups.

The corporate recovery and reconstruction teams aim to solve the very specialised problems that occur when clients encounter financial difficulty in either their own business or that of a trading partner or debtor. In some cases the firm acts as the receiver of a company and undertakes to run the business – managing cash flow, purchasing goods, liaising with suppliers and filing statutory details.

The privatisation and emerging markets group apply their skills on a macro basis, dealing with major elements of developing economies or countries in economic crisis. This is big stuff. Several UK consultants are responsible for designing privatised welfare systems for the former communist countries. Then there is the real estate consulting arm, which focuses primarily on assisting clients in the management of real estate assets and developments.

In this chapter we focus on the core taxation services.

TAXATION

Clearly, taxation is the core function of the more traditional chartered accountant. If this is your primary interest, when you join one of the mega-firms you can expect to train and specialise in one of the following areas:

- Corporate tax consulting
- Indirect tax
- Private client services
- Tax depreciation
- Technology solutions
- Transfer pricing

TRAINING

The financial rewards for a successful tax adviser can be very high. Starting salaries for graduates will depend on location, size of firm and whether the employer is in industry or commerce. However, as an example, a graduate Association of Taxation Technician (ATT) trainee in London would start on a salary of approximately £19,000, although it could be as high as £28,000 for top graduates with the major firms. Salaries should increase substantially after success in the ATT and ATII (Chartered Institute of Taxation) examinations and as experience is gained. Exams are a big commitment in this field but, if it's any consolation, recruitment consultants report that UK accountancy qualifications are highly respected throughout the world.

This is a very important component in your package. Charlotte, a human capital analyst, who joined Arthur Andersen (not to be confused with the management and IT consultant Andersen Consulting, now known as Accenture) in July 2000, says, 'The training is incredible. I spent three days in the office and then went to the Chicago training centre for two weeks. I'm already studying for my tax qualifications, starting with ATT, after which I'll move on to the ATII exams.'

Like all of the big firms, Arthur Andersen gives graduates a lot of support for the relevant qualifications – for example, if you join the corporate tax planning department you will be encouraged to study for the Chartered Accountancy (ACA) qualification. Once qualified, you have the option to study for the Chartered Institute of Taxation qualification (ATII) and an MBA. Graduates in Private Client Servicing study for the Association of Taxation Technicians (ATT) qualification, as well as the Financial Planning Certificate. More advanced qualifications will depend on your chosen specialisation but could include the Chartered Institute of Taxation qualification (ATII), the Pensions Management Institute (PMI) qualifications, the Advanced Financial Planning Certificate or an MBA.

The following descriptions were provided by Arthur Andersen.

CORPORATE TAX PLANNING

As companies achieve greater access to global markets through mergers, acquisitions and alliances, tax is no longer an afterthought; it is an integral part of an organisation's forward planning. As ownership and operations cross borders, the complexity of tax grows exponentially.

Managing this complexity goes well beyond tax compliance planning. Capitalising on different tax rates across multiple jurisdictions can have a direct impact on a company's valuation. How tax is treated in a transaction can be critical in determining the success or failure of a new venture. Corporate tax consulting helps companies develop innovative, effective tax strategies to support their business objectives. Projects may include:

● Mergers and acquisitions
● International investment and foreign exchange
● Setting up businesses in the UK and abroad
● Employee remuneration planning
● Negotiating with the Inland Revenue

Jason, a graduate trainee in corporate tax consulting, says, 'I chose tax because I like solving problems. The environment here is fast-moving and you're constantly learning. I enjoy having the opportunity to think in a business context, not an ivory tower. For example, I advised a US client buying a UK business. The original structure didn't work, and in presenting an alternative we won the client's trust. After that, we worked so closely we became part of their team and we had a big celebration when it was over.'

INDIRECT TAX

In the new economy, global operations are the rule rather than the exception. Indirect taxes affect virtually every aspect of our lives. An indirect tax practitioner says, 'Stop and think about the last time you bought Jaffa Cakes – have you ever wondered whether they are cakes or biscuits? One carries value added tax (VAT), the other does not: a factor of 17.5 per cent is about three times greater than the average retailer's profit margin.

'Or consider a can of fruit cocktail imported from California. The tin was manufactured in Germany, the peaches are from California, the cherries are from Italy. With different rates of tax depending on the point of origin, what is its "imported value" on which duty should be calculated?'

Businesses need pragmatic advice on how to minimise the costs of indirect taxation, which can add thousands of pounds to a transaction. VAT is a key consideration at all levels of business, and there may be duty liabilities any time goods cross a border.

Whether it is helping with the implementation of a supply chain management strategy, or assisting an Internet start-up, in this line of business you could be advising on the VAT and customs implications of your clients' current operations and on possible strategies for the future. You will be involved in negotiating with Customs and Excise on behalf of your clients and attending tribunal hearings, and you will act as a VAT and customs expert within the firm, advising people from other practices on any indirect tax issues relevant to their clients. With the introduction of VAT in all European Union countries and in most countries outside the EU, you can expect to work closely on projects with colleagues from offices round the world.

Marc, a graduate in the indirect tax department, says, 'I have really got to grips with how and why businesses make decisions. There is far more to this job than tax advice. I have to be a salesman, a lawyer and an economist. The variety really keeps me on my toes. If it crosses a border, I deal with it.'

PRIVATE CLIENT SERVICING

Like the investment banks, the professional services firms offer a comprehensive financial service to wealthy individuals. Whether your clients are senior executives of FTSE 100 companies or owners of small start-up companies with great potential for growth, they need personalised advice on tax and financial planning.

It's more than a numbers game: you are dealing with people's lives and livelihoods. This means getting to know all clients in turn and developing an understanding of their objectives, needs and preferences. Private client services help clients meet their long-term financial objectives – whether they are starting out in business, planning to sell their company or building a nest egg. Your job is to advise clients on how to minimise their income and capital tax liabilities, and to help them make informed decisions on pensions, life assurance and transfer of assets. In this department you will gain experience across a range of areas, including personal tax, personal financial planning and shareholder planning.

Mark, a graduate trainee in PCS, says, 'During my first year there were no "typical days". Generally we deal with very high-net-worth individuals ranging from directors of large multinationals to lottery winners. Our work brings us into daily contact with stockbrokers, fund managers, providers of pensions and life assurance and occasionally lawyers. As we are essentially in the business of broking large sums of money, we are seldom short of lunch invitations!'

TAX DEPRECIATION

Any business that makes capital investments – from high-street retailers to property investment companies or power station operators – can benefit from advice on tax depreciation. Tax depreciation is a form of tax relief on expenditure such as buying properties, constructing or refurbishing buildings or leasing fixtures or equipment.

If you work in this department your job will be to help clients benefit from substantial tax savings, in both the UK and overseas, through the identification of tax relief and proactive consultancy. The advice must be provided in the context of overall business plans.

You will accompany consultants and managers on capital allowances surveys of a wide variety of client properties. You can also expect to liaise with clients, professional consultants and building contractors, and gradually develop surveying skills to include knowledge of construction technology and building costs. Part of your role includes advising clients and architects on the most tax-efficient building designs and agreeing capital allowances claims for clients with the Inland Revenue.

Nathan, a graduate in the tax depreciation department, says, 'I was attracted to tax depreciation work by the diverse nature of the job and the responsibility that graduates are given from day one. Despite my non-surveying background, the breadth and diversity of training brought me up to speed very quickly. I have worked on projects relating to factories, retail units and offices, bringing me into contact with clients from the leisure, manufacturing, retail and healthcare sectors. Site surveys have meant frequent travel around Britain and occasionally abroad.'

INFORMATION TECHNOLOGY

While off-the-shelf software may meet the needs of some businesses, others need more tailored applications. This division of the Arthur Andersen consultancy, for example, provides a wide range of IT services to the firm's tax practice and to its clients. 'Working together, we provide innovative and individual solutions across a wide range of tax and technology issues. You could be working on on-line tax returns or accounting system integration projects from bespoke website design to employee administration systems. You could be using programming languages ranging from C++ to HTML. One of our proprietary tax software products available to clients is "Abacus", which is used for tax compliance work by many of the FTSE 100 companies.'

Rachel, a graduate trainee in the IT department, says, 'I had no previous knowledge of tax but the induction training was excellent. My work over the last three years has been extremely varied and my computer skills have improved dramatically. I have been involved in programming, client training, software support and demonstrating software to new clients. The great thing about working here is the variety and nature of the work.'

TRANSFER PRICING

Arthur Andersen's Transfer Pricing group, based in London, is an international team of dedicated economic consultants operating throughout the UK, Europe, the Americas and Asia Pacific.

Within companies, there may be a number of transfers between divisions and countries. For example, a US subsidiary of a UK company may manufacture a new wonder drug that it 'sells' to the UK parent company. The US subsidiary may also own the worldwide patent rights. Therefore, there is both a transfer of the physical product (the drugs) as well as the intellectual property associated with the patent rights (intangibles).

Your job in this department is to advise clients on the international tax laws determining how these transfers should be priced for tax purposes. Geoff, a graduate trainee in the transfer pricing department, says: 'I've worked on a large intangibles valuation project aimed at deriving an appropriate royalty rate back to the owner of intangible goods. This project was very different to anything I had done. I had my own segments of the analysis and, being closest to the data, had a lot of input in the way the analysis was carried out. The tight deadline required hard work, but the knowledge that I had contributed significantly to the project, which was very rewarding.'

QUALIFICATIONS AND SKILLS

The major recruiters of tax trainees are the traditional accountancy practices, now known as 'professional services' organisations. These recruit in London and around the UK and generally require a 2:1 degree and a high number of UCAS points (often 24). 'Top 20' firms offer fewer places, as their tax departments are smaller, but they may be more flexible on entry requirements.

While the quality of your academic record is of primary importance, if you want to enter the more technical areas of taxation, for example, you will need a good understanding of economic theory and the ability to apply that knowledge, as there are no clear-cut answers to the problems that clients face. Applicants for certain areas of business must have studied economics (for all or at least part of their degree). PhD or Masters students are also very welcome.

TIPS

In the early postgraduate days, experience with the right type of firm is crucial – more so than the starting salary and benefits. Tell that to a starving graduate crippled by student debt, you might say – but even the recruitment consultants agree that the right firm and training are more important than the golden hello.

SOURCES OF INFORMATION ON CAREER

All the major firms have good websites, and you will find sources for these in Chapter 6. If you are expecting to get a good degree (2:1 or first) make sure you check all the relevant sites, and ideally contact a recruitment agency to get comparisons of working conditions and training at the different firms.

● Try the specialists
www.prospects.csu.man.ac.uk and www.doctorjob.com

● For details about the Association of Graduate Careers Advisory Services

(AGCAS) publications 'Legal Profession' and 'Careers for law graduates outside the legal profession', see page 36.

THE PROFESSIONAL BODIES AND QUALIFICATIONS

There are five Recognised Qualifying Bodies (RQBs) statutorily recognised in the UK for company auditors under the Companies Act 1989. These are provided on page 38. A prospectus and comprehensive careers literature are available free of charge from the Institute and Association of Taxation. The Chartered Institute of Taxation has over 11,000 members, including most of the country's top tax experts. The ATII qualification denotes associate membership of the Institute.

The Association of Taxation Technicians is the Institute's sponsored sister body, founded in 1989 to provide the qualification of 'Taxation Technician'. Membership of the Association provides a qualification in its own right; however, many progress to sit the examinations of the Institute. Neither the Institute nor the Association employs tax trainees themselves. The ATT and ATII qualifications are held in high regard by employers and undoubtedly contribute to career progression.

SOURCES

● Arthur Andersen is at www.arthurandersen.com

31
MANAGEMENT CONSULTANT

k **MONEY:** £26,000–£28,000 but can be as high as £30,000 for graduate trainees. Plus a sign-on bonus, typically £3,000–£5,000. The highest sign-on at present is £10,000, but this is exceptional.

h **HOURS:** Officially 9–5.30 but we are talking seriously long hours here, folks, to the point where the major employers see fit to organise social events to make sure you have a life outside work! Remember, a lot of your time will be spent at client sites and these could be a very long way from home, so serial secondment is the name of the game.

PRESSURE RATING: 8–9/10. About as bad as it gets. Deadlines are tough, although they may not be daily, but then there's all the travel on top.

C **GLAMOUR RATING:** 8/10. Management consultancy has a definite 'made it' feel to it. Good intellectual rating.

l **TRAVEL RATING:** 8/10. Most consultancy jobs involve on-site work where you virtually live with the client until the job is finished. Your travel programme, therefore, will depend on where the clients are based.

SUMMARY

Management is all about change and getting results through people. Management consultancy is primarily concerned with initiating and implementing change, whether this is a change in the technology a company uses, in its management or organisational structure, or in the attitude and behaviour of staff.

Your job is to:

● Identify and investigate problems relating to strategy, policy, markets, organisation, procedures and methods
● Make recommendations
● Agree with the client the most appropriate course of action
● Help implement the plan

The job can involve very sensitive or downright unpleasant situations the company itself can't sort out. 'Company doctor' and the old-fashioned term 'troubleshooter' are synonyms you may come across.

ON THE MOVE

The job involves a lot of travel, although the locations will depend on your client base. The point to remember is that most of the time you will be working at client sites, so even if your office is in the City you may not experience as much City life as those of your friends who went in for investment banking.

According to the Institute of Management Consultants, to do this job well you need:

● Objectivity, impartiality and independence
● Knowledge of management organisation and techniques
● Consulting skills – that is, analytical, fact-finding, solution-building skills
● Practical experience
● Technical expertise

Good analytical skills are essential, as management consultants tend to break problems down into bite-sized chunks and then build appropriate solutions. Many consultants spend two or three years post-graduation working in the field and then do an MBA.

One of the biggest areas for management consultancy in the City is in information technology, so we took a look at the type of career you might find at the Cap Gemini Ernst & Young Group, a world leader in IT services and management consultancy with global revenues of 7.7 billion Euros in 1999. The company employs over 55,000 people internationally and has offices in most European countries, as well as in the Far East and the USA. It was voted European Company of the Year 1999 by the European Business Press Federation.

Services include management and IT consulting, systems integration, technology development, design and outsourcing capabilities on a global scale to help traditional businesses and dot.com companies continue to explore growth strategies in the new network economy.

The company also provides technical or business consultancy in most economic sectors, builds new or develops existing systems and applications, and can run a company's entire IT system if required. It has particular strengths in:

● EMU
● Customer Relationship Management (CRM), including call centres
● The Internet and electronic commerce
● Supply chain management, including package-based solutions
● Applied knowledge management (AKM) and
● Applications management

When you look at a potential employer you can tell a lot from its client base. Cap Gemini Ernst & Young's customer list includes household names like Virgin, BT, Axa Sun Life, General Motors, British Steel, Scottish Power and B&Q.

IT

A company like this would recruit graduates into IT, strategy consulting and the consultant development programme. Cap Gemini says, 'Wherever you want to go in your career you will need to have an understanding or interest in the role of IT within business, a thorough grounding in technology, along with sound business and interpersonal skills.'

Training at Cap Gemini starts with an intensive induction programme that runs all year round, so there are no application deadlines. After induction you will be directly involved with clients, and this will involve working at client sites. Your IT training will focus on one or more of the following:

- Programming
- Systems development
- Testing
- Technical support

CONSULTANT DEVELOPMENT PROGRAMME (CDP)

The two-year Consultant Development Programme run by Cap Gemini aims to transform top graduates into first-class consultants. As a new or recent graduate joining the CDP, you will have the opportunity to work in a wide variety of roles, which may be based in the UK or overseas across a wide range of industries and services (strategy, business transformation, supply chain, systems development and technology, financial services and manufacturing) before choosing where to specialise at the end of the CDP. Examples of roles might include project planning, risk management, training, workshop facilitation or design of change management programmes.

A good employer like Cap Gemini will provide you with a wide range of learning opportunities including on-the-job experiences, course-based events and access to a huge range of flexible learning materials. Counsellors form an important part of the supportive environment. Upon joining the CDP, each Assistant Consultant is assigned to a counsellor who will play an active role in personal development and performance measurement and offer active support in defining a career path.

'We need people who are sufficiently confident to be themselves and help the company progress and succeed,' Cap Gemini says. Your skills must include:

- A high level of self-awareness
- Good listening skills
- Confidence
- A rigorous approach to work
- Analytical thinking
- The ability to assimilate and interpret information quickly and arrive at balanced arguments and credible solutions
- Strong and proven team-working skills
- A strong interest in business

TELL IT HOW IT IS

Amaya joined the company in September 1998. 'I had a six-month work placement at Coca-Cola Madrid, a three-month work placement at Metaleurop Commercial [Paris] and a four-month work placement at the MBA Center [Paris], before joining the Consultant Development Programme.

'Since joining the CDP, I have worked on a variety of projects ranging from a couple of weeks to several months. My first project involved development of a new service to improve the efficiency of the supply chain for a major international logistics company. I participated in the development of the strategy as well as in the more technical phase where the system was being built and tested. I have also gained experience at the forefront of electronic commerce, working with our solutions team to deliver sales presentations for our major global clients. My current project is an e-commerce pan-European market entry strategy for a major international company.'

Amaya describes the CDP as 'An excellent launch pad into the world of business. It is a group of highly motivated and competent graduates with varying skills, backgrounds, nationalities and experiences. Members of the CDP are always willing to help each other, particularly in our first weeks in the firm, as we have all been through it before. We are also really good at getting together after work and organising formal and informal social events.

'My current role is particularly exciting because I am responsible for developing a market entry strategy for Spain and I am able to apply my language skills and knowledge of Spanish culture, as well as flying to Spain on a regular basis.'

Norton joined Cap Gemini in March 1998. He already had a year's experience working as a management consultant in Poland. 'My time in the CDP has given me a wide variety of experiences ranging from a global telecoms billing implementation project in Hampshire and Paris to organising the pan-European logistics of an office products company. I have also spent three months in an analytical team as part of the Strategy group, providing up-to-date company and industry analysis in a fast-paced environment for senior strategists.

'One particularly enjoyable experience was when I was working in Ghent on a European logistics cost reduction project. I worked with client staff right across Europe on a daily basis and managed to practise my language skills – although trying to remember Polish grammar at two a.m. when in the bar with a client proved challenging!'

The lifestyle can be tough, Norton warns. 'You are likely to find yourself working long hours away from home at the client site. However, we also try to enjoy ourselves with a Team Development Event once a year, as well as regular social events where the group gets together.'

E-COMMERCE CONSULTANCY

One of the major management consultants that specialises in IT is Accenture. It describes itself as follows: 'With more than 65,000 people in 48 countries and worldwide revenues of US$8.9 billion, Accenture is a dominant global force committed to transforming the e-commerce marketplace. Eighty-five of the Fortune Global 100 companies and nearly 75 per cent of Fortune's most profitable firms are our clients.'

Accenture allocates graduates to four different areas of business, or 'competencies'.

Processes

The Process Competency creates ways to help clients stay competitive. You help analyse a client's business processes and apply technology to develop more efficient ways of operating, from streamlining a particular business function to rethinking how an entire organisation works. Process professionals come from many backgrounds, but share analytical and problem-solving skills.

Technology

The Technology Competency focuses on the use of technology in business to create a competitive edge.

Change Management

This helps clients derive additional business value by focusing on the individual performance aspect of their organisations. A background in business, psychology or organisational development provides the foundation for developing tools and strategies that increase employee productivity and maximise business results.

Strategy

This is the strategy consultancy to the e-economy. 'We envision and define the industries and economies of the future.' Here you would work with senior executives on the problems most critical to the success of their organisation.

FINANCIAL SERVICES INDUSTRY CONSULTANCY

Tillinghast Towers Perrin provides management consulting to financial services companies, including banks, investment managers, insurance companies and securities firms. Its range of consulting services includes:

● Strategic restructuring
● Financial management and measurement
● Organisational planning
● Merger and acquisition evaluations
● Product development and distribution strategy

BUILDING A NEW ORGANISATION CULTURE

For example, Towers Perrin was involved with the merger of nine financial regulatory bodies in the UK. The work had to be done within a tight time frame and under intense government scrutiny. Its success depended on creating an entirely new culture, rather than trying to blend existing cultures. 'We worked with integration teams from all the organisations to develop a new strategy, vision, mission and values, and designed the full range of people systems necessary to implement the new culture. The merged regulatory body became fully operational in the required time frame, and 98 per cent of the staff signed on with the organisation.'

When two global banks merged to create one of the world's largest financial organisations, the geographic complexities paled next to the challenge of integrating an investment-oriented bank with a largely retail bank. A consultant says, 'We began with a comprehensive cultural assessment, interviewing each organisation's top management team and using a culture profiler tool to conduct focus groups with twelve hundred employees around the world. The findings helped launch a new training and coaching programme for leadership and lay out a detailed change-management strategy for integrating the new business.'

RE-ENGINEERING KEY BUSINESS PROCESSES

A global oil company wanted to improve the management of its corporate staff functions. Working with the CEO and a team drawn from across the business, Towers Perrin:

● Established benchmarks for best practices for corporate centres
● Delineated corporate roles and

services
● Evaluated opportunities for shared services
● Devised clear lines of accountability for delivery and cost

The project achieved savings of $220 million through process re-engineering, reconfigured service levels and resulted in a new performance framework for the company.

REINVENTING THE COMMUNICATION FUNCTION

A credit card company that was moving into new markets and technology asked Towers Perrin to help reinvent its communication process, especially in terms of involving employees in the business and helping them focus on key priorities and performance-related behaviours. 'We began with a gap analysis that looked at a range of communication capabilities in terms of both their importance to achieving business strategy and their current performance vis-à-vis their competitors. The gaps that emerged were in areas such as counselling leaders, building business literacy among employees and measuring communication programme effectiveness. We helped shift its focus to those activities that provided the most value to the business.'

QUALIFICATIONS AND SKILLS

This is definitely an area for the intellectuals. The minimum require-ment is a 2:1 degree and 24 UCAS points, but if you are on track for a first or are studying for a second degree

you stand an even better chance. Languages are a real asset.

TIPS

A large management consultancy will cover just about every business operation, but depending on your background you are likely to specialise from an early stage. Check the consultancy's client list in the areas in which you are interested. As most firms claim to offer just about everything, if you dig around you will find that each has its particular specialisations. These might be in:

● Communications – for example, electronics and media
● Financial services – for example, insurance and banking
● Government departments
● Products – for example, retail, industrial, cars
● Resources – for example, chemicals, energy, natural resources, utilities

SOURCES OF INFORMATION ON CAREER

● An excellent source of career information is the Institute of Management Consultancy.
TEL 020 7242 2140, www.imc.co.uk.

The organisations that helped in particular with this chapter were:
● Cap Gemini Ernst & Young Group www.cgey.com
● Accenture www.accenture.com
● Towers Perrin www.towers.com

32

INVESTMENT CONSULTANT

Money: £25,000–£30,000 with benefits, plus possible sign-on bonus or interest-free loan to clear your student debt.

Hours: Expect a significant chunk of overtime on top of the standard 9.30–5.30.

Pressure rating: 8/10. You are responsible for winning and maintaining pension fund clients worth billions of pounds. A screw-up *will* be noticed.

Glamour rating: 8/10. This is the glam side of the professional services, actuarial and employee benefits industry. Lots of good lunches and conferences in exotic places.

Travel rating: 9/10. If you work for one of the large City firms your clients will have global operations – and you will need to visit them, of course. There will also be international conferences.

SUMMARY

All the major UK pension funds and the larger charity funds use an investment consultant to help the trustees determine the investment objectives and asset allocation of the pension fund, and to appoint the right investment managers. Once contracted, the consultant is responsible for monitoring the performance of the managers and recommending replacements where appropriate.

Investment managers complain that in the UK the consultants control the entire manager appointment process to the pension funds, which are their biggest clients. You can turn this into an interesting debate at your interview, but always remember – the investment managers are absolutely right.

Outside the UK the going is much tougher. Investment consultants are working hard to build up business in the European pension markets, where the trustees (or foundation boards) are much more used to choosing their own managers without the added expense of an intermediary. However, as the investment management structures become more complicated, the need for consultancy increases, so an important part of your job is to encourage the most complicated investment arrangements possible.

WHO'S WHO?

Pension fund investment is a massive subject in its own right. In the UK, company pension funds hold assets worth £850 billion. Together, life assurance companies and pension funds own two-thirds of the UK stock market. So now you know who really runs the economy.

The organisations involved in investment consulting tend to be the big actuarial firms like Watson Wyatt, William M. Mercer and Towers Perrin, and the professional services firms like PricewaterhouseCoopers (see Chapters 30 and 37).

As an investment consultant your

job is to help clients achieve their objectives in the most efficient way. Your first task, therefore, is likely to be helping your clients discover what those objectives should be. In some cases they may not have thought about this very much.

The Investment Consulting Practice at William M. Mercer breaks down the consultancy process as follows:

● Establish the investment objectives
● Draft statements of investment principles
● Devise investment strategy using asset/liability modelling where appropriate
● Design the investment manager structures
● Select the investment managers and custodians
● Establish a comprehensive monitoring system including performance measurement, manager monitoring and portfolio analysis

TELL IT HOW IT IS

Alan graduated with a degree in mathematics from Balliol College, Oxford, and joined William M. Mercer in 1998. He is an actuary in the investment consulting practice. 'Our main activity is advising clients – mostly pension fund trustees – on a variety of investment issues and monitoring the performance of the fund's investment managers. I help to produce quarterly and annual investment reports for clients. Daily contact with fund managers helps me gain a deeper insight into the workings of the financial markets.'

David, an economics graduate from Oxford, works at a major actuarial firm in the investment consulting department. He explains, 'Our first task is to assess the investment objectives and making sure the statement of investment principles [Sip] is accurate.'

To do this you need to consider what the pension fund is there to achieve. Essentially, the pension fund's aims are to pay out to scheme members the benefits promised by the employer's pension scheme. Apart from the pensions themselves, these include death-in-service benefits and retirement lump sums. The list may also include disability payments. 'The fund must generate a substantial regular income stream to pay all the retirement pensions and it must have a sufficient number of liquid assets in order to pay the lump sum benefits,' David points out.

ACTUARIAL CALCULATIONS

The actuarial calculations are complex, and clearly the age profile of the workforce is a significant factor in the amount of capital and income required to pay benefits. A new scheme for a company with mainly young people will not expect to pay out pensions for many years and so can afford to invest predominantly in equities (UK and overseas) in order to generate the maximum capital growth. By contrast, a 'mature' scheme, for a company with many retired members and an ageing work force, as is common among some of the depressed industrial sectors, will need a high income stream. To achieve the target income the fund will need to invest heavily in income-producing assets such as gilts and bonds.

To assess the proportion of the fund that must be invested in each asset class, the consultant carries out an asset-liability model (ALM) exercise. This makes sure the fund is invested in the right sort of assets to match the scheme's liabilities in terms of benefit payments.

ETHICAL VIEWS

The statement of investment principles sets out any specific requirements for investment managers – for example, what ethical constraints managers should take into consideration when stock-picking. By law, pension funds must have an ethical or socially responsible investment policy. In some cases this might require the investment manager to avoid all companies that include certain unethical practices or products in their brands. Typical exclusions include companies that engage in alcohol, tobacco and gambling activities.

Jane, a history graduate from Liverpool University, works in the investment consultancy department of a professional services firm. 'I enjoy discussing socially responsible investment with clients. It is very thought-provoking and far more complicated than I imagined. For example, if the trustees want to exclude alcohol and gambling, do they ban the supermarkets that sell alcohol and lottery tickets? Most of the larger UK companies will include something unethical somewhere along the line, and this can cause problems because we would not want to see a fund weighted too heavily towards smaller, more volatile companies. It is important for the trustees to decide how far they want to take their ethical views. If they are not careful they will find that the only ethical asset left to invest in is property!'

MULTI-MANAGER STRUCTURES

The selection of investment managers for UK pension funds is a huge business in its own right. What trustees are looking for is an asset management structure that reduces short-term volatility against their benchmark and produces consistently good long-term results. To achieve this, most consultants now recommend a multi-manager structure as opposed to the traditional 'balanced' manager, who might have been responsible for investing across all the asset classes.

Under a multi-manager structure different managers are appointed for different asset classes. Where the fund is really big, the consultant might even divide the fund's exposure to a major asset class between two investment managers with different styles. So, for example, the UK equity mandate might be managed partly by a passive manager to provide low-cost exposure to the All-Share, and partly by a specialist active manager who would aim to add value through careful stock-picking.

Once the managers are appointed, the consultant must monitor performance carefully. This does not just involve checking that the annual returns are on target. It is also important to analyse performance attribution to see why a manager performed the way he or she did. 'Our job is to see that the managers we appoint stick to their brief. If performance was particularly good but was achieved by a manager investing outside the brief, then we would be very concerned and might even sack the manager,' David says.

GLOBAL CLIENTS

With the increase in cross-border mergers and acquisitions, investment consultancy is no longer confined by national boundaries. Western European pension fund assets are estimated at some US$3.3 trillion by William M. Mercer – hence the considerable interest among investment consultants in advising these funds.

Private company funds are increasing as demographic changes are imposing intolerable strains on overburdened state pension schemes, most of which are being cut back by European governments.

Where a client has operations in several European countries, the consultant needs to consider all the factors outlined above but within the context of the different tax and regulatory regimes. Pension funds are governed by extraordinarily complex rafts of tax legislation to prevent money being invested badly or being stolen by cash-strapped employers.

At the time of writing it is impossible to establish one fund for several European operations. Instead each country has to have its own fund governed by its own laws. Here the consultant's aim is to co-ordinate the investment policy as much as possible and where appropriate to establish a list of preferred managers who are recommended throughout the company's operations.

QUALIFICATIONS AND SKILLS

The minimum is a 2:1 degree and 24 UCAS points. You must be able to demonstrate a keen interest in investment. Languages are a definite plus and may be compulsory in some of the international consultancies.

TIPS

Some of the top investment consultants started life as fund managers, so you might want to consider this route if you are particularly interested in the practical aspects of investing.

SOURCES OF INFORMATION ON CAREER

● The best places to find out about investment consultancy are on the employers' websites (see below, and also the recruitment websites).

● The National Association of Pension Funds is the trade organisation for the medium- to large-sized pension funds in the UK, and its website is at www.napf.co.uk

● A good publication for sources of information is *Pension Funds and their Advisers*, issued by AP Information Services (www.ap-info.co.uk). It lists all the UK pension funds and consultancies as well as investment managers. Try the following for starters:

● Aon Consulting www.aon.com

● Bacon & Woodrow www.bacon-woodrow.com

● Hewitt Associates www.hewitt.com

● Hymans Robertson www.hymans.co.uk

● William M. Mercer www.wmmercer.com

● PricewaterhouseCoopers www.pwcglobal.com

● Towers Perrin www.towers.com

● Watson Wyatt www.watsonwyatt.co.uk

33
IT/IT CONSULTANCY

k **MONEY:** £26,000–£28,000 but can be as high as £30,000. Plus a sign-on bonus of up to £10,000.

h **HOURS:** Officially 9–5.30 but as in most areas of consultancy we are talking seriously long hours here. Again, remember that a lot of your time will be spent at client sites which could be a very long way from home, so expect to spend a good part of the year living out of a suitcase.

PRESSURE RATING: 8/10. You will be working on multimillion-pound projects. Get them wrong and your company ain't gonna like it. This can be very high-profile work if it is a government project or installing a system for a major financial institution. The press love it when big systems crash.

c **GLAMOUR RATING:** 8/10. This is the sexy side of IT work.

l **TRAVEL RATING:** 6–8/10. Opportunities depend on the client base location. Most consultancy jobs involve on-site work where you virtually live with the client until the job is finished. However, we're talking largely UK travel, so don't get too excited.

SUMMARY

Key to the smooth running of City institutions is the IT support network. Screen-based trading is backed by seriously clever settlement and security systems. 'Real time' information is pumped out by analysts and wired to clients in milliseconds. A dealer in the main markets will have maybe half a dozen such screens on his or her desk.

One of the key functions behind the scenes is to support the 'back office' systems, which are also known as 'operations' and 'support functions'. This is where all the settlement of trades takes place.

Systems are developing so rapidly that obsolescence is a serious problem. If computing is your strength, your work could involve designing systems for a major exchange or for a derivatives specialist. Inside an insurance company or professional services firm you might design the intranet or Internet site, or build the technology required to drive its client servicing department. Pensions administration is another huge area for IT consulting, particularly as more and more employers are outsourcing this whole function to specialists.

As a very broad guide, you are likely to be involved at the maintenance and security level, which is known as systems analysis, or you may prefer to go in for systems analysis, which focuses on new projects or redesigning an existing system.

IT IN FUND MANAGEMENT

Investment banks have large IT departments. If you work for a large investment house this function would typically cover:

● Analysing business processes and systems to recommend improvements
● Defining and carrying out systems testing on upgraded software
● Developing and co-ordinating the IT intranet site
● Configuration management, to ensure all systems and user acceptance testing is carried out to the correct specifications
● Assessing the requirements of the business and translating them into a functional specification
● Acting as the link between the business and programmers to ensure that technology meets the business need

Shryash, an IT manager at Schroders, says, 'Schroders is basically run on information technology. Providing the means to store and then make the best use of that information is our responsibility.

'Graduates joining us become involved in a range of activities from actual installation of hardware and support of hardware and networks, through to application development and areas such as testing and configuration management. There are project management roles, and a range of work on architecture and technology strategy.

'Whether you are interested in specialising in a particular area of technology, or more interested in a management role, good communication skills are essential if you are to provide effective technological solutions to meet the needs of the business.'

Graduate trainees are thrown straight into the business. Even if you work in the more technical roles you will find you are talking to internal clients. IT is the life-blood of any financial institution and there are plenty of career choices and opportunities.

OPERATIONS/SUPPORT

Also part of the IT scene are the 'back office' functions. This term covers a range of jobs that relate to the administration and settlement of the functions of an investment bank, for example. The key task is to ensure that any deals carried out by the traders and dealers (see Chapter 28) have been settled, and that the money has changed hands.

Typically you might be involved in creating and maintaining the IT infrastructure to run the business – for example, to ensure payments are made, deals are settled, and the database of market intelligence is maintained and kept secure from hackers – as well as in telecommunications, and running the intranet for the global operation. Where the company outsources a specific project or function to one of the major IT consultants, your job is to provide the interface between your company and the consultant.

The more hi-tech the business, the more sophisticated the IT and the more likely it is you will need a technical background. John, for example, works for convertibles and equity derivatives specialists KBC Financial Products, where he is responsible for developing the IT environment for networking to European exchange and clearing systems. He joined the financial products team straight from graduate studies at City University, where, following his undergraduate computer science studies at Imperial College, he gained a Masters in business systems analysis and design. 'I started with the company in 1997 as a line member of the helpdesk, and since early 1999 I have progressively taken on more development-oriented responsibilities.'

One of John's colleagues, Tim, builds convertibles and warrant trading systems. He joined KBC in 1996. 'I've been instrumental in the development and improvement of the firm's real-time trading software.' Tim has a degree in computer science from Manchester University and held intern positions at Texas Instruments and ICL. Before he joined KBC, he worked for an investment bank, where he spent three years developing the financial analytics and trading platforms.

PENSIONS ADMINISTRATION

Pensions administration is a huge area for IT. Many employers now outsource this function to specialist consultancies or invite them in to build new systems. Even government departments use private sector consultants.

QUALIFICATIONS AND SKILLS

A minimum of a 2:1 degree applies. It is helpful to have a technical qualification or experience in an IT role before you join a consultancy. These employers are looking for problem-solvers, mathematicians and logicians. You also need good teamwork and communication skills.

TIPS

Check the consultancy's client list to get an idea of its size and scope. Find out if you will get the chance to specialise. Accenture, for example, encourages staff to specialise in a particular line of business that might cut across industry segments. These include:

● Customer relationship management
● Enterprise business solutions
● Finance and performance management
● Strategic IT effectiveness
● Supply chain management

SOURCES OF INFORMATION ON CAREER

● Go to the employers direct through their websites or contact the major recruitment agencies, including the specialists:
www.prospects.csu.man.ac.uk and www.doctorjob.com
● Look at the specialist press – for example, *Financial Sector Technology*, www.perspective-publishing.co.uk
● Accenture is at www.accenture.com
● Schroders is at www.schroders.com

34
RISK CONSULTING

Money: £25,000–£40,000 (PhDs required for the top end of this scale) plus possible sign-on and banking benefits.

Hours: 9–5.30 and then some! Like all consultancy jobs this one can entail seriously long hours. Remember, a lot of your time will be spent at client sites which could be a very long way from home. Add 'smart suitcases' to your graduation gifties list.

Pressure rating: 7/10. Lots of tough deadlines and you may be living out of a suitcase.

Glamour rating: 8/10. More glam points than other areas of assurance/insurance owing to its international nature. Good intellectual rating.

Travel rating: 8/10. Risk consultancy is aimed very much at global corporations, so there should be excellent travel opportunities.

SUMMARY

Traditionally, risk was classed as an insurance business. However, the risks faced by today's global corporations go far beyond the traditional narrow definitions of insurance. Risk consulting today can involve, for example, forecasting the risks and potential returns for banks dealing in a huge range of markets.

You need to be a bit clever for this job. As the AGCAS publication 'City Institutions and Financial Markets' points out, 'The underlying mathematics and programming of such forecasting is extremely complex and mathematicians and computer scientists (often PhD level) are actively sought to fill the comparatively small number of positions available.'

WHO'S WHO?

Risk services are offered by the professional services firms (see Chapter 30) and the management consultants (Chapter 31). The Assurance and Business Advisory practice is one of Arthur Andersen's largest departments. The firm says, 'Confidence is the foundation of economic activity. Businesses need confidence in the information that they rely on to run their business and that others rely on to invest in it. However, in the new economy traditional methods of providing assurance are not enough. Not when business risks are increasing in number, scale and frequency and the capital markets have no tolerance for disappointments.

'Our approach to Business Assurance and Risk Consulting is based around our Business Risk Model™, which we designed for these complex, dynamic times. It gives us a framework for helping our global clients identify and understand their business risks – the root causes of financial reporting surprises, misstatements and errors. We then focus on assuring the quality of key controls. We have developed the Business Audit, which is our risk-focused approach to providing assurance on financial statements.'

Chris works in the risk consulting division of Arthur Andersen. He says, 'When I first joined I was sold on the ethic that if you worked hard you were rewarded well. This has been the case for me. Recently I worked closely with a client to develop a solution to a very technical accounting issue. There was a steep learning curve and some long nights but we got there in the end. The client was impressed with our work and I received a performance bonus.'

Chris's colleague Douglas adds, 'My projects have ranged from testing the security of websites to correcting errors in a scheduling and payroll system. There is plenty of flexibility in my work, and as much responsibility and independence as I've wanted from early on. Every few weeks I join a new team, often with a different manager. What makes it satisfying is that managers acknowledge a job well done.'

RISK AND TECHNOLOGY

In the new economy, technology is no longer just a matter for the IT director – it is a boardroom issue of strategic importance. The growing sophistication of technology means that businesses are moving into unfamiliar markets, forming unexpected alliances and investing in uncertain futures. New risks arise as quickly as new

technology is introduced. 'The ability to maintain a balanced perspective on IT-related risk can give a business a significant competitive advantage,' says Arthur Andersen. 'Our role is to help clients manage the business risks they face arising from their use of technology. This involves both working as part of the assurance team and advising on specialist technology consulting projects. As a member of the assurance team, you support colleagues applying the Business Audit, our innovative and integrated audit approach, by focusing on IT risks. This will help you build a broad understanding of how businesses are run and managed, and further your development as a business risk adviser. Consulting projects range from implementing secure IT processing environments to running successful systems development projects to helping clients manage the risks and maximise the benefits of e-business.'

Towers Perrin Reinsurance, part of the Towers Perrin organisation, provides a wide range of consulting services to a variety of insurance and reinsurance companies. Teams of reinsurance professionals, including actuaries, collaborate on client engagements. These projects may involve:

● Analysing financial positions, on-going operations and long-term business objectives
● Counselling the client after the devastation of a tornado or hurricane
● Reviewing the client's aggregate exposures to determine a reasonable

amount of protection against losses from a single catastrophe

For example, a new reinsurance company wanted to use new modelling technology to manage its exposure to catastrophic losses. The company's management turned to Towers Perrin Reinsurance for an innovative approach. 'We applied modern portfolio theory to the problem and helped the company develop an underwriting system that has helped optimise the diversification of its exposure. The system has allowed the company to consistently outperform its peer group by making more efficient use of capital.'

In January 1998 a freezing rainstorm in the Province of Quebec produced an estimated insured loss of more than $1 billion – the largest catastrophe in Canada up to that time. Towers Perrin Reinsurance negotiated a payment arrangement with the reinsurance markets, whereby their cash reimbursement essentially matched Towers Perrin's clients' projected payout to those they had insured. 'As a result, the negative impact of the storm on our client companies' cash flow was effectively minimised.'

QUALIFICATIONS & SKILLS

A minimum of a 2:1 degree applies and a technical background is helpful. Risk consultancies are looking for problem-solvers, so good analytical skills are essential. You also need good teamwork and communication skills.

TIPS

● To get a good feel for this area of consulting, read the specialist publications and contact the professional and trade bodies for risk and insurance (see Chapter 6).
● A good place to start is The Association of Insurance and Risk Managers in Industry and Commerce (AIRMIC), www.airmic.co.uk

SOURCES OF INFORMATION ON CAREER

● Go to the employers direct through their websites or contact the major recruitment agencies, including the specialists www.prospects.csu.man.ac.uk and www.doctorjob.com

SOURCES FOR THIS CHAPTER

● Arthur Andersen
www.arthurandersen.com
● Towers Perrin
www.towers.com

35
THE LAW

k **Money:** £22,000–£28,000 with benefits, plus possible sign-on bonus or interest-free loan (to clear your student debt). If you are going into law as a career then you will be looking at the lower end of the salary range to start with owing to the training commitment.

h **Hours:** Depending on position, expect a significant chunk of overtime on top of the standard 9.30–5.30. Expect also to work hard for exams in your free time.

Pressure rating: 6–8/10. Varies depending on the department. Higher rating for those on the front line dealing with corporate clients.

C **Glamour rating:** 4–8/10. Depends on the organisation you join. Jobs in the big City law firms are very highly sought after.

1 **Travel rating:** 4–8/10. If you join a major firm you should get plenty of travel, particularly if you are working for international clients. On the other hand you could be working as a solicitor for a UK financial services company and not budge from your office.

SUMMARY

If you join a big law firm you could get involved with any one of over a dozen different specialisations. Dibb Lupton Alsop, for example, offers services in the following areas, among others:

- Aviation
- Banking
- Business services (debt recovery and repossessions, for example)
- Business support and restructuring (insolvency, liquidations)
- Edicts from Brussels such as competition law, e-commerce
- Communications and technology
- Corporate taxation
- E-commerce
- Employee incentives
- Human resources
- Insurance
- Litigation
- Marine insurance and shipping
- Public policy developments
- Real estate
- Regulation
- Reinsurance

WHO'S WHO?

Jobs with law firms are not just limited to solicitors. Far from it. In a useful booklet, *The Legal Profession*, AGCAS states, 'The knowledge and skills acquired from studying law are widely applicable in many employment sectors. Transferable skills include problem-solving, logical thinking, research skills, an ability to assimilate large amounts of material and to communicate ideas effectively both verbally and in writing.'

For this reason, if you have a law degree you will find that good opportunities exist in finance, accounting, banking and insurance, so do read the relevant chapters in this part of the book. It's worth noting that accountancy firms are particularly keen to employ law graduates in their tax practices. You might also consider personnel work, as this can involve employment law, health and safety regulations, and industrial relations.

If you are set on joining a legal firm, then the important features to consider are its size, client base, reputation, and the training. In fact you will spend your first few years training, so make sure the programme is comprehensive and will set you up for a better job within the firm or outside if you choose to move on.

Big isn't necessarily best, but the major law firms do tend to pay the highest salaries – and make the most money. Clifford Chance LLP, for example, is now the world's largest law firm, and at the time of writing was on target to generate £800 million in fees in 2000 – a record £200 million increase on the previous year. This reflects the global boom in legal services as well as the firm's three-way UK–German–US merger at the start of 2000 (see below).

In addition, the large firms tend to encourage business travel and secondments overseas in other offices.

THE MAJOR FIRMS

To get a feel for what it is like on the inside of a law firm, we looked at a couple of top employers – Clifford Chance LLP and Baker & McKenzie. Even if you don't expect to join a leading firm, it is worth considering what these employers offer in the scope and range of their training. This provides a good benchmark against which you can measure your more likely prospects.

In January 2000 Clifford Chance, Rogers & Wells LLP and Pünder, Volhard, Weber & Axster merged to create Clifford Chance LLP. The firm describes itself as follows: 'Our aim is to be judged by our clients as the premier global law firm. As one of the largest law firms in the world with over 3,000 legal advisers we can provide clients with high-quality legal advice on major transactions and litigation. We are uniquely equipped to deliver co-ordinated legal services in every major financial market.'

Like most other financial services organisations, law firms are either going global or developing a niche presence. If you are just starting out you might be better off going for a large integrated firm. The big law firms recruit top graduates from a wide variety of backgrounds and universities. You can find out which firms offer genuine opportunities to qualified graduates by the retention numbers. For example, in 1999 over 95 per cent of Clifford Chance's trainees stayed with the firm on qualification.

So what opportunities will you get with a major international firm? This type of organisation should offer:

● Financial advice to some of the world's largest international and

domestic financial institutions
● A cross-border mergers and acquisitions, competition and funds practice
● Private equity practice
● Technology practice
● Integrated US antitrust and EU competition law capability
● International litigation teams
● Global regulatory expertise
● Intellectual property capabilities in all major jurisdictions
● Real estate practice in Europe and the US
● Tax capabilities in all key jurisdictions

Let's get practical. What does this mean for your career? Clifford Chance LLP says, 'It means that you will work on some of the best deals – both international and local – for the best clients alongside some of the most talented minds in the commercial world.' The firm's 3,000 legal advisers represent more than 50 nationalities, and the lawyers are backed up by the same number of support professionals.

'The Academy' is Clifford Chance's training programme. 'Our aim is to develop lawyers who can work very closely with our clients, be they governments, banks or businesses, regardless of nationality or location. And who understand marketplace events, their impact on clients and the commercial and political context of transactions. They must develop personal and legal skills to advise clients in highly complex situations.'

At the time of writing the firm was introducing the Profile, a career development guide to help trainees improve performance and develop by:

● Setting objective benchmarks for the skills, knowledge, experience and training – legal, managerial and interpersonal – that you will need at different stages of your career
● Enabling you to keep a record of your experience and development, including feedback from partners and senior lawyers on your job performance, the deals you've completed, training courses and non-fee-earning activity like pro bono work (work for the public good) or business development
● Providing you with practical information which you can use in conjunction with your annual performance review to set development goals, such as taking on new types of work or additional training

Initially, the firm runs induction courses that provide a general introduction to a specialised area of law and practice. These are followed by foundation programmes of talks and workshops that explore in-depth technical aspects. These programmes include updates on current law and practice, talks by specialists in particular areas, and lectures from lawyers in other legal disciplines.

You also get plenty of help with non-technical skills – for example, presenting, negotiating, and legal writing. About three to four years post-qualification (the timing varies according to jurisdiction), you will attend the Lawyer's Development Centre, an off-site residential educational facility at which your non-technical skills will be assessed. The purpose of this is to identify your strengths and weaknesses in those areas critical to meeting a client's legal and commercial needs. Subsequently, each lawyer drafts a development plan to be achieved over the next 18 to 24 months.

INTERNATIONAL OPPORTUNITIES

One of the options Baker & McKenzie offers is an international clerkship programme. The idea is for you to compare legal practice in two jurisdictions and become familiar with a different legal culture.

James, a graduate trainee with Baker & McKenzie, describes his experience in London and Hong Kong. 'In London I spent time in the IP [intellectual property], IT, banking and corporate departments, which gave me a well-rounded view of how the firm operates, the calibre of the lawyers and the work they handle. The fact that for different parts of the programme I was sitting with a trainee, junior associate, senior associate and head of department also meant that I was able to see what the lawyers did and the level of responsibility they handled at different levels of experience. Throughout I was given a range of interesting assignments, including a research report on the impact a government white paper would have on a range of IT clients if passed.'

In Hong Kong James spent the six-week assignment in the IP department and soon became immersed in the operations. 'Hong Kong does have a reputation for IP infringements. Although the promised raid on an infringing factory on the Chinese mainland never materialised, I was able to follow through from start to finish several cases. One of the most interesting I was involved in concerned fake video CDs and the resulting action by the patent owner.'

LIFE AS A TRAINEE

The amount of time spent in the office varies, but the reality of City life is that there is no such thing as a nine-to-five job – you will have to work long hours when the demands of the job require it. In terms of facilities, don't expect a smaller firm to match those offered by Clifford Chance, where the on-site facilities include a restaurant, shop and fitness centre featuring pool, gym, squash court and exercise studio.

QUALIFICATIONS AND SKILLS

For full-time positions, Dibb Lupton Alsop says it is looking for candidates who possess 2 Bs and 1 C at A level, and a 2:1 degree in any discipline. It stresses that throughout the recruitment process it will be seeking applicants who demonstrate the following skills and qualities:

● Written and oral communication skills
● Teamwork
● Analytical skills: handling complex data
● Commercial awareness
● Organisational skills
● Attention to detail
● Resilience
● Loyalty
● Ability to work to deadlines

TIPS

While you are at university, do take a look at the summer vacation placements. These will give you a really good insight into the firm and whether you want to join full time. Dibb Lupton Alsop, for example, operates a formal Summer Vacation Placement Scheme between June and August in all its UK offices. Students are invited to spend one week in a department, shadowing a trainee or an assistant solicitor, and taking part in group activities.

The scheme also features presentations from departments about the work they do, and a social event with the firm's trainees, giving you the opportunity to look at the firm from different perspectives. There are approximately 175 places available across the firm as a whole. All vacation placements are paid. The figure for the London office was £185 per week in 2000. Applications for the scheme must be submitted on the firm's own application form by 28 February each year.

SOURCES OF INFORMATION ON CAREER

● For details about the Association of Graduate Careers Advisory Services (AGCAS) publications 'Legal Profession' and 'Careers for law graduates outside the legal profession', see page 36.
● Read *The Lawyer* (weekly), *The Law Society Gazette* (weekly) and *The Times* (Tuesday's edition). See below and pages 37 and 38 for websites.

WEBSITES

● **Sites listing vacation placements, pupillages and training contracts:**
www.chambersandpartners.com/student
www.lawcareers.net
www.prospects.csu.man.ac.uk
www.studentlaw.com

● **Publishers' sites for vacancies and legal articles:**
www.guardian.co.uk
www.independent.co.uk
www.lawgazette.co.uk
www.the-lawyer.co.uk
www.the-times.co.uk

● **Sites providing information on firms and the latest legal developments:**
www.gti.co.uk
www.icclaw.com
www.venables.co.uk/legal

● **Professional bodies:**
www.barcouncil.org.uk
www.ilex.org.uk
www.lawsociety.org.uk
www.TSG.org

● **Sources for this chapter**
Dibb Lupton Alsop www.dla-law.co.uk
Clifford Chance
www.cliffordchance.com
Baker & McKenzie
www.bakerinfo.com

c) Pensions and Insurance

36
THE JARGON

ACTUARIES AND EMPLOYEE BENEFITS FIRMS

We have put the firms of actuarial and employee benefits consultants in this section because of their strong links with the insurance world. However, much of the information on consultants in the previous section applies.

Although the big firms tend to cover both aspects, we have divided the range of jobs on offer into two broad sections. In Chapter 37 we deal with pensions and actuarial work, and in Chapter 38 we look at the wide range of jobs in employee benefits.

Employee benefits grew out of pension schemes. Once upon a time an employer offered a salary and a pension. And that was it. These days the non-cash remuneration elements of employee benefits typically account for 20–30 per cent of the total bill. For senior employees the non-salary elements can exceed the salary itself, particularly where there are valuable stock options.

BENEFITS BUZZWORDS

You'll find there are a lot of buzzwords in this industry. Benefits consultants have become much grander in recent years, and you will be hard pressed to find anyone who uses the term 'personnel'. 'Human resource' or HR management is about as user-friendly as it gets. People are 'human capital' these days, and benefits are 'compensation' or 'reward' schemes. Frankly it's all about the same thing, but if you get allocated to the human capital and reward department or the people strategy and human resource management department you must fiercely defend your particular specialisations and learn to curl your upper lip at personnel.

INSURANCE

When it comes to insurance companies there are two important definitions to remember:

Insurance usually refers to **general insurance**. Here you are protecting against certain events such as fire, theft, storm damage, wars, and so on.

Life assurance is all the stuff that relates to personal protection, such as life assurance itself and various types of income protection insurance. Think of it as the 'what if' scenarios for people who depend on their earnings. What if they fall ill and can't work? Well, in this case they need an insurance policy that provides either a regular income or a lump sum that, when invested, can generate a regular income. What if they die? In this case the employee's dependants need the lump sum for the same reasons.

Life assurance also covers investments. What, you might wonder, has life assurance got in common with investment? Logically the answer is nothing, but life offices (as the life assurance arms of insurance companies are known) have little to do with logic. In fact they have a taxation system all of their own that nobody but the actuaries who run them really understands. This makes some of their investments very tax efficient for certain types of investors – but not usually the ones who get sold the policies.

INSURANCE BUZZWORDS

● **Defined benefit (DB)** (also known as '**final salary**') This is a type of pension scheme where the pension is based on the employee's salary and number of years in the scheme. The employee usually makes a contribution but the investment risk and guarantees are backed by the employer.

● **Defined contribution (DC)** (also known as '**money purchase**') This is a more modern type of pension scheme where the employee's fund is used at retirement to purchase an 'annuity' from an insurance company, which provides a regular income. The value of that annuity will depend largely on the fund size, which in turn depends on investment returns: there are no guarantees.

● **Endowment** This is a type of long-term investment that is typically linked to a capital debt such as an interest-only mortgage. During the term of the investment the borrower pays the interest (hence the term interest-only mortgage) and at the end of the term (maturity) the investment is used to repay the capital. The key feature of the endowment is that it includes life assurance, so that if the investor dies before the end of the term the gap between the fund built up through the investment and the capital owed is covered by the life policy.

● **Flex** is short for flexible benefits. These are employee benefits subsidised by an employer and offered as a menu from which employees can choose up to an annual monetary limit.

● **Life office/life assurance company** The life assurance and investment arm of general insurance companies – or it can be a stand-alone company with no general insurance link.

● **Voluntary benefits** are low-cost deals arranged by employers for employees to buy on a voluntary basis – for example cheap insurance, package holidays, car purchase and legal helplines.

37
ACTUARY

k **MONEY:** £22,000–£28,000 for graduate trainees with top firms. £18,000+ elsewhere.

h **HOURS:** Depending on position, expect a significant chunk of overtime on top of the standard 9.30–5.30. And as in accountancy and law, allow a sizable amount of free time for study.

PRESSURE RATING: 5–7/10. Varies depending on the department, but the work involves method and precision rather than the competitive deadlines of corporate finance.

C **GLAMOUR RATING:** 4/10. Sorry. However, it is good to know that behind the scenes actuaries are quietly running the country and possibly the world. Think of the actuaries as the Clark Kents of this world and you've got the picture. Once you're fully qualified you'll be able to afford that Batmobile and run the Porsche-driving derivatives traders off the road.

1 **TRAVEL RATING:** 4–8/10. Depends on the type of job and the location of the clients. There are big travel opportunities for those who deal with global corporations, but if your clients are Midlands-based manufacturers then you may have to settle for a return to Crewe.

SUMMARY

This is a job for the maths swots. Pure actuarial work involves extremely good mathematical abilities and the skill to assess probability and risk. All insurance companies must have an appointed actuary, who is responsible for assessing and maintaining the company's solvency in relation to potential claims and, in the case of investors, the 'reasonable expectations' of policyholders.

The underwriting departments of insurance companies require actuaries to assess non-standard risk to enable the company to price premium rates at a competitive level. Actuaries also have to review the standard priced products in the light of claims experience.

For example, life assurance rates may be reduced when actuaries take account of the general increase in life expectancy. At the same time it is possible to create new products that reflect 'lifestyle' features. The cost of annuities (which provide a regular income for life) for those who smoke or are significantly overweight can be cut because actuaries know that the statistics are right when they tell us we will die early if we do not look after our health. All in all, it's best not to be squeamish if you want to be an actuary.

On a broader scale, company pension schemes need actuaries to make a wide range of predictions that will affect how much of the fund must be kept in liquid assets to make payments other than the expected retirement pensions, such as death-in-service benefits where employees die before retirement. If you join a pensions department you will get involved with the investment management team.

WHO'S WHO?

Most of the major international actuarial and employee benefits consultants – William M. Mercer, Watson Wyatt, Towers Perrin, for example – started life as actuarial firms but today offer a wide range of services which aim to meet all the needs of the global corporation. In many fields these firms are direct competitors to the professional services organisations (see Chapter 30) and offer similar graduate training programmes.

We provide details of some of the major firms below.

IN DEMAND

Actuarial work is in great demand and the profession is expected to double in size (from 7,000) by 2020. Lots of actuaries are still employed by insurance companies following the review of sales of personal pensions in the late 1980s and early 1990s, when many employees who were in good company pension schemes that guaranteed a salary-linked pension at retirement were persuaded to transfer out of their scheme and invest the money in a personal pension plan. With this type of plan there are no guarantees – your retirement income depends to a large extent on stock market returns.

On the government's insistence pension companies have had to review thousands of plans to see whether the individual would have been better off staying in a company pension scheme. Where this has proved to be the case, actuaries are used to calculate a fair compensation for the missold pension plan or, where possible, to calculate what the rogue insurance company should pay the employer's scheme for reinstating the employee for the period during which he or she opted out.

Most insurance companies have been unable to cope with the volume of work and have outsourced reviews to external firms and individuals, including senior students. Sources report that actuaries working full time in this field can earn over £10,000 per month.

TRAINING

Edward joined William M. Mercer in 1997 after graduating from Durham University with a degree in physics. 'I wanted a career that would allow me to use my mathematical background. An actuarial career offers the security of a professional qualification and it's a highly respected profession.'

Edward has found that there are three elements to the training programme followed to become an actuary:

● Professional exams
● Practical on-the-job training
● 'Soft skills' like letter and report writing, project planning and presentation skills

Training is a key factor in selecting your first employer, so do check that you get full support for studying towards your professional exams (see 'Tips' below). This doesn't necessarily mean working for one of the major firms. There are smaller firms of actuaries and employee benefits consultants that offer opportunities to young people, while some of the life offices are also big players in the occupational pensions markets and are significant employers of actuaries.

Trevor, who has a maths degree from Portsmouth University, joined a medium-sized firm of actuarial consultants in the City in September 2000. 'I like the people and the fact that I can get involved in all aspects of the work. We don't have any global clients but some of the companies we deal with are at the cutting edge of technology, and the pension arrangements have to reflect the expectations of the high-fliers they employ.'

A graduate trainee's training schedule at one of the employee benefits giants will probably be similar in scope to those offered by the professional services firms. Jan left Sheffield University in 1999 with an economics degree and joined one of the big firms of international consultants. 'The training for the actuarial exams is demanding and thorough and my firm gives me all the help I need. While I am training I get to work with international clients who want to develop pension schemes for thousands of employees around the world. The regulations that affect these schemes and the tax treatment of the funds in all the different regimes are mind-bogglingly complicated. It's no wonder these companies call in the experts!'

As the world's largest employer of actuaries, Towers Perrin offers a variety of professional services that require actuarial expertise. 'We seek individuals with strong analytical and quantitative skills, and the ability to forecast future events and financial results that support our clients' business goals,' the firm says.

The firm provides support for those preparing for actuarial exams, including paid study time and the payment of exam registration fees and the cost of study notes, textbooks and outside seminars. During training you can expect to work on a variety of client assignments, and you will also receive formal and informal training in-house, as well as coaching and mentoring. On successful completion of exams you should receive a salary increase and bonus. 'Entry-level actuarial associates go on to pursue careers as actuarial specialists, team leaders and consultants, and may, over time, become client relationship managers,' Towers Perrin says.

Employees with undergraduate degrees typically begin in supporting roles on project teams, and take on increased project and client relationship management responsibilities over time. Experienced employees normally begin as project and/or client relationship managers.

PENSIONS AND ACTUARIAL CONSULTING

You are going to have to learn a lot about pensions if you want to make it as an actuary.

The provision of a substantial pension can be the ultimate incentive when attempting to recruit the best employees. Pension schemes are a costly, important and sensitive part of any competitive compensation package.

Occupational pensions are not limited to single-employer schemes. An increasing number of employers belong to industry-wide arrangements where a scheme is set up to cater for all employees within a specific sector for example, broadcasting, chemical engineering, civil engineering, hotels and leisure groups, and so on.

Group arrangements generally offer economies of scale that cannot be achieved by individual plans. For this reason, from April 2001 the government extended the availability of such schemes through 'stakeholder' pensions so that the self-employed and employees who do not have access to a company pension can still join a group scheme.

TYPES OF PENSION SCHEME

There are two types of pension scheme – defined benefit (DB) and defined contribution (DC) – and you should understand the difference. With DB (also known as 'final salary') the pension is based on the employee's salary and number of years in the scheme. The employee usually makes a contribution but the investment risk and guarantees are backed by the employer.

With a DC pension (also known as 'money purchase') the investment risk falls fairly and squarely on the employee's shoulders, as his or her fund is used at retirement to purchase an 'annuity' from an insurance company, which provides a regular income. The value of that annuity will depend largely on the fund size, which in turn depends on investment returns: there are no guarantees. Not surprisingly, money purchase schemes are proving very popular with employers.

MORE THAN JUST ACTUARIES

Your job in pensions could embrace a wide range of issues, including:

● Assessing the funding requirements for defined benefit schemes – that is, the amount the employees and employer need to contribute to enable the scheme to pay the promised benefits
● Scheme design – for example, should it be DC or DB, or should the employer offer both? DB is considered more flexible for younger employees because there is an identifiable pot of money he or she can take from job to job
● Asset management
● Communication and administration

Arthur Andersen says, 'As a member of the Pensions and Actuarial Consulting team you will advise clients on retirement, health, welfare, actuarial, investment and other risk management services. On a day-to-day basis your work will vary from the mathematics of pension valuations to creating the best method of communicating pension information.

'The team works on projects, the majority of which involve offering advice to companies, although you could also be working with individuals and pension scheme trustees. A large part of our work requires us to provide solutions to issues arising from acquisitions and mergers, for example advising on the post-merger integration of pension schemes. However, you will be working on many other projects, such as pension scheme reviews, or comparison of executive pension schemes with the competition. You will also help clients formulate pension and benefit packages for key appointments in the company.'

Remember that the pensions department has to work closely with the other areas of 'human capital' and personal tax. Arthur Andersen says, 'You will learn about tax issues, share schemes and compensation strategy, giving you knowledge beyond the scope of the actuary, helping you to develop into a multidisciplined consultant.'

QUALIFICATIONS AND SKILLS

The big firms will be looking for a minimum of a 2:1 in an academic subject. For graduates joining the pensions and actuarial consulting group of a major consultant, it is usually a requirement of the Institute and Faculty of Actuaries that student members possess at least a grade B in A-level maths.

TIPS

As with accountancy, actuarial exams require a great deal of study time, so look for an employer that allows you plenty. William M. Mercer offers each graduate a bank of 60 study days to be used as required – for example, one day per week. When you pass an exam the firm adds extra days to your bank to replace those used. Mercer also finances your first attempt at the exams, and this includes study materials and attendance at external tutorials.

SOURCES OF INFORMATION ON CAREER

● The Institute and Faculty of Actuaries (see page 39) offer lots of information on the actuarial profession.
● The best source book for firms that operate in this field is *Pension Funds and their Advisers* (known in the industry as the Blue Book), published by AP Publications; website www.ap-info.co.uk.

SOURCES FOR THIS CHAPTER

● Arthur Andersen
www.arthurandersen.com
● William M. Mercer
www.wmmercer.com
● Towers Perrin
www.towers.com

38
EMPLOYEE BENEFITS CONSULTANT

k **Money:** £22,000–£28,000 plus possible sign-on bonus.

h **Hours:** 9.30–5.30 plus overtime.

Pressure rating: 6/10. Possibly higher for those on the front line dealing with corporate clients.

C **Glamour rating:** 5/10. Not a very sexy image. Can be more glam if you advise on executive remuneration schemes like chunky share options.

1 **Travel rating:** 6/10. Travel opportunities depend on the type of job and the location of the clients. Good prospects if you deal with global corporations.

SUMMARY

The days when employers appointed a personnel officer to look after salaries are long gone. These days it's 'total reward' or 'total compensation'. Salaries represent only one element of this, and often the simplest. Big employers reward employees through very elaborate benefit schemes that involve a wide range of providers and advisers.

With all the buzzwords it is easy to forget the whole object of this exercise. The aim of an employee benefits package is to attract, retain and motivate staff without costing the company an arm and a leg. Well,

actually, it does cost an arm and a leg, but a lot of it is tax deductible and frankly it's the only way to get good staff in competitive markets.

The important point is that the benefits should achieve their purpose. Your job, therefore, is likely to involve designing – or in most cases redesigning – the most appropriate benefits scheme for a client, negotiating the most competitive deals with providers of the benefits, and communicating the benefits to the workforce.

We dealt with pension schemes in the previous chapter. On top of this employers offer everything from annual bonuses, company cars and medical insurance to stock options, extra holiday and nursery vouchers.

THE MODERN PACKAGE

Some employers have a fixed range of benefits to which everyone is entitled whether they want them or not. The approach favoured by most US employers – and increasingly popular here – is to provide a core benefits scheme covering the essentials like pension, life assurance and disability insurance, and then allocate a percentage of salary to each employee (typically 5 per cent) and let them choose which benefits they want from a 'menu' up to this annual monetary limit. This is known as a flexible benefits scheme, or just 'flex'.

To confuse matters, employers

might also offer 'voluntary' benefits. With voluntary benefits there is no automatic inclusion and no subsidy from the employer. The attractions of a well-organised scheme are the convenience of being able to buy in the workplace, a discounted price or premium (due to the bulk negotiating muscle of the employers), and the backing of top providers. To give you an example, Towers Perrin is a member of, and arranges benefits for, the Benefits Alliance, a group of employers that includes Asda, British Airways, the BBC, BT, the Royal Bank of Scotland, SmithKline Beecham and Whitbread. The voluntary benefits negotiated by the group include:

● Annual travel insurance
● Electrical goods
● Health insurance – for example, dental, eye care, lump sums for critical illness
● Financial products – for example, loans, mortgages and saving schemes
● Personal car purchase (new and second hand)
● Gas and electricity supplies
● Package holidays
● Property conveyancing
● Retail vouchers
● Will writing

If you get involved with this sort of negotiation, you are not just looking for the cheapest deal. Martyn, a consultant with the Benefits Alliance, says, 'Naturally, the cost of the benefit is important, but while we look for a competitive premium or price, we will not necessarily choose the cheapest. Equally important is the standard of service. Before we select a provider we investigate their administration and service track record and may visit their call centre. Some of the providers we use offer a dedicated helpline for each member company in the Benefits Alliance.'

TELL IT HOW IT IS

Anna joined Mercer's in 1997 with a degree in Business Administration and Social Science from Aston University. 'As a graduate joining HR Consulting at William M. Mercer you have immediate involvement in client projects so that consulting skills and technical knowledge can be developed quickly.' Even in her first year, Anna was involved in several high-profile client projects including:

● Employee attitude surveys
● Flexible benefits consulting, design and implementation
● Expatriate remuneration policy design
● Job evaluation and salary structure work

'A large part of my job involves the use of computers for client work and keeping myself informed via Mercer's intranet and, of course, the Internet. The company regularly sends me on IT training courses to ensure my skills are up to date and I am expected to put these to good use.'

Stephen works in the human capital department at a major firm of consultants. 'In the past many employers offered great benefits but the impact of the package was undermined or lost completely because employees didn't know they had these benefits or didn't understand them. Part of my job is to make sure the benefits are communicated in the right way to the employees. This might involve designing a program for the company's intranet system, if the employees have good access to computer screens. In low-tech industries we may recommend regular seminars where benefits are explained, plus an attractive notice-board near the staff rest room in each site.'

INTERNATIONAL EMPLOYEES AND BENEFITS PLANS

Today's global business environment requires workforces to be internationally mobile. 'We help our clients with the many HR issues that need to be addressed when moving executives around the world,' says an Arthur Andersen consultant. 'It is challenging work, designing relocation packages that are flexible enough to deal with the cultural and tax variables of overseas employment.'

As part of such a team you will find yourself assisting clients in the design of compensation strategies for expatriates which are culturally compatible, tax efficient and cost effective, and then helping the client implement these policies. Alternatively you may be required to advise a client on the more practical issues that expatriates and their families face – not only tax considerations, but personal issues like finding schools for the children, or questions of culture.

The work does not stop there. The International Employment Solutions (IES) team at Arthur Andersen is constantly updating clients on tax regulation changes, which also means devising innovative strategies to maximise after-tax compensation. You have to ensure international compliance with individual and corporate tax-reporting requirements, and when a leading global organisation or a confused expatriate has a query, you will become their first port of call.

Dan, a graduate in IES, comments, 'I didn't really know what to expect when I joined, but I've found the people very friendly and supportive. Everyone works hard but there's still a relaxed atmosphere. The training has been great – after I joined, I was immediately sent to Washington, DC, for a course on International Employment Solutions.'

MERGER WORK

With all the recent merger and acquisition activity, benefits consultants have been busy integrating different schemes and cultures. 'When two global energy giants merged, the scope of change was too great for conventional media,' a consultant at Towers Perrin says. 'With our help, the new organisation looked to the Web as its primary communication vehicle. On the first day of the merger, an intranet site appeared on the desktops of all employees, offering detailed information on what it would mean to work for the new company, including:

● The recruitment process
● Pay scales
● Benefits
● Career development opportunities
● The work environment

'At the same time, we helped develop an Internet site for employees' families to acquaint them with the new organisation and the details of relocation policies. In the first month, the hits to the intranet site exceeded the combined hits to the intranets each company had previously offered.'

COMPENSATION AND EQUITY INCENTIVES

An increasingly common way to ensure employees give their best is to link their rewards to the company's success through a share scheme. If you work in Arthur Andersen's Compensation and Equity team, for example, you would be involved in the design and implementation of innovative, cost-efficient incentive schemes that will motivate employees and promote the enhancement of shareholder value while complying with tax, legal and accounting regulations.

This type of work is as varied as the client base. 'One day you could be working on individual executive pay levels, the next consulting other Arthur Andersen offices across the world about issues relating to a worldwide share scheme for a global organisation,' a consultant says. 'As regulations change, we are constantly developing new strategies to help our clients create the most efficient compensation and equity schemes. You will see our clients returning time after time because we can offer them the latest, most innovative and cost-effective solutions available.'

QUALIFICATIONS AND SKILLS

Any good degree, but you will need at least a 2:1 for the top firms. Look for jobs that give you the chance to study for professional qualifications – for example, the Chartered Diploma in Accounting and Finance, MSc in Human Resource Consultancy, MBA, Association of Taxation Technicians (ATT), Associate of the Chartered Institute of Taxation (ATII).

TIPS

The big benefits firms are a good place to start, but you may prefer to join a major blue-chip corporation that offers training for its in-house benefits department. With a few years' experience, you might consider joining a recruitment consultancy, a specialist function in the City.

SOURCES OF INFORMATION ON CAREER

● A good publication for sources of information is *Pension Funds and their Advisers*, published by AP Information Services (www.ap-info.co.uk), which lists all the main benefits consultants.
● *Employee Benefits* is a specialist publication dedicated to this field. **TEL** 020 7292 3719 or e-mail employee-benefits@centaur.co.uk
● The Institute of Personnel and Development website is very informative: www.ipd.co.uk

SOURCES FOR THIS CHAPTER

● Arthur Andersen www.arthurandersen.com
● William M. Mercer www.wmmercer.com
● Towers Perrin www.towers.com

39
INSURANCE/RISK MANAGEMENT

MONEY: £16,000–£18,000 for general insurance, where good A levels may be enough to get you in; £20,000–£24,000 for the more specialist roles which require a good degree.

HOURS: 9.30–5.30. Occasional overtime which will increase with seniority.

PRESSURE RATING: 5/10. Depends on the department but again will increase with seniority. There can be job insecurity with the current spate of mergers between insurance companies.

GLAMOUR RATING: 4/10. Sorry, this is not the glam side of City life, but it's less stressful than investment banking.

TRAVEL RATING: 0–7/10. This is totally dependent on the nature of your work and whether it involves visiting clients in the UK or overseas.

SUMMARY

Insurance covers a wide range of jobs, from underwriting and claims management to product design and marketing. For standard risks the actuary will provide fixed or flexible guidelines, but the underwriter will be called upon to assess specific non-standard risks. This can involve a wide variety of skills. For example, if you want to insure a space shuttle you will need to consider the engineering technology and the technical expertise of the organisation building the shuttle. You will also need to consider what competitors might charge and why. The underwriter will liaise with reinsurers if he or she thinks that the risk is too great for the insurance company alone to bear.

An international operation would be split into several divisions, including:

● Life assurance – group protection for employers
● Non-life or general insuring corporations, local governments and other authorities against fire, theft, storm, war/civil disturbance
● Reinsurance – covering the top layer of financial risk for a self-insured organisation like a business or insurance company
● Personal lines – individual policies for both life assurance and general, such as car, home protection

WHO'S WHO

There is considerable overlap between jobs in corporate insurance, risk management and risk consultancy, so do look at the services provided by actuarial consultants and professional services firms (see Chapters 34 and 37).

As far as mainstream general insurance goes, many of the big names have moved out of the City, if indeed they were ever there in the first place.

If you want to work at the headquarters of Pearl, Axa Sun Life, Co-operative Insurance or Royal & Sun Alliance, then it's off to the leafy suburbs with you (if you are lucky), or to the industrial towns.

Following a frenzied period of takeovers and mergers, you will find that several major international insurance companies now own many of the formerly independent insurers and investment companies. The Swiss-based company Zurich, for example, owns Allied Dunbar in the life assurance market, and in the investment sector owns Scudder Kemper Investments (New York) and Threadneedle Asset Management, based in London. If you are looking for a varied career that involves travel and overseas secondments, then the major global firms are worth considering. The Zurich Financial Services Group is represented in over 60 countries and is particularly strong in the UK, US, Australia, Canada and China.

Insurance companies dominate the Edinburgh and Glasgow financial centres, which are home to the likes of Standard Life and Scottish Widows. You will find, however, that most of the Scottish life offices also have a London presence for press and other communications purposes.

Insurance or assurance in the City is more likely to involve one of the major actuarial consultancies than an insurance company. This type of work might involve:

- Actuarial services
- Product design
- Underwriting
- Risk management and reinsurance
- Investment management

Details about consultants – for example, Bacon & Woodrow, Watson Wyatt and William M. Mercer can be found in Section A. Many of these services are also offered by the professional services firms (see Chapter 30). We describe the specialist Lloyd's underwriting market in Chapter 13.

INSURANCE AND RISK MANAGEMENT

Insurance has a much wider role than simply spotting a potential risk and buying a policy to cover it. Commercial organisations employ risk management techniques as an important element in their business development plans.

If you are interested in risk management, take a look at the Association of Insurance and Risk Managers in Industry and Commerce (AIRMIC) website. The association explains, 'The risk manager's role in most leading companies is much wider than buying insurance. Sophisticated risk modelling techniques now proliferate. The trend among companies is to take an integrated approach to risk. Risk managers are becoming involved in areas that previously were outside their remit, such as human resources (see Chapter 38), corporate governance and brand value. In one dramatic example, a major US auto manufacturer scrapped its plans to build a new plant extension after receiving the risk manager's evaluation of the business risks associated with the concentration of assets.' (See also 'Risk consulting', Chapter 34.)

PRODUCT DESIGN

Product design is a growth area for the assurance departments of actuarial firms. Retail products need to comply with a great many regulations these days, and must also be appropriate for the target market. Specialists in the insurance services department at firms of actuarial consultants are well placed to spot the gaps in the markets and to put a product through its paces before launch.

Marian, a mathematics graduate who works in the insurance services department of an actuarial firm, says, 'Some of the products insurance companies want to launch in the retail market are very complicated. For several years it has been fashionable to offer investment and savings products that are either guaranteed in some way or at least "protected". This involves buying derivative contracts to achieve the guarantee of, for example, ninety-five or even a hundred per cent of the investor's original capital. The cost of the derivative contract is an important factor in the pricing for the insurance company.'

William joined the assurance division of a major firm of actuaries and has helped design several savings products for well-known insurance companies, banks and building societies. 'We have to look at the tax implications for the target market – for example, life funds are taxed at broadly the equivalent of basic-rate tax, so this makes them unsuitable for non-taxpayers. However, some of the bonds sold by insurance companies offer a yield that is considerably higher than a non-taxpayer could get through National Savings, for example, and this outweighs the tax disadvantage.

'We get asked to design products for a lot of offshore life assurance companies that want to sell to the expatriate community. It is really important that these companies understand the tax treatment of the expatriate and how their products fit into the existing market for savings and investments.'

Insurance companies have large investment management divisions that run the funds for the companies' retail products, such as independent savings accounts (ISAs), pension funds, unit trusts and insurance bonds. Life offices (the life and investment arms of general insurance companies) also play a major role in providing pooled fund management to the institutional pension funds.

WHICH COMPANY?

Given the rationalisation of the industry, it is important to look for a company that has a strong financial base. The troubles experienced by Equitable Life in 2000 revealed that strong performance and a first-class client base are simply not enough to guarantee a future role in this competitive industry. Equitable ran into trouble when it challenged a court ruling over the way it planned to treat certain policyholders. The court costs were crippling, and because the company's liabilities towards its policyholders could not be measured accurately, the original line-up of prestigious buyers dropped out one by one.

Look for strong independent organisations and those that have merged to strengthen the company's market position as well as its financial base. For example, against a background of increasing competition and consolidation in European financial services, the combination of CGU (itself a merger of General Accident and Commercial Union) and Norwich Union means that greater scale and improved efficiency can be used to deliver competitive products and better levels of service to an increasingly international customer base. The new company – CGNU – will have an improved competitive position in Europe and the financial strength to develop further in international markets.

QUALIFICATIONS AND SKILLS

Insurance companies offer jobs at all levels, but if you have a degree consider the positions that give you professional training. If you have or are likely to get a 2:1 or higher, then try for the City-based firms of actuaries and employee benefits consultants or professional services organisations, as the money and training are likely to be of a higher standard.

TIPS

Insurance today is inseparable from the boom in financial services products, so take a look at Chapter 40 on the independent advisers who sell financial products.

SOURCES OF INFORMATION ON CAREER

● Most large insurance companies have a graduate recruitment programme, so if you are interested check the websites, although it has to be said that the insurance companies' sites are no match for the investment banks'.

● You can get access to the main City employers through the major recruitment agencies, including the specialists www.prospects.csu.man.ac.uk and www.doctorjob.com

● A good source of information on insurance is the Association of British Insurers (ABI). Their site provides a great deal of information and also includes a list of members: www.abi.org.uk

Useful publications (see Chapter 6) include:

● Insurance Day
www.insuranceday.com
● Global Insurance Bulletin
www.rirg.com
● Insurance Age
www.insuranceage.com
● AIRMIC is at www.airmic.co.uk
● Zurich is at www.zurich.com

40

INDEPENDENT FINANCIAL ADVISER

k **MONEY:** Larger firms £18,000–£22,000.

h **HOURS:** 10–6. Possibly an earlier start if you deal with the investment markets.

PRESSURE RATING: 5/10. Depends very much on your client base. It will get very busy towards the end of the tax year.

C **GLAMOUR RATING:** 4–6/10. Much depends on the profile of the company you work for.

1 **TRAVEL RATING:** 4/10. Unless you work for a firm that specialises in international client work, your travel opportunities are likely to be limited to the UK.

SUMMARY

The term independent financial adviser (IFA) can be used to describe some of the top financial consultants in the country – and some of the cowboy firms that get fined whenever there is a misselling scandal.

Generally, IFA describes those who operate primarily in the retail insurance and investment markets and give advice to the public. The Financial Services Act regulates over 27,000 independent financial advisers and over 70,000 company representatives, but very few actually work in the City. Those who do are likely to specialise in investment and tax advice

and deal with wealthy clients. In this respect there are many similarities between the top IFAs and private client services (see Chapter 27).

WHICH TYPE OF IFA?

The posh end of financial advice is financial planning. These are the advisers who charge fees and give 'holistic' financial planning advice to cover all areas of your life. They are not interested in making money by selling insurance products that generate large sales commissions. Financial planners work in independent firms and also in the private client services departments of the major professional services firms. We give the website for the Institute of Financial Planning at the end of the chapter.

You might also consider a firm that specialises in investment research for the retail market. John Spiers, managing director of Bestinvest, explains, 'The job of the fund research analyst is to look beneath the glossy veneer provided by the marketing departments of fund groups and assess whether a fund is really capable of being a top performer in the future. Since investment is a mixture of science and art, the analyst needs a combination of logical reasoning and the ability to make accurate character assessments.' Bestinvest has a high profile in the market and it is well worth looking at its website to get a feel for the services offered by a specialist firm of IFAs.

If you want to make money and you have an entrepreneurial spirit, you could consider becoming a company representative. As the name implies, reps are employed by – and work solely for – one company. Some of the best financial products – as well as some of the worst – are sold in this way. The important point to remember is that if you work as a representative you are restricted by law in what you can do as you are only permitted to sell the products of the company you represent and through which you are authorised. You will also find that a significant chunk of your remuneration is through sales commission, so you need to feel comfortable with that prospect.

The type of firm and its ethos will dictate your working environment – so do choose carefully and consider how well you will fit in.

FINANCIAL PLANNING

Jenny is a certified financial planner with a City firm. 'We get a lot of people coming to us who have had a bad experience with financial advisers and have been sold a lot of products that might have generated commission for the sales person but did little to improve our clients' financial positions.

'My first job is to sift through the uncoordinated financial baggage clients bring with them. This is likely to include an assortment of investments and insurance plans, some of which might be good quality but others will represent poor value. I evaluate all these and then spend a lot of time helping clients to clarify their financial goals. This might be to retire early or to earn enough to leave the rat race and start a business or go back to college or travel. Wealthy clients are particularly concerned about inheritance tax and passing on their wealth to their children in the most tax-efficient way.'

Jenny spent several years studying to become a certified financial planner and hopes longer term to become a fellow of the Institute. She feels strongly about her profession. 'I think it's a shame that there are so many "advisers" out there who do not offer a good service. People rarely have the time or interest to really get to grips with their finances, and if they choose the wrong type of adviser they can be ripped off very badly. Although the regulators will act if they think a firm has sold an inappropriate product for a client's needs, provided the firm can demonstrate the client needed a personal pension, for example, there is nothing to stop them selling a product that is expensive, inflexible and offers very poor asset management.'

QUALIFICATIONS AND SKILLS

A degree is certainly helpful but not essential if you want to get into a firm of financial advisers.

TIPS

If you are serous about this as a career, then consider firms that offer training towards professional qualifications as well as the obligatory regulatory exams (see Chapter 8).

To find out about the different types of adviser, visit the websites of member firms of the associations below. Also take a look at Bestinvest, the company quoted in the text, as this is a good example of the specialist investment services certain firms offer.

Bestinvest is at www.bestinvest.co.uk

SOURCES OF INFORMATION ON CAREER

The professional multidisciplinary organisation dedicated to training financial planners is

● **The Institute of Financial Planning:**
www.financialplanning.org.uk

There are several sources of independent financial advice:

● **The Association of Private Client Investment Managers and Stockbrokers** Many of APCIM's members provide a full financial planning service: www.apcims.co.uk

● **The Association of Solicitor Investment Managers** (ASIM): www.asim.org.uk

● **The Institute of Chartered Accountants in England and Wales** Many accountants offer a full financial planning service: www.icaew.co.uk

● **The Society of Financial Advisers** Part of the Chartered Insurance Institute and a major examiner of independent advisers and life assurance company sales staff: www.sofa.org

● **Solicitors for Independent Financial Advice** (SIFA): www.solicitor-ifa.co.uk

41
FINANCIAL REGULATION

k **MONEY:** £18,000–£22,000.

h **HOURS:** 9.30–5.30.
Occasional overtime but generally fairly steady.

PRESSURE RATING: 4/10.
Moderate – this is not the sharp end of City life.

C **GLAMOUR RATING:** 4/10. More of a worthy than a glamorous role.

l **TRAVEL RATING:** 3/10. You are likely to be deskbound most of the time, perhaps occasionally visiting firms in the UK.

SUMMARY

The financial services markets are self-regulated. This means that those who sell their services and products pay an annual levy to the financial services regulators who effectively police the City and beyond.

Regulation may appeal to those who want to be involved in the City but from a public service rather than private enterprise point of view. In other words, you need to be a little more altruistic than the money-grubbers in investment banking. If big money and fast living appeal, then abandon altruism right here.

The regulators employ people with administration, accountancy and legal backgrounds, and also need people to deal with the media. The aim of the job is to vet companies to ensure that they comply with the regulations and to investigate complaints.

THE FINANCIAL SERVICES AUTHORITY

To get an idea of what's involved in regulation, we took a look at the chief regulator, the Financial Services Authority (FSA). The role of the regulators in the City is also discussed in Chapter 17.

The FSA has a graduate development programme, so if regulation appeals to you it is worth visiting their website for more details. This and the websites for the other regulators are provided on page 38.

So what does the FSA do? Well, from the horse's mouth, 'The FSA is committed to protecting consumers, enhancing understanding of financial products and promoting market confidence and the highest standards of practice throughout the financial services industry. We strive to be adaptable, forward-looking, fair, open, responsive, rewarding and fun.

'We know that, in order to succeed, we must recruit people who share our vision and values. Our staff are drawn from a wide range of backgrounds, including the financial services industry, the legal and accountancy professions, the Civil Service and other regulatory bodies. This diversity of experience, skill and talent is effectively combined in order to achieve our primary goals, not least because we seek to manage, train and reward our people well.'

TRAINING

The FSA (which is based at Canary

Wharf) expects to recruit 15–20 graduates to enter the Graduate Development Programme in the autumn of 2001. The majority of opportunities tend to be in authorisation, supervision and enforcement.

Before you join your first team, you follow a four-week induction course, and get to meet the key members of the business plus the chairman and members of the senior management team. You also have a line manager, who sets objectives, a mentor, who is an experienced employee, and a 'buddy', who is a recent graduate.

The training includes a comprehensive introduction to the financial services industry, involving an interactive and practical look at the major markets. The FSA says, 'You'll examine the main products traded in the cash markets, foreign exchange, money markets, bonds and equities, and develop an understanding of the main derivative products and how they are traded on the market. You will also gain knowledge of the life assurance, insurance and retail financial product markets, and financial markets and institutions. By the end of this course, you will understand the role of the City of London in the context of the global trading economy.'

INVESTMENT

Chris is 27 and works in the Investment Business division. 'I joined the FSA's graduate programme in October 1999. I had left university four years earlier. I did a degree in French and Latin at Oxford and then went to Japan to teach English. After returning to the UK I decided I wanted to work in a dynamic area of business but one with a public rather than private sector background. The Financial Services Authority fitted the bill perfectly, combining the excitement of the financial services sector with the public good.

'After a month-long induction, I joined a team in the Investment Business division. We supervise about one hundred and twenty firms, ranging from large pension funds to small venture capital companies. Our work is split between visiting the firms (about a quarter of my time is spent out of the office) and doing desk-based supervision, reporting on visits, checking firms' finances and approving changes to firms' business and senior staff.

'Although my background was not in finance or economics, I became fully involved from day one and got stuck in straight away. The team I work with and the visits I have been on have given me a great introduction to the financial services industry. The on-the-job training from my team has supplemented the formal training I have received in the months since I joined. I am now about to move on to my next post as part of the graduate programme. This time it will be a policy role, helping the FSA adapt its structure to the requirements of the new financial services legislation.'

BANKS AND BUILDING SOCIETIES

Suzanne is 23 and works in the Banks and Building Societies division. She has a joint honours degree in

Economics and Business Law from the University of Strathclyde. 'I saw the job advertisement for the FSA graduate programme in the *Sunday Times* when I was visiting my parents in Houston, Texas, after graduating in 1998.

'The main attraction was that I would join the FSA in its inceptive form. I would have the opportunity to be part of the organisation as it responded to the challenges posed by the changing shape of the UK financial services sector. I started work at the FSA in Canary Wharf in October 1999 as one of eleven graduate trainees. The scheme involves four placements, three of which are within the FSA while one is external, probably to a regulated institution.

'My first placement was in a team of six in the Banks and Building Societies division. You are quickly given real responsibility; initially I had two Swiss branches to supervise and I was then given two additional Australian branches. I have decided to extend my first placement in banking supervision by an extra six months, and as part of this I have recently taken on three Japanese banks. The international dimension to my department has been one of the most enjoyable and interesting aspects of working here.'

Suzanne says her university course has been useful in her work. 'Not all my graduate intake have a business or economics background; one read English, for example, another geography; but it is important to have an understanding of the financial services industry.'

The FSA encourages its staff to gain industry qualifications, so Suzanne is studying for the Securities Representative exam. Some of the other graduates are also studying for the Financial Planning Certificate (see Chapter 8).

The placements provide plenty of experience of regulation and the City. In your first placement, you may be involved in working with a firm that is either applying for authorisation or requires supervision. Alternatively, you may be in a team that has responsibility for the enforcement of the FSA's statutory objectives. The second is also within the FSA, but for the third you will be placed on an external secondment for a six-month period to gain valuable industry experience.

QUALIFICATIONS AND SKILLS

For this work you will need a good degree and a keen interest in financial services. Excellent communication skills and attention to detail are vital.

TIPS

Training with a regulator will give you a good start to a City career. Every firm in financial services must have a compliance department that deals with regulation. Training as a gamekeeper is excellent experience if you want to turn poacher later on.

SOURCES OF INFORMATION ON CAREER

Look at the regulators' websites listed on page 38.

42
THE JARGON

Financial journalism is an excellent career if you have good writing and investigative skills. Similar skills are used in public relations, but here you have to be much more polite and you get paid a lot more.

Increasingly the financial press incorporates on-line news and information services. If you get a job on the research side of this type of organisation, your work will be similar in many respects to that of an analyst, trying to spot news, corporate changes and trends before everyone else.

BUZZWORDS

Leak If a company or the government wants information released but does not want to go through the official channels, then they organise a leak to the press so that one or more newspapers can break the story without those close to the events taking an official line.

Off the record This is information given to a journalist that cannot be attributed in print but can be used as background to a story.

43
FINANCIAL PR

k **MONEY:** A graduate would probably start with a PR agency on £15,000–£17,000 as an account assistant, rising to £18,000–£22,000 as an account executive. In-house PR may pay more but it depends on the size of the company and the seniority of the position.

h **HOURS:** Typically 10–6, but you need to be very flexible. The job involves deadlines which must be met, so you could end up starting early – for example, if you need to check early morning share prices – and working on into the night. Most agencies are flexible, however, so you would probably get time off in lieu on an informal basis.

PRESSURE RATING: 8/10, depending on the agency and the clients. Deadlines are stressful, as is dealing with irate clients and bored or uncooperative journalists. People are definitely in your face with this job. It's not a comfortable thought knowing that your success in dealing with a client could make or break the contract and that if you screw up in a press release, for example, *everyone* will know.

C **GLAMOUR RATING:** 9/10. This obviously depends on the clients, but if you are City-based you should get to see some fine places as venues for client lunches, conferences and 'get to know the press' meetings. It's a dress smart/talk smart environment.

l **TRAVEL RATING:** 5–8/10. Depends entirely on who your client is. If it's an American investment manager you will get to see the US headquarters, if it's a London operation you might get as far as the West End.

SUMMARY

Financial PR is enjoying a boom. City companies no longer regard this function as a luxury but as a necessity. A good relationship with the financial press can make or break a company's plans to launch a new product or service aimed at the retail or institutional financial market.

PR agencies act as an interface between the companies that want to present a good public image to encourage new business and the press, who usually prefer to dish the dirt. If you work in-house as part of the press department your 'client' will be your own company.

Your job is taking a message, honing it into elegant prose or an exciting presentation, and then persuading the press to come along and hear it. The more coverage you get in the press for a client the happier that client will be.

The other side of the job is damage limitation. A client screws up – for example, it gets caught by the regulators for misselling products – and you will be hauled in to repair a tarnished image.

PRESS RELATIONS

A big part of the PR business involves getting to know the press. This can be the best and worst part of the job. Some journalists are fair-minded and helpful, but others are aggressive and cynical. Actually, most of them are aggressive and cynical.

When you take on a client, you need to build up a detailed profile of what the client does, the area of the financial services market in which the client works, and a good profile of what the competitors are up to. The best PR managers will be so knowledgeable about the industry that they will come up with ideas to promote their clients – not just respond to the client's own suggestions.

If you are responsible for a media campaign, you will have to:

● Write press releases
● Distribute written material for use by the media
● Research special editorials and surveys in which the client can participate
● Arrange press lunches, meetings and press briefings
● Arrange photo calls
● Prepare press packs
● Liaise with press cuttings agencies and broadcast monitoring services
● Analyse and submit reports on coverage obtained during day-to-day activity and campaigns
● Liaise with outside agencies and

the client – for example, the client's internal PR and marketing departments and advertising agencies
● Maintain accurate media mailing lists
● Monitor, maintain, research, update and improve individual clients' media databases in order to maximise coverage, ensuring all new journals, publications and broadcast programmes are included

TELL IT HOW IT IS

Lucy is an account executive at Polhill Communications, a specialist financial PR agency built up by former financial journalists. She started out as an account assistant in 1995 after graduating from Goldsmiths' with a degree in German. As a rule, if you are good at your job you can expect to move up from account assistant to account executive after about twelve to eighteen months.

Lucy was attracted to the good atmosphere and friendly staff at Polhill. 'The job offers tremendous flexibility and diversity. Given the wide range of clients, no two days are the same. Here we work as a team and you are made to feel like you are a valuable member. It's important to me to feel that my ideas are welcomed. I was always interested in the use of language and I've certainly found my translating skills very useful here.'

The hours can be long but they are flexible. 'If I have to work late on a client's presentation, for example, I can usually leave early to take a long weekend once the project is completed.' You do have to be available, though. 'As in journalism there are deadlines that must be met. This is not a straight nine-to-five job.'

INTERNAL OR IN-HOUSE PR

The skills required here are similar to those needed in PR agency work, but there is a very important difference. With internal PR you will only have one 'client' – that is, the company for which you work. Needless to say, it helps if you actually like the company and its people.

If you go for in-house PR, check how much authority you have to discuss issues with the press and what authority you have over senior staff, who may be contacted by the press and will want to talk, perhaps dangerously. Journalists report that a successful in-house PR manager will make sure the right person is available very quickly.

QUALIFICATIONS AND SKILLS

A degree in virtually any subject is acceptable but good communication skills – both written and verbal are essential. Languages are a real plus point. You also need accurate typing (minimum 45 wpm RSA/Pitman qualifications) and computer literacy (Microsoft Office – Word, Powerpoint, Excel). Agencies are looking for graduates who are good organisers and who will not be fazed by having to handle several projects at different stages of development simultaneously. The ability to work accurately under pressure is vital. Excellent present-ation skills are also important.

Direct entry into a City PR agency would usually require a degree, although good A levels might get you into an in-house PR department and allow you to work your way up. Knowledge of the City and its institutions will boost your chances. Languages are very useful and may be essential for some in-house jobs with foreign banks, for example.

TIPS

For your first job – for example, as an account assistant – it is important to choose a PR firm with a good client list offering a variety of work. Equally important, check the company's track record in terms of retaining clients *and* staff.

Once you have established yourself, if internal promotion doesn't happen then consider moving to another PR firm or taking a position as an in-house press/public relations officer.

SOURCES OF INFORMATION ON CAREER

● Good recruitment agencies that specialise in media jobs are keen to talk to graduates in particular.
● You should read *PR Week* and *Marketing Week* regularly.
● The *Guardian* on a Monday advertises jobs in the media (see page 34).
● The Association of British Insurers (ABI) publishes an annual *Media Contact Directory*. This costs £60 but should be available in public libraries, particularly in the City. The ABI's website bookshop is at www.abi.org.uk
● Polhill Communications' website is at www.polhill.com

44
FINANCIAL JOURNALIST

k **MONEY:** £16,000–£21,000.

h **HOURS:** 10–6 but will vary considerably depending on your deadlines.

PRESSURE RATING: 6–9/10. Depends on frequency of publication. Daily deadlines take their toll, particularly if you are on the news desk – the battle equivalent of the front line. Weeklies are also pretty fraught but at monthlies the pace is more relaxed.

C **GLAMOUR RATING:** 9/10. Even the fund managers tend to be nice to journalists, particularly if you work on a national. There's just something about it.

1 **TRAVEL RATING:** 4–8/10. If you are covering UK companies your opportunities are limited. International news can involve travel, but you are more likely to get a posting overseas than lots of short-term trips. Press trips to foreign climes are regarded as a bit of a luxury these days, and few journalists can afford to be away from their desks for more than a few days.

SUMMARY

Fleet Street isn't what it used to be. The former Street of Shame, as it was dubbed by *Private Eye*, is home today to a load of foreign investment banks.

The infamous El Vino's has no trouble enforcing its dress code, and the Japanese bankers make for a polite clientèle compared with the rowdy hacks of the past. All the newspapers have long since fled to Canary Wharf, the Isle of Dogs or, in the case of the *Financial Times*, to Southwark Bridge.

So what's involved? Well, you'll be following stories that relate to companies, markets and sectors. You may specialise in investment funds, in which case you will follow the fortunes of the fund management houses and of the individual star managers, tracing their rise and – quite often – their fall.

You'll be talking to chief execs of FTSE 100 companies, and you will build up your contacts in all the most important institutions. If you want to work on companies and markets coverage you will need to develop an in-depth knowledge of your sector and the businesses within it. You need to know how companies are analysed and how to read the annual report and accounts. Some of the stories will be routine – analysing a typical corporate event such as a dividends announcement and seeking comments from the economists and investment analysts – others will be dynamite. Those who follow financial services must have a good grasp of financial regulation and how it affects the design and marketing of products to consumers.

You need to write quickly and fluently with an eye always on the clock and your word count. Don't forget that there's a boom in on-line financial information (see Chapter 45), which requires regular updates by the hour as opposed to the daily or weekly deadlines familiar to the printed press.

RESEARCH COMES FIRST

Good writing skills are pointless without the research to back them up. 'Above all else,' says Jackie, a graduate who joined a City weekly paper, 'you need to know how to research a story. A good story is based not so much on *what* you know as *who* you know. It is impossible to keep completely up to date with all of the technical issues – for example, the development of the rules for the new stakeholder pension schemes or the finer points of the derivatives market. What you can and must do if you want to succeed is be prepared to find out who the experts are in each of the main City organisations and build up a relationship so that you can find out the news and the stories behind the news.'

Getting people to talk is not always easy. A lot of employees in the City are not allowed to talk to journalists, although some of these will be good sources of 'off the record' information – that is, non-attributable news and background. Off-the-record conversations are usually behind press statements that start 'A source close to the company/regulator ...'

Don works on the City desk of a national. 'Your contacts have to trust you and this means you follow a strict code of conduct. When someone is talking off the record you *never*

attribute these comments, no matter how exciting. This could blow the relationship for good and word will get around that you can't be trusted.'

Some companies have a relaxed attitude to the press. 'These are the best,' says Georgina, a freelance journalist who covers personal finance for a national newspaper. 'If I need a comment or some background, I can phone the person I want directly. It's much more difficult dealing with companies that are press-phobic. These tend to forbid any but the chosen ones from speaking to the press. You can get ridiculous situations like the one I had recently with a FTSE 100 company that should have known better. I spoke to the right person and got what I needed. Then he told me apologetically I'd have to check with the press officer if it was OK to use the material. The press officer didn't know anything about the subject so I had to explain it all to her. Then she passed me on to the corporate communications manager and I went through the same process. Three days later they decided that the person I should speak to was the bloke I had contacted in the first place. Nightmare!'

You also need to deal with public relations agencies (see Chapter 43). 'Be nice to them,' urges John, who also works on the City desk of a national. 'They have files on all of us journalists and I dread to think what they say about me! But good PR people will make your life easier by putting you in touch with the right person quickly. The new recruits can get on your nerves because they tend to phone you up every day with details of wonderful new companies or products that have no bearing on your area of specialisation. It's best to be straight with them rather than do what I did and think of a dozen different excuses for not meeting their precious new client.'

SPECIALIST SUBJECTS

Some newspapers assume you will find your area of specialisation and stick with it. This can be quite restrictive. Others – the *Financial Times*, for example – will expect you to develop first-class research skills so that you can change position within the company every few years. 'The idea behind this is to stop you getting stale or cynical, which can happen if you cover just one area of the markets year after year,' an *FT* writer explains. 'It's much more stimulating to know that after two or three years on, say, the personal finance desk, you might be able to move to cover education or companies and markets.'

The hours will vary, but be prepared for long days if your area of expertise is in demand. If you have a law degree and there's a legal battle brewing, you may suddenly find yourself filling a space on the front cover. 'February and March are always extra busy here,' says Phil, who works on a trade weekly that covers the independent financial adviser market. 'Budget time is a nightmare. You spend days preparing drafts of possible stories and lining up your experts. Then, when the Budget papers are released, you get about an hour to write six pieces on topics you know

nothing about. It's like going into an exam totally unprepared.'

LIFESTYLE

The camaraderie can be good but this is a very aggressive environment, and when deadlines loom tempers can get frayed. Press lunches, dinners and jollies abound – but you have to listen to the presentation as well as eat and drink. Young journalists from different papers tend to get to know each other quickly, and there's plenty of opportunity to mix and make friends – usually at the expense of the public relations agencies, whose job it is to get to know journalists and to bend their ears about their clients.

TELEVISION

● For jobs in television we recommend you start with the BBC's website, which is at www.bbc.co.uk, and look under careers.

Journalism opportunities exist in the following areas:
● Broadcast assistants
● Broadcast journalists
● News editors
● Features editors
● On-line news

The BBC also offers broadcast journalism and network news trainee schemes.

QUALIFICATIONS AND SKILLS

Most of the big papers – including the nationals – offer places to a limited number of graduates each year. However, if you have experience in a particular sector and you have good communication skills, you should apply. You must be able to write quickly and accurately, and feel comfortable phoning top professionals and asking them awkward questions.

TIPS

If you can't get on a national straight from university, try one of the weekly trade publications like *Financial Adviser*, *Money Marketing* or *Investment Week*. Features writers might be better with a monthly publication like *Money Management*, or a consumer publication like *Bloomberg Money* or *Moneywise* (see page 35). Take a trip to the City Business Library and read all the financial publications to get a feel for which style suits you. Write direct to the editor of any publication you particularly like the look of – editors usually made it through the ranks the hard way and will be impressed by initiative and flair.

Jobs are always advertised in-house, so if you join a major organisation – like the Financial Times Group – there are lots of opportunities to move internally. A minority of journalists do manage to move across from the *FT* magazines to the *FT* itself, although this is unusual.

Once you've done a few years as a journalist, if you want to add £5,000–£10,000 to your salary, get a job in PR.

SOURCES OF INFORMATION ON CAREER

● Research all the financial press at a main library like the City Business Library, or use a media directory like the ABI's *Media Contact Directory*

(www.abi.org.uk) or the *Media UK Internet Directory* at www.mediauk.com/directory
● A list of websites for the main publications is provided in Chapter 6.

45
ON-LINE INFORMATION SERVICES

k **MONEY:** £17,000–£21,000.

h **HOURS:** Very variable – this is shift work.

PRESSURE RATING: 9/10.
Deadlines can loom on an hourly basis – more frequent when you are covering a major development.

C **GLAMOUR RATING:** 8/10.
As for journalists.

1 **TRAVEL RATING:** 8/10.
There are usually good opportunities to work in overseas offices on short-term secondments.

SUMMARY

Several organisations – Bloomberg, Reuters and the *Financial Times*, for example – are dedicated to providing news and information on-line to the investment community. Depending on which part of the organisation you work for the job can be a cross between that of an analyst (see Chapter 23) and that of a journalist (see Chapter 44). Information services also design the electronic systems to execute trades (see Chapter 33 on IT consultancy).

WORLDWIDE OPPORTUNITIES

Reuters is perhaps the best-known news service, providing private investors with the information and tools with which to trade and manage their portfolios. The group developed an early computer system in the 1960s to distribute information to market players. That provided the foundation for the Monitor, a computer-based information distribution and dealing service for equities, foreign exchange, commodities and bonds, which transformed Reuters' finances.

Today Reuters operates 184 bureaux in 154 countries. While news still lies at the heart of the business, the 150-year-old group, which started life dispatching information by carrier pigeon, is now a major technology player. It provides information, analytical and trading tools to financial markets on its own electronic network and has successful businesses across the technology, media and telecoms industries. It is also tackling the wider retail market as part of a new Internet strategy.

The company sells its news to websites. More than 40 million viewers now call up its news services at more than 900 websites each month, and sales to websites have leapfrogged sales to newspapers in the United States.

Reuters is currently teaming up with a host of big technology, media and telecoms (TMT) names to promote its content via new technologies. In the mobile phone arena, Reuters has set up a joint venture with US wireless software group Aether to deliver information to mobiles, while a Multex.com partnership will offer research and trading to European private investors.

The group focuses on three key business areas: the core business under Reuters Financial; the electronic brokerage business Instinet; and Reuterspace, encompassing the group's Internet-related ventures.

TELL IT HOW IT IS

Rajiv joined Reuters Financial TV in London in 1999. He explains why he was attracted to the world of on-line media as opposed to the printed page. 'I'd worked for a business newspaper in the US for three years, but the parochial nature of the work was killing me. I wanted to do something that was broader in scope, more international. Reuters fitted that description, and, while it covers economic and financial news, there's also a big general news element to it.

'After a three-week induction programme, I started on the two-month intensive journalism classroom training in London. Even though I had a degree in journalism and three years of work experience on a business newspaper, Reuters' style is very, very different. You need to be quick and accurate at the same time – a hard combination to achieve. I got a thorough grounding in economics – it seemed as if I got a mini-MBA in those two months – along with a crash course on covering coups, earthquakes and civil wars.

'After classroom training finished, I worked on Reuters Financial TV, learning how to book guests and prepare and do TV interviews. After a brief spell on the sports desk, I joined General News for eight weeks, where the adrenaline was high and the pace fast. During the assignment, I spent four nights at London's Stansted Airport covering the hijack of an Afghan airliner. It was not only a mental but also a physical challenge – sometimes you couldn't even go to the bathroom, because if something happened and you were the only Reuters journalist present, then your competitor would probably get the story!

'I then went back to the States for six weeks, as Reuters America graduates usually do, spending two weeks at each of the Washington, New York and Toronto bureaux. A highlight was covering the spring meeting of the International Monetary Fund in Washington. The anti-IMF demonstrators were creating havoc, and we were trapped inside the IMF building because the police said they were going to use tear gas! But it was a brilliant learning experience and I got to write a couple of byline stories, too.'

At the time of writing, Louise, who works in Reuters' Information Marketing Communications department, was just off to Sydney to start on a project that involved working with consultants to devise sales and marketing strategies. 'In my first assignment I project-managed the largest internal presentation ever held, following the chief executive, Peter Job's, announcement to analysts and the media of the company's new Internet strategy. It involved two and a half thousand staff either face to face or via teleconferencing.'

For graduates who feel they might

find the confines of a traditional City firm rather restrictive, the media has much to offer. Tony works on marketing and business development with Reuters, and describes one of the reasons he joined. 'After meeting several current graduates, I knew Reuters was for me. They were smart, came from all facets of both the private and public sector, and had a sense of humour. Being raised in a diverse area, I looked for a company with employees from all over the world.'

QUALIFICATIONS AND SKILLS

A good degree in finance, technology or an economics subject is ideal.

TIPS

Check out the websites for the information services. They include career opportunities. Be ready to explain why you prefer on-line journalism rather than the printed variety.

Once you have some training and experience under your belt, it is possible to move between the two media, and also possibly into television.

SOURCES OF INFORMATION ON CAREER

- Bloomberg www.bloomberg.co.uk
- Dow Jones Newswires www.dowjones.com
- Reuters www.reuters.com

APPENDIX:
JARGON BUSTER

● **AAA** A top credit rating. The credit rating of a company or financial institution indicates its ability to service any bonds it issues and to repay the capital when a bond matures. As a rule, the lower the credit rating the higher the yield (interest rate), but also the higher the risk of the company defaulting.

● **Acid test** The ratio of a company's current assets (excluding stock) to its current liabilities.

● **Active management** In contrast to what happens in **passive investment** or **index tracking**, the active manager selects sectors in the light of expected economic conditions and individual stocks on the basis of research into a company's prospects.

● **Advisory management** Under an advisory stockbroker or private client service the adviser discusses investment opportunities with the client and will not take any action without the client's prior approval. Under a **discretionary** arrangement the adviser makes all the decisions for the client. An **execution-only** service is where the adviser acts on the client's instructions but gives no advice or opinion.

● **AKM** stands for Applied Knowledge Management – a management consultancy term.

● **ALM** Investment consultants carry out an asset/liability modelling exercise to ensure that a pension fund is invested in the right sort of assets to match the scheme's liabilities in terms of benefit payments.

● **Alternative Investment Market** (AIM) is for small, fast-growing companies. Can be a springboard to the **Official List** (the main stock market).

● **Annual report and accounts** Companies that trade on the Stock Exchange or Alternative Investment Market must provide shareholders and the Exchange with an annual report and accounts that include financial details of the past trading year.

● **Arithmetic average** This is a simple arithmetic calculation – the sum of the total returns for a given category of shares, divided by the number of companies within the category.

● **Assets** A catch-all phrase which refers to different types of investments, for example UK **equities**, overseas equities, property, fixed-interest securities (**gilts** and **bonds**), and **cash**.

● **Association of Investment Trust Companies (AITC)** The main trade body for **investment trusts**.

● **Association of Unit Trust and Investment Companies (AUTIF)** The main trade body for **unit trusts** and **open-ended investment companies**.

● **Authorised unit trust** Unit trusts sold to the public must be authorised by the **Financial Services Authority (FSA)**, the chief regulator for financial services in the UK.

● **Balance sheet** Produced with the **annual report and accounts**. Shows what the company owns and owes.

● **Bargain** The term used when a purchase or sale agreement is struck.

● **Bear market** Where share prices are falling over a prolonged period.

● **Beauty parade** The final interview process for a major fund management appointment, usually in the pensions field, although it could be for a major charity fund. The investment consultant puts together a short list and the investment managers are called on in turn to make a presentation to the trustees of the pension or charity fund.

● **Beneficial owner** The real owner of shares held in a **nominee** account.

● **Beneficiaries** Those who benefit from a trust. With a **unit trust**, the trustees run the fund on behalf of the beneficiaries – in this case the unit-holders. With a pension fund the beneficiaries are the scheme members and their dependants.

● **Bid/offer spread** The full initial cost of an investment in a collective fund, including administration, sales commission, if applicable, dealing costs and **stamp duty**, among other items. Typically the spread is about 6 per cent, but where the initial charge is reduced or abolished it could be as low as 0.5 per cent.

● **Bid price** The price at which investment managers buy back units in a **unit trust**. They sell at the **offer price**.

● **Big Bang** (1986) Major changes which opened up the London Stock Exchange to greater competition, including foreign ownership of member firms and the abolition of minimum commissions.

● **Blue chip** Large, well-established company – for example, a **FTSE 100** company. Named after the highest-value chip in a poker game.

● **Bonds** UK bonds are issued by borrowers – for example, the government and companies – which undertake to repay the principal sum on a specified date, similar to an IOU. During the time the bond is outstanding a fixed rate of interest is paid to the lender, which might be an individual or a financial institution. Not to be confused with insurance company bonds, which are collective investments sold by insurance companies.

● **Broker/dealer** In the broad sense a broker is an intermediary who sells financial products to consumers on behalf of the institutions. A dealer (or broker-dealer) is involved in the marketing and the buying and selling of securities. See **market maker**.

● **Bull market** A market in which share prices are rising over a prolonged period. See **bear market**.

● **Call option** See **options**.

● **Capital gains tax** CGT is the tax on the inflation-adjusted increase in value of an asset when it is sold, compared with its value at the time of purchase.

● **Capital growth** An increase in the value of shares or assets.

● **Carpetbaggers** People who become members of mutual societies (building societies or life offices, for example) in the hope of a windfall of shares when the mutual converts to a plc.

● **Cash** As an asset class, cash usually refers to deposit accounts.

● **Cash management** Balancing the day-to-day cash flow and making the most of money on short-term deposit.

● **Chartist** An investor who uses charts of company price movements to determine investment decisions.

● **Chinese walls** Invisible information barriers that separate two different parts of a bank to avoid conflicts of interests and regulatory problems.

● **Collective/pooled fund**. Investors buy units in a collective fund such as a **unit trust** or **open-ended investment company (Oeic)** in order to gain access to a wider range of assets than they could otherwise afford through direct investment. In this way, pooled funds spread risk. They also reduce the dealing transaction costs.

● **Commission** 1. The fee that a stockbroker charges clients for dealing on their behalf. 2. The remuneration an adviser receives from a financial institution for selling you one of its products. See **fee-based adviser**.

● **Commodity** is a term usually used to refer to raw materials or foods like coffee beans, wheat and pork bellies, which are traded on commodity exchanges. Futures contracts are common in commodity trading; here a buyer agrees a fixed price in advance for delivery and takes a risk on, for example, the weather that might affect a grain harvest and drive the actual price up or down at the time of delivery.

● **Convertible** A type of equity that is more akin to a bond in that it pays

a regular income and has a fixed redemption date. The owner can convert it to an ordinary or preference share at a future date.

● **Corporate banking** Banking to medium-sized companies: cash and currency management, custodial services.

● **Corporate bond** An IOU issued by a public company. In return for borrowing an investor's money, the company pays a fixed income (**coupon**) for a specified period and guarantees to return the original capital (**nominal**) on a predetermined future date.

● **Corporate finance** A synonym for investment banking.

● **Coupon** The rate of interest as a percentage of the nominal price that is paid by a **bond** or **gilt**. The purchase price may be different from the nominal price.

● **Credit rating/risk** If you are a bank lending money to businesses you need to assess the likelihood of a borrower not being able to service the loan (the regular interest payments) or repay the capital at the end of the loan period. A borrower's credit rating will dictate the terms of the loan, including the cost. AAA is the highest rating.

● **CREST** An electronic service that handles the mechanics of settling share transactions.

● **CRM** stands for Customer Relationship Management, a management consultancy term.

● **Cum dividend** With dividend. The purchase price of the share includes the value of the dividend. If you buy **ex-dividend**, the dividend is paid to the previous owner.

● **Current ratio** The value of a company's current assets divided by current liabilities. Used as a measure of liquidity.

● **Custody** The safe-keeping of assets. The biggest custodians offer global custody to the multimillion-pound pension funds.

● **DCMs** The debt capital markets, where big companies issue **bonds** to raise finance.

● **Debenture bonds** are issued by UK companies, and are secured on the company's underlying assets – for example, property. Unsecured bonds are known as loan stocks.

● **Defined benefit (DB)** (also known as 'final salary') A type of pension scheme where the pension is based on the employee's salary and number of years as a member of the scheme. The employee usually makes a contribution but the investment risk and guarantees are backed by the employer.

● **Defined contribution** (DC) (also known as 'money purchase') This is a more modern (but not better) type of pension scheme where the employee's fund is used at retirement to purchase an 'annuity' from an insurance company, which provides a regular income. The value of that annuity will depend largely on the fund size, which in turn depends on investment returns: there are no guarantees.

● **Demutualisation** The process by which a mutually owned building society or life office becomes a public limited company. Members of the former **mutual** usually receive

windfall or free shares.

● **Derivatives** Financial instruments are referred to as derivative securities when their value is dependent on the value of some other underlying asset. See **futures**, **options** and **warrants**.

● **Discount** If the share price of an **investment trust** is lower than the value per share of the underlying assets (**net asset value**), the difference is known as the discount. If it is higher the difference is known as the **premium**. As a general rule a share trading at a discount often represents good value.

● **Discretionary management** This is where a stockbroker makes all the investment service decisions for the client. See **advisory management** and **execution-only.**

● **Distributions** Income paid out from an **equity** or **bond** fund.

● **Dividend** The owner of shares is entitled to dividends – usually a six-monthly distribution to shareholders of part of the company's profits.

● **Dividend cover** The number of times a company could pay its annual dividend out of earnings.

● **Dividend yield** See **gross yield**.

● **Due diligence** An investigation into the financial position of a company. It may be carried out by investment banks as part of the research on a merger or acquisition.

● **Earnings per share** The amount of profit earned for each ordinary share of the company.

● **Endowment** A type of long-term investment that is typically linked to a capital debt such as an interest-only mortgage. During the term of the investment the borrower pays the interest (hence the term interest-only mortgage) and at the end of the term (maturity) the investment is used to repay the capital. The key feature of the endowment is that it includes life assurance, so that if the investor dies before the end of the term the gap between the fund built up through the investment and the capital owed is covered by the life policy.

● **Equities** The ordinary share capital of a company.

● **Equity risk premium** The higher risk/reward characteristic of equities when compared with, for example, **cash** and **bonds**.

● **Eurosterling bond** A **corporate bond** issued in pounds sterling by a company that wants to borrow money on the international markets rather than just in the UK.

● **Ex-dividend** The period of about six weeks before a fund or equity pays out its dividend/income. If you buy during this period you are not entitled to that dividend. See **cum dividend**.

● **Execution-only** Under execution-only terms the investment manager/stockbroker simply buys and sells at your request without offering any advice. See **advisory management** and **discretionary management**.

● **Exit charges** A charge deducted from some collective funds if the investor pulls out early – usually within the first five years.

● **Fee-based adviser** Professional advisers do not accept sales **commission**. Instead they usually charge a fee calculated on an hourly basis and/or an annual percentage of your funds under management.

● **Final dividend** Paid at the end of a company's financial year when the final report is made setting out its financial position. See **interim**.

● **Financial gearing** The ratio between a company's borrowings and its capitalisation – i.e. a ratio between what it owes and what it owns.

● **Financial Services Act 1986** The act that established the system of self-regulation for financial services and a series of self-regulatory organisations (SROs) that administer different types of financial institutions and the advisers and representatives who sell their products.

● **Financial Services Authority (FSA)** The chief regulator for financial services in the UK (which replaced the Securities and Investments Board in 1997). See **Financial Services Act 1986.**

● **Fixed-interest securities** Another term for **fixed-rate bonds**. See **bonds**, **corporate bond**.

● **Fixed-rate bonds** Bonds that pay a fixed rate of interest (the **coupon**) for a predetermined period.

● **Fledgling** An index covering about 680 companies that are too small for the **All-Share**.

● **Flex** is short for flexible benefits. These are employee benefits subsidised by an employer and offered as a menu from which employees can choose up to an annual monetary limit.

● **Floating rate notes** An FRN is a **Eurobond** that has its interest rate linked to a base rate (for example, the London Interbank Offered Rate or Libor). FRNs usually have a **maturity** of between seven and fifteen years.

● **Flotation** The initial offering in the **primary market** of a company coming to the Stock Exchange for the first time.

● **FTSE 100 Index** The index that covers the top 100 companies on the UK Stock Exchange measured by market capitalisation (the number of shares times the share value).

● **FTSE All-Share Index** The yardstick for professional investors. The All-Share contains about 770 companies listed on the UK Stock Exchange.

● **FTSE Mid 250 Index** The index that measures the 250 companies below (by market capitalisation) the FTSE 100.

● **FTSE SmallCap** The All-Share minus the top 350. See **Fledgling**. Together, the SmallCap and Fledgling are known as the All-Small index.

● **Futures** A type of **derivative**. A futures contract is a legally binding agreement to buy or sell a number of shares (or other instruments) at a fixed date in the future at a fixed price.

● **Gearing** In company terms, the ratio of long-term borrowing to assets. High gearing means that there is a large proportion of debt in relation to the assets held.

● **Gilts** Bonds issued by the UK government. Conventional gilts pay a fixed percentage of the **nominal** price. The value of **index-linked** gilts rises each year by a fixed percentage above the rate of inflation.

● **Gross yield** A method of assessing income from an investment. It is the annual gross dividend (as currently declared or forecast by the directors of the investment trust) as a percentage of current market price. This shows the rate of gross income return a shareholder would receive on an investment at the share price on the date specified – much as one might describe the interest received on a deposit account.

● **Human capital** Employees. A variation on the term human resources. You might also come across the terms 'human strategy', 'compensation' and 'reward', used by employee benefits consultants who advise on benefits packages.

● **Index-linked** An investment (e.g. a **gilt**) whose value increases each year in line with retail price inflation or by a fixed percentage. See **Retail Price Index (RPI)**.

● **Index tracking** With a tracker fund, the investment manager uses a computer model to select stocks to simulate the performance of a specific stock market index. In some cases all the shares in an index will be held. Index tracking is also known as **passive management**.

● **Individual Savings Account (ISA)** Tax-exempt investment accounts launched in April 1999 (replaced PEPs and TESSAs).

● **Inflation** An increase in the general level of prices over a prolonged period, which forces down the real value or purchasing power of money. There are various measures of inflation, the most common being the **Retail Price Index (RPI).**

● **Inheritance tax (IHT)** A tax on the value of your estate above a certain limit when you die.

● **Insider information** Market-sensitive knowledge that is not available outside the company or its advisers. To invest on the basis of this knowledge is illegal.

● **Institutional banking** Another term for corporate banking.

● **Intangibles** Assets that have no physical form – for example, royalties and patents (aka intellectual property).

● **Interest cover** The number of times profits can cover the interest payments on a company's debts.

● **Interim** A statement by a company which sets out its financial position half way through its financial year. An interim dividend is also paid. See **final dividend**.

● **Internship** Formal work experience which usually takes place in the summer holidays before your last year at university. This is a key recruitment activity for City employers and gives you a chance to see if you will like working for a company full time.

● **Investment banking** Advising companies on major changes to their corporate structures through loans and issuing shares, supervising the financing of mergers and acquisitions. Aka corporate finance.

● **Investment trust** A UK company, listed on the Stock Exchange, which invests in the shares of other companies in the UK and overseas. See **discount** and **premium**.

● **Jobbers** The original traders through whom the old-style **brokers** made their sales and purchases. Replaced by **market makers** in 1986.

● **Joint stock companies** The forerunners of today's public limited companies.

● **Liabilities** What a company owes to suppliers and lenders.

● **Life office/life assurance company** The life assurance and investment arm of general insurance companies – or can be stand-alone companies with no general insurance link.

● **Liquidation** When a company is wound up and its assets, if any, are distributed to its creditors.

● **Loan stocks** Unsecured **bonds** issued by UK companies. Bonds secured on a company's underlying assets (property, for example) are known as **debentures**.

● **Long-dated bond** A bond or **gilt** with fifteen years or more to go to **redemption**, when the **nominal** capital is repaid to the holder.

● **Market maker** A dealer who can buy and sell shares, replacing the previous **brokers** and **jobbers**.

● **Maturity** Another word for **redemption**, when the investment period ends and, in the case of a **bond**, the **nominal** capital is repaid.

● **Medium-dated bond** A bond or **gilt** with five to fifteen years to go to **redemption**, when the **nominal** capital is repaid to the holder.

● **Mutual** A savings or insurance institution owned by its members.

● **Net asset value (NAV)** The market value of an **investment trust**'s underlying assets. This may be different from the share price since the latter is subject to market forces and supply and demand. See **discount** and **premium**.

● **Net yield** The return on an

investment after tax has been deducted. See **gross yield**.

● **Nominal** Usually refers to a price or value that has not been adjusted for inflation, for example. Nominal value is the face value of a security, rather than the market value, which may be higher or lower depending on supply and demand.

● **Nominee account** An account for your shares, held in the name of your stockbroker.

● **Offer price** The price at which a security is offered for sale. In the case of a **unit trust**, for example, the offer price will be higher than the bid price (the price at which the broker will buy) as it reflects the broker's commission, among other costs.

● **Official List** Where shares are listed after their initial launch on the exchange.

● **Offshore funds** For UK investors this usually refers to funds in the Dublin International Financial Centre, the Isle of Man, the Channel Islands or Luxembourg. Offshore locations are not subject to UK tax law, although usually, if you are UK resident, when you repatriate money to the UK you must pay the appropriate income and capital gains tax.

● **Open-ended investment companies (OEICS)** were launched in 1996. They are similar to **unit trusts** but have a corporate structure and a single price rather than a **bid/offer spread**, so in some respects also resemble **investment trusts**.

● **Operations/support** Used to be known as the 'back office' function,

where all the settlement and risk management takes place.

● **Options** A type of **derivative**. A call option gives the buyer the right (but not the obligation – hence *option*) to buy a commodity, stock, bond or currency in the future at a mutually agreed price struck on the date of the contract. Put options give you the right, but not the obligation, to sell.

● **Over-the-counter (OTC)** In the UK this refers to a security that is not listed on a recognised exchange. In the US the OTC market is for smaller companies that do not qualify for a full listing on the main markets like the New York Stock Exchange (NYSE).

● **Passive management** See **index tracking**.

● **Personal Investment Authority (PIA)** Under the **Financial Services Act 1986**, the PIA is the regulator for companies that market and sell retail investments such as ISAs, pensions and life assurance savings plans. This is being merged with the **Financial Services Authority (FSA)**.

● **Pitch** The investment banking term for a proposal put to a client regarding a corporate development – for example, to acquire a rival company that is going cheap.

● **Placing** A new issue of shares sold privately through a group of financial institutions.

● **Pooled funds** Another term for collective or mutual funds, which invest in a range of different shares and other instruments to achieve diversification for the smaller investor who buys units in these funds.

● **Portfolio** A collection of assets.

● **Preliminary results** A report to

the Stock Exchange on the company's annual results. This is issued about six weeks before the annual report and accounts are published.

● **Premium** If shares are trading at a premium this means that the going price is higher than the value of the underlying securities or the **nominal value**.

● **Pre-tax profit margin** A company's trading profit (before the deduction of depreciation, interest and tax) as a percentage of turnover.

● **Price/earnings ratio (PE)** The market price of a share divided by the company's earnings (profits) per share in its latest twelve-month trading period.

● **Primary market** Used for flotations of new companies and for further raising of capital under a **rights issue**.

● **Pro bono** A legal phrase that describes work done for the public good.

● **Profit and loss account** Contained within a company's annual report and accounts, together with the **balance sheet**. It sets out what the company has sold (turnover) during the past twelve months and its expenses in terms of salaries, raw materials, etc.

● **Proprietary trading** Where a trader uses the bank's own funds to invest to make a profit.

● **Public sector borrowing requirement (PSBR)** The amount by which government spending exceeds the income from taxation and other revenues.

● **Put option** See **options**.

● **Ratio analysis** Used by investment analysts as a way of comparing different companies or the same company at different times in its history. May be used to analyse companies in various ways, for example in terms of accounts, performance and quoted profits/dividends.

● **Real-time** means, er, real time, as in now. Real-time trading is buying and selling at the current price rather than at yesterday's closing price, for example.

● **Redemption** The date at which a bond becomes repayable. Also known as the maturity date.

● **Redemption yield** The current dividend or interest rate increased or decreased to take into account the capital value if the bond is held to maturity.

● **Retail banking**, also known as high-street banking, is banking (loans, current and deposit accounts) to individuals and small partnerships and companies that do not need a fancier service.

● **Retail Price Index (RPI)** The main measure of consumer inflation.

● **Rights issue** An issue of shares to raise additional capital. Usually offered to existing shareholders at a discount.

● **Running yield** The current dividend or interest payments on a fund.

● **Secondary market** Where shares are bought and sold on the Stock Exchange after the initial **flotation** in the primary market.

● **Securities** The general name for all stocks and shares. Broadly speaking, stocks are **fixed-interest securities** and shares are the rest. The four main types of securities listed and traded on the UK Stock Exchange are UK **equities**, overseas equities (i.e. those issued by non-UK companies), UK **gilts** (bonds issued by the UK government) and **bonds**/fixed-interest stocks (issued by companies and local authorities).

● **Securitisation** The process whereby financial contracts – mortgages, for example – are bundled together so they can be bought and sold.

● **Self-regulatory organisation (SRO)** The organisations established by the **Financial Services Act 1986** to authorise sales and marketing of financial services and products.

● **Settlement** The transfer of shares from the existing owner to the new owner and the corresponding transfer of money.

● **Short-dated** A **gilt** or **bond** with up to five years to go to **redemption**. See **long-dated bond** and **medium-dated bond**.

● **SIP** Statement of investment principles – the document that sets out socially responsible (ethical) investment principles, among other features, for a pension fund.

● **Spot market** is where currencies or commodities are traded on their **spot price** for delivery within two days, as opposed to the forward market, where deliveries and rates are quoted for some future date.

● **Spot price** The immediate price of a currency or commodity rather than a future delivery price.

● **Stamp duty** A tax on the purchase (but not the sale) of shares, currently

0.5 per cent.

● **Stockbroker** Aka private wealth manager or private client services manager. A member of the Stock Exchange who can buy and sell shares on behalf of a private investor.

● **Stock Exchange Automated Quotations (SEAQ)** A computer-based system that allows stockbrokers to see share price information anywhere in the UK. The Stock Exchange Alternative Trading System (SEATS) was introduced in 1993 for less liquid securities.

● **Stock Exchange Trading Services (SETS)** Introduced in October 1997 to speed up order-driven trading, initially in the FTSE 100 companies. Allows sales and purchases to be matched electronically.

● **Stock market** The place where shares, bonds and other assets change hands.

● **Stock market indices** An index is a specified basket or portfolio of shares, and shows how the prices of these shares are moving in order to give an indication of market trends. Every major world stock market is represented by at least one index. The **FTSE 100** index, for example, reflects the movements of the share prices of the UK's largest 100 quoted companies by market capitalisation.

● **Tax avoidance** Saving tax by using loopholes in the law. This is legal but may be frowned upon by the Inland Revenue.

● **Tax depreciation** is a form of tax relief on expenditure, such as buying properties, constructing or refurbishing buildings, or leasing fixtures or equipment.

● **Tax-efficient investments**
Investments – for example, pension plans – that offer an element of tax exemption, reduction or deferral.

● **Tax evasion** A deliberate attempt to reduce your tax bill by withholding information or lying. This is illegal.

● **Tax mitigation** Tax saving encouraged by the law, for example by saving through a pension plan.

● **Tax year** 6 April to the following 5 April.

● **TMT** The technology, media and telecoms sector.

● **Tracker funds** See **index tracking**.

● **Transfer pricing** involves transferring goods or intellectual property, for example, between subsidiaries of the same company.

● **Treasury services** cover a wide range of currency and interest rate exposures for corporations that have overseas markets and operations.

● **Trust deed** The legal document on which a unit trust or pension is based, for example. The use of a trust separates the fund from the management or sponsoring company's assets.

● **Trustee** You can't have a trust without a trustee who, as legal owner of the fund, looks after the assets on behalf of the beneficiaries. UK pension funds are established under trust, as are **unit trusts**.

● **Underwriting** In insurance terms this means agreeing to cover the costs if things go wrong. In banking terms it usually refers to the agreement (in cases where the bank has advised on a share or bond issue) that the bank will buy any remaining securities not bought through public subscription. Where the issue is very large the lead bank may organise a syndicate of banks to underwrite the public offering, and so spread the risk.

● **Unit trust** A collective fund where assets are pooled and investors buy units, the value of which will rise and fall in line with the value of the underlying securities.

● **Voluntary benefits** are low-cost deals arranged by employers for employees to buy on a voluntary basis – for example, cheap insurance, package holidays, car purchase and legal helplines.

● **Warrants** Risky and volatile investments which give the holder the right but not the obligation to buy investment trust shares at a predetermined price within a specified period. This type of share confers no voting rights and holders do not normally receive dividends.

● **Windfalls** Free shares given to members of a building society or mutual life office when it demutualises to become a public limited company.

● **Yield** The annual dividend or income on an investment expressed as a percentage of the purchase price. See **gross yield**.